GO AHEAD

8

Cornelsen

Go Ahead 8

für die Jahrgangsstufe 8 an sechsstufigen bayerischen Realschulen

erarbeitet von	John Eastwood, Street, Somerset
	Klaus Berold, Kulmbach
	Elke Zahn, Bayreuth
	Cheryl und Daniel Davy, Tillamook, USA
unter beratender Mitarbeit von	Gerlinde Eberhardt, Traunreut
	Werner Epp, Kempten
	Gisela Fiedler, Nürnberg
	Günter Geiß, Weiden
	Renate Grieshaber, Kempten
	Renate Heidemeier, Eichstätt
	Konrad Huber, Maisach
	Jürgen Kanhäuser, Rain
	Reinhold Schnell, Frickenhausen
Verlagsredaktion	Stefanie Gröne
Projektleitung	Helga Holtkamp
redaktionelle Mitarbeit	Jill Kitchen, Fritz Preuss, Barbara Swayne
Design und Layout	David Graham (*Units*) James Abram (*Anhänge*)
Bildredaktion	Béatrice Collette, Uta Hübner
zum Schülerbuch sind erhältlich	**Workbook, CDs**

Hinweise zu weiteren Bestandteilen im Lehrerhandbuch.
Bild-, Text- und Musikquellen auf Seite 161.

www.cornelsen.de

1. Auflage, 7. Druck 2009 / 06

Alle Drucke dieser Auflage sind inhaltlich unverändert
und können im Unterricht nebeneinander verwendet werden.

Um die Wiederverwendbarkeit zu gewährleisten, darf in dieses Buch
nicht hineingeschrieben werden.

© 2002 Cornelsen Press GmbH & Co. KG, Berlin

Das Werk und seine Teile sind urheberrechtlich geschützt.
Jede Nutzung in anderen als den gesetzlich zugelassenen Fällen bedarf der
vorherigen schriftlichen Einwilligung des Verlages.
Hinweis zu den §§ 46, 52 a UrhG: Weder das Werk noch seine Teile dürfen ohne
eine solche Einwilligung eingescannt und in ein Netzwerk eingestellt oder sonst
öffentlich zugänglich gemacht werden. Dies gilt auch für Intranets von Schulen
und sonstigen Bildungseinrichtungen.

Druck: CS-Druck CornelsenStürtz, Berlin

ISBN 978-3-464-02697-7

 Inhalt gedruckt auf säurefreiem Papier aus nachhaltiger Forstwirtschaft.

CONTENTS / INHALT

Page	Unit		What we learn in this unit

 NEW YORK, NEW YORK

Page			
5	W & P		
6	Intro 1	Sit 1–2, Ex 1–3	*can, can't, could, couldn't, be able to*
8	Text 1	**Almost a New Yorker**, Ex 4–7	Negative questions
10	List	Ex 8	Infinitive with *to* for purpose
11	Act 1	**New York**	
12	Intro 2	Sit 3–4, Ex 9–11	*can, may, be allowed to*
14	Text 2	**The bright lights**, Ex 12–16	Present tenses for the future
17	Act 2	**Hip hop**	
18	Com	**International spelling alphabet**, Ex 17	
18	TYE	1–4	
20	Read	**Public Enemy Number One**	

2 THE AMERICAN WAY OF LIFE

Page			
21	W & P		
22	Intro 1	Sit 1–2, Ex 1–3	The passive: present, past
24	Text 1	**Jennifer's year**, Ex 4–7	The passive with *by*
26	List	Ex 8	
26	Pair	Ex 9	
27	Act 1	**Thanksgiving**	
28	Intro 2	Sit 3–5, Ex 10–13	Personal passive
30	Text 2	**The Super Bowl**, Ex 14–18	The passive: present perfect, modal verbs
33	Act 2	**Get in touch**	
34	Com	**When you don't understand**, Ex 19	
34	TYE	1–5	
36	Read	**Which way now?**	

 LOOKING BACK

Page			
37	W & P		
38	Intro 1	Sit 1–2, Ex 1–2	Simple past – past perfect
40	Text 1	**Pocahontas**, Ex 3–6	Past perfect (positive, negative, questions)
42	List	Ex 7	
43	Act 1	**Native Americans**	
44	Intro 2	Sit 3–5, Ex 8–10	Reflexive pronouns
46	Text 2	**Front of the bus**, Ex 11–16	Emphatic pronouns
49	Act 2	**African-American people**	*each other*
50	Com	**Interviewing people**, Ex 17	
50	TYE	1–4	
52	Read	**Ellen's diary**	

CONTENTS / INHALT

Page   Unit   What we learn in this unit

4 STARS AND STRIPES

53	W & P	
54	Intro 1	Sit 1–2, Ex 1–4
56	Text 1	Florida vacation, Ex 5–8
58	List	Ex 9
59	Act 1	Grizzly!
60	Intro 2	Sit 3–4, Ex 10–12
62	Text 2	Rattlesnake! Ex 13–16
64	Pair	Ex 17
65	Act 2	USA Quiz
66	Com	Making a request, Ex 18
66	TYE	1–5
68	Read	Blizzard

If … simple present, *will / can / …*
  (Revision)
If … simple past, *would / might /*
  could / …
Prepositions in questions
Subject / object questions

EXTRA PAGES

69	Unit 1	Guns in school
72	Unit 2	Smokejumpers
75	Unit 3	Gone with the Wind
78	Unit 4	Headfirst into America

81	Proj	Project pages
84	Rev	Revision exercises 1–15
90	Read	American Literature
92		Tips – How to present a paper
94		Pair work
95		Grammatical terms
98		Grammar
113		English sounds
114		British and American English
116		Unit vocabulary list
138		Irregular verbs
140		List of names
147		Index
		Activities vocabulary list
		Extra Pages vocabulary list

Lerntipps
Partnerübungen
Grammatikalische Fachausdrücke
Grammatikanhang
Erklärung der Lautschriftzeichen
Britisches / amerikanisches Englisch
Wörterverzeichnis
Unregelmäßige Verben
Liste der Namen
Alphabetisches Wörterverzeichnis
Wörterverzeichnis **Activities**
Wörterverzeichnis **Extra Pages**

Act = Activities   **Com** = Communication   **Ex** = Exercise   **Intro** = Introduction   **List** = Listening   **Pair** = Pair work
Read = Reading   **Rev** = Revision   **Sit** = Situation   **TYE** = Test your English   **W & P** = Words and pictures

4 four

UNIT 1
NEW YORK, NEW YORK

WORDS AND PICTURES

01

It's the biggest city in the United States and the most exciting city in the world, and it has the most famous skyline. It's New York City, in New York State. It has the Statue of Liberty, the Empire State Building, Central Park and a whole lot more.

New York City is really five cities in one. The five parts are all called boroughs. Manhattan is the center of everything. The four other boroughs are Queens, Staten Island, the Bronx and Brooklyn.

New York is home to people from all over the world. More than 150,000 Chinese speakers live in Chinatown, at the southern end of Manhattan. There's also Little Italy, Little India and Little Korea. Many Jews live on the Lower East Side, a lot of Hispanic people live in El Barrio, and Harlem is America's most famous black community.

Most people in Manhattan live in apartments. The other boroughs have houses as well as apartment blocks. Some New Yorkers live in nice homes, but others have to live in very poor conditions. There are slums in parts of the Bronx, for example.

five 5

Unit 1 — INTRODUCTION 1

🔵 SITUATION 1

02

Anna and Sarah Miller live in Harrisburg, the capital of Pennsylvania. Their 16-year-old cousin, Daniel from Bavaria, is visiting them.

Sarah We're glad you were able to come, Daniel.
Daniel Me too. I couldn't miss an opportunity to come to America.
Sarah Did your parents pay for your ticket?
Daniel Well, I had a spare time job, so I was able to pay some of the money.
Anna I earned two hundred dollars at Christmas. I worked in a clothing store. I took the job so that I could buy a new stereo.
Daniel I've got some heavy metal tapes with me. Can I play them on your stereo?
Anna Sure. Mom and dad will be out tonight, so we'll be able to play them really loud.

If you fall over, will you be able to get up again?

EXERCISE 1

Look at the table and make sentences.

Can and be able to	→ page 98-99
Present	I **can** pay for my ticket. Anna **can't** send a text message because her phone isn't working.
Past	I **could** hear heavy metal music. Anna **couldn't** send a text message yesterday. I **was able to** pay for my ticket. She **wasn't able** to get a message to you.
Future	In the vacation we **will be able** to do what we like. I **won't be able** to go out with you tomorrow. I have to help my dad.

▶ Daniel got a spare-time job,
1 Sarah is going to borrow my map,
2 Brittany is a good singer,
3 Mike has decided to record the movie,
4 Tom is going to work on his project at the weekend,
5 We didn't have a camera,
6 My friend Lauren was ill,
7 The girls didn't have tickets for the concert last week,
8 There were horses on the farm where Kirsty was staying,

| so | he <br> she <br> we <br> they | was <br> wasn't <br> were <br> weren't <br> will be <br> won't be | able to | go on the trip last week.
 find the way.
 take photos of the view.
 earn some money.
 see their favorite band.
 go to the beach with us.
 go riding.
 play a part in the musical last year.
 watch it tomorrow. |

▶ Daniel got a spare-time job, so he was able to earn some money.

We sometimes use *could* instead of *was / were able to*.
▶ Daniel got a spare-time job, so he could earn some money.

Now write sentences 6, 7 and 8 with *could / couldn't*.

INTRODUCTION 1

SITUATION 2

Mrs Miller is planning to take Daniel and the girls to New York City.

Mrs Miller We haven't forgotten our trip to New York, Daniel. We booked a hotel for next week. We'll take you in the car.
Daniel Oh, that's great. I'd love to go – if you're sure it's no trouble. Isn't it a long way?
Mrs Miller It's only about 180 miles. And it's certainly no trouble.
Sarah Haven't you been to New York before, Daniel?
Daniel No, I haven't.
Sarah We like going to New York. We shop till we drop.
Mrs Miller Well, Daniel might want to do some sightseeing, you know.

Positive questions	Why **are** you working now? **Does** Sarah like burgers?
Negative questions	Why **aren't** you working now? **Doesn't** Sarah like burgers?

→ page 101-102

EXERCISE 2

Complete the conversation. Make negative questions from the notes.

▶ *Anna* We haven't got the kind of music you like, Daniel.
  Daniel **Don't you like heavy metal?** (you / not / like / heavy metal)
  Anna No, not really.
1 *Mrs Miller* It's cold today. … ? (you / not / bring / coat)
  Daniel Yes, I did. It's in my room. I'll go and get it.
2 *Anna* Hurry up, Sarah. … ? (why / you / can / not / walk / faster)
  Sarah I'm walking as quickly as I can. … ? (this / is / not / fast enough)
3 *Sarah* I'm going to watch 'Titanic' on TV tonight.
  Daniel … ? (you / not / see / it / before)
  Sarah Yes, about five times.
4 *Sarah* I can't understand what you've written here, Daniel.
  Daniel … ? (you / can / not / read / German) … ? (you / not / learn / it / school)
  Sarah No, we learn French.
5 *Mrs Miller* … ? (it / is / not / time / go / bed) It's eleven o'clock.
  Anna Oh, mom. … ? (we / can / not / stay up / bit / longer)
  Mrs Miller … ? (you / are / not / tired)
  Sarah No, we're OK.

EXERCISE 3

What negative questions can you ask? Use these words in your questions: *cold, dangerous, money, swim, win.*

▶ I don't need a coat.

▶ Aren't you cold?

1 I can ride a bike with no hands, look.

2 I'm not going to jump in the water. I'll just sink to the bottom.

3 I want to buy this CD, but I can't.

4 I watched the New York Yankees today. They weren't very good.

seven 7

Almost a New Yorker

'Look, kids, this is the most famous city skyline in the world!' said Barbara Miller. It was almost dark now. Daniel looked out the window of the car at the millions of lights on the hundreds of skyscrapers in the city center. He could hardly believe that he was in New York City. Just one of those skyscrapers could hold everyone who lived in his home town back in Bavaria. And as they reached midtown Manhattan, the buildings looked even bigger.

Daniel was with his cousins Anna and Sarah on a trip from Harrisburg. 'Where will we go first?' he asked. He wanted to see everything. 'To the hotel, of course,' said his aunt Barbara. 'It's called the Howard Johnson. Aren't you tired after the journey?' Everyone agreed that sightseeing could wait until tomorrow.

'I'm going to leave the car in the hotel garage,' she said as they left the hotel the next morning. They took a taxi to the Empire State Building. 'Aren't there a lot of taxis on the streets?' said Daniel. Anna told him that most people in New York don't have their own cars; they use taxis, buses, or the subway. 'It's too hard to find a place to park a car,' she said.

At the Empire State Building there was a line of people who were all waiting for the elevator. But the line was not very long and the family only had to wait 15 minutes. They had to change elevators twice before they reached the 102nd floor. The building was once the tallest in the world, and the view from the top was spectacular. They could see all of Manhattan, across the river to Brooklyn, and west into New Jersey, the state next to New York. 'We're lucky that we were able to come in spring,' said Mrs Miller. 'In summer it's more crowded, and the tourists make the wait much longer.'

The next stop was the Statue of Liberty. First they took the subway to Battery Park, at the southern end of Manhattan.

The subway wasn't as dirty as it looks in movies, where they always show litter and graffiti. From Battery Park they went on a small boat over to Liberty Island. They went inside the huge copper statue and climbed the 354 steps up to the crown, where they got another marvelous view of the city. There were even some steps up to the torch, but visitors couldn't go up so far.

The next day it was shopping. There were clothing stores, shoe stores, and stores with every CD you can imagine. Daniel soon got bored with clothes and was glad when they stopped for lunch. 'I'd like to find a guitar store,' he said. He and his friends back home liked to play heavy metal music. 'I'll meet you back at the hotel at 5 P.M.' 'OK,' said his aunt, 'but be careful. Don't go too far.'

After only a few minutes Daniel found what he was looking for. So many guitars and other instruments, too! He had a good look at everything. When at last he finished, he went out the door onto the sidewalk. Should he go left or right? Did he need to cross the street? He couldn't decide. He was afraid of losing his way. There were all kinds of people and everyone seemed to be in a hurry. A woman came out of the music store.

'Excuse me.' Daniel asked for directions to the hotel. The woman spoke very quickly and Daniel didn't understand what she said. He walked to the corner and looked down all four of the streets. They were so long and straight, and the tall buildings all looked the same. He stood there for what seemed like a long time, and then he saw two police officers. They were walking slowly along the sidewalk. Daniel needed all his courage.

TEXT 1

'Excuse me,' he began again. 'Can you tell me the way to the Howard Johnson Hotel and can you please speak slowly?' The
5 officers smiled and told him which way it was and how many blocks he should go. He reached the hotel just before 5 P.M.
 'Did you have any trouble finding
10 your way back?' asked Anna.
 'Of course not!' said Daniel.
 He almost felt like a New Yorker after two whole days in the city.

EXERCISE 4

Answer the questions.

1 Which sentence in the text tells you that New York is much bigger than the town where Daniel lives?
2 Why didn't Mrs Miller drive them around the city in her car?
3 Why is New York City better for tourists in spring than in summer?
4 How did Daniel feel about all the clothing stores? Did he enjoy shopping?
5 How do you think Daniel felt when he was standing on the sidewalk?
6 Which sentence best describes Daniel's adventure?
   a) Two heads are better than one.
   b) Don't cross a bridge till you come to it.
   c) All's well that ends well.

EXERCISE 5

Complete this summary in your own words. Sometimes you need more than one word.

Mrs Miller and the three … arrived in … City in the … , when they could see all the … on the skyscrapers. They went straight to … .

On their first day in the city, they took … to … . They went up in … and looked at … . After that they took the … and then a … to the … of Liberty. Here there was no … , so they had to … to the top.

On the second day they looked around … . In the … Daniel went on his … to a … , where he looked at … and other … . When he left the store, he didn't … to the hotel. But luckily two … gave him … , and he soon found the hotel, where … glad to see the others.

EXERCISE 6

Look at these sentences.

➤ Daniel went to America to see his cousins.
➤ Anna got a job to earn some money.

 (They tell us the purpose of Daniel's journey and Anna's job.)

Use *to* and a verb and complete each sentence. You can use the information in the text.

1 The girls went to New York … .
2 They all went to the top of the Empire State Building … .
3 They went to Liberty Island … .
4 They shopped all morning and then went to a café … .
5 Daniel went to a music store … .

Now complete these in your own words.
6 I phoned my friend … .
7 I sometimes go out … .
8 I use a computer … .

nine 9

Unit 1   TEXT 1

EXERCISE 7

Look at the map of part of Manhattan and read the information.

Most streets on Manhattan go in a straight line, so they make a simple pattern. Those that go north to south are called avenues, and those that go east to west are called streets. Most avenues and streets have numbers, not names. One of the most famous avenues is Fifth Avenue, where there are lots of big stores. Fifth Avenue divides Manhattan into East and West. So if you're on West 47th Street, you're west of Fifth Avenue. If you walk along Fifth Avenue from 47th Street to 48th Street, you've walked a distance of one block.

In America, 'downtown' means the city center or business district.

In Manhattan downtown is the business district around Wall Street, and midtown is the area south of Central Park which includes Rockefeller Center, the Empire State Building and the Chrysler Building.

Find these places on the map and say what you can do if you go there.

➡ Central Park – right in the … of Manhattan – take a boat on the lake
'If you go to Central Park right in the middle of Manhattan, you can take a boat on the lake.'

1. Chelsea Piers – on the Hudson … – do all kinds of sport
2. Rockefeller Center – south of … Park – see a show at NBC
3. Chinatown – at the … end of Manhattan – eat some real Chinese …
4. the Intrepid – on the … River – see some ships and planes
5. the Empire State Building – on 5th Ave at 34th St …

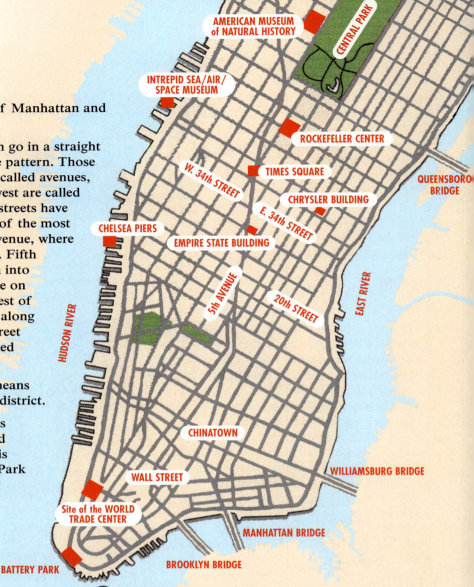

 05

EXERCISE 8

Listening

Alice is on vacation in New York City. She and her friend Natalie are staying at a hotel on W 20th St. They want to go to the American Museum of Natural History to see the dinosaurs. Alice is asking the desk clerk for directions.

Imagine you are Alice. Listen to the directions and take notes. Write down the following information.

- where the museum is
- why it's best to go on the subway
- how you get to the subway station
- the number or letter of the lines you have to use
- where you have to change
- where you get out and how far you have to walk

10   ten

ACTIVITIES 1

1 NEW YORK, NEW YORK

SONG 06

Start spreading the news, I'm leaving today
I want to be a part of it – New York, New York
These vagabond shoes are longing to stray
Right through the very heart of it – New York, New York

I want to wake up in a city that doesn't sleep
And find I'm king of the hill, top of the heap

These little town blues are melting away
I'll make a brand new start of it – in old New York
If I can make it there, I'll make it anywhere
It's up to you – New York, New York

words → page 159

2 THE CITY THAT NEVER SLEEPS
07

When the Millers and Daniel were in New York, they went on a sightseeing tour. Mrs Miller told them lots of things that even Anna and Sarah didn't know. Listen to the conversations and find the places they are visiting. Form groups of three people. Make a list and write down the names of the places.

➤ Statue of Liberty   1 … 2 … 3 … 4 … 5 … 6 …
Which place is the most interesting? Which sight wouldn't you like to visit and why?

Long Island
Broadway
Empire State Building
Madison Square Garden
Manhattan
Statue of Liberty
Brooklyn Bridge

eleven 11

Unit 1 **INTRODUCTION 2**

SITUATION 3
08

Daniel There's so much traffic in New York, isn't there?
Sarah Yes, it's terrible. That's why it's better to use the subway to get around.
Anna I'll be able to drive soon.
Daniel Already? But you're only 15, aren't you, Anna?
Anna That's right. But here we can learn to drive at 15, so I was allowed to start in January. And we're allowed to get a driver's license at 16. If I pass my test next year, I'll be allowed to drive my mom's car. Freedom!
Daniel You're lucky. In Germany we aren't allowed to drive until we're 18.

Are we allowed to rap here?

EXERCISE 9

Complete the second part of each sentence. Use a form of *be allowed to*.

➡ If you live in Europe, you – allow – enter – US – without a visa (now)
   If … , you're allowed to enter the US without a visa.

1 If you go to the US as a tourist, you – allow – stay – for ninety days (now)
2 If you take food with you, you – not – allow – take – it– into – US (next month)
3 When Daniel and the girls climbed up inside the statue, they – not – allow – go up – to the torch (yesterday)
4 If they are with an adult, kids under 3 feet 8 inches tall – allow – travel free – New York subway (now)
5 If you see the sign 'Don't walk', it – mean – you – not – allow – cross – road (now)
6 When I last went to Central Park, people – allow – cycle – there (last year)
7 It's nice there at weekends because cars – not – allow – drive – through the park (now)

Be allowed to	➡ page 100
Present	We're allowed to take photos in here.
Past	We were allowed to go to the fairground last week.
Future	We'll be allowed to leave school early tomorrow.

12 twelve

INTRODUCTION 2

SITUATION 4

09

Mrs Miller Are you doing anything special when you get back home, Daniel?

Daniel No, the new term starts only three days after I get back. There won't really be time to do anything.

Sarah I'm going to Niagara Falls next week with my friend Carol. Her parents are taking us.

Niagara Falls is really two waterfalls. One is called the Horseshoe Falls or Canadian Falls and the other is called the American Falls. Every second 195,000 cubic feet of water pours over the falls.

EXERCISE 10

Bus services Harrisburg – Washington		A.M.			P.M.	
Harrisburg		6:05	8:15	11:45	4:35	7:20
York		6:45	8:55	12:25	5:15	8:00
Baltimore	arr.	7:55	10:05	1:35	6:25	9:05
	dep.	8:05	10:15	1:45	6:35	9:10
Washington		9:00	11:10	2:40	7:35	10:10

There are several people at Harrisburg bus station. Read this paragraph about Joshua.

▶ Joshua is in Harrisburg, and he's taking a bus to Washington. The bus leaves at 8:15 A.M. It stops at York at 8:55. It gets to Baltimore at 10:05 and leaves at 10:15. It arrives in Washington at 11:10.

I'm flying to Venus. My spaceship leaves in ten minutes.

Now complete these paragraphs.

1 It's quarter past four, and Erica is waiting for the bus to Washington. The bus leaves at … .
2 It's early evening, and Michael is getting on a bus in Harrisburg. The bus … .
3 Lauren is hoping her bus will be on time because she's meeting a friend in Washington at quarter past three. …
4 Scott needs to get to Washington as early as possible in the day. …

EXERCISE 11

➔ page 102-103

This is Ashley's diary for next week. Say what she is doing.

▶ On Monday she's doing trampolining.
▶ On … meeting Nicole and …

What about you? Draw a diary page in your exercise book and note down some things that you are doing next week. Choose at least two of the things and make a sentence about each of them.

Notes

Mon Sept 30
Trampolining 4:00

Tues Oct 1
Meet Nicole and Amber at Chelsea Piers 6:30

Weds Oct 2
Math test

Thurs Oct 3
Movie with Chris

Fri Oct 4
Basketball 7:30

Sat Oct 5
Amber's party 8:00

Sun Oct 6
Show my cousin Lindsey some of the sights

thirteen 13

Unit 1 **TEXT 2**

🟡 **The bright lights**

Before Daniel went to New York City, he agreed to send e-mails about the trip to his classmates and English teacher. His teacher wanted to put the reports on the school website. So Daniel wrote about what he did and then Sarah corrected a few mistakes for him.

Yesterday we went to Central Park, where we looked around a little zoo and then did some in-line skating. It was fun. For lunch we went to another fast food place. This time it was the Hard Rock Café, where the hamburgers are the biggest I've ever seen.

While we were eating our lunch, we discussed what we're going to do during the rest of our stay in the city. Later today we're going to Rockefeller Center to look around the NBC Television studios. And we've got tickets for a show in the evening. We're seeing the musical 'Chicago' at a Broadway theater.

On Friday we're driving back to Harrisburg, and next Wednesday I fly home. My visit to America is almost over already!

In the evening I went out with my cousins. We were allowed to go out on our own to a nightclub for teenagers. (Aunt Barbara really is my favorite aunt.) But of course we had to stay together, she told us. We got directions from the desk clerk at the hotel, and we were able to walk to the club because it wasn't far. There were bright lights everywhere and as many people on the sidewalks as during the day. New York is 'the city that never sleeps'.

Some of you asked me about the night life. Well, this club was a great place, with loud music and flashing lights. We drank soda – in most American states you aren't allowed to drink alcohol until you're 21. If you ask for alcohol, you need a passport or a driver's license, something that shows you are over 21.

So we sat in the club and drank soda and ate a plate of nachos and listened to the music. It was great. There was a black couple at the next table, and somehow we started talking to them. Their names were Robert and Jasmine. I told them about my trip from Germany to visit my cousins. Then we talked about the music – it was hip hop.

They said that hip hop really belongs to black Americans, even though lots of white teenagers like the music and buy the CDs. In fact it's now the most popular kind of music in the US. Hip hop began in the Bronx, where Robert and Jasmine live. It was music for poor young black people, something that could truly be theirs. Robert and Jasmine can both rap, they told us. They each started a couple of years ago, when they were 14, and now they do it together. They've performed in different places – parks, churches and high schools. 'If you want to rap, you have to believe in what you're saying,' said Jasmine. 'You have to stand up and look people in the eye.' Robert told us that hip hop is a whole way of life for many black people. 'It isn't just music, it's break-dancing, too, and it's hip-hop magazines, and it's graffiti on concrete and on subway trains, and it's the kind of clothes you wear.'

'What about all the crime?' asked Sarah. 'Isn't there a lot of drugs and violence that seems to go with hip hop and rap?' 'We don't like that side of it,' said Robert. 'We don't do violent gangster rap. We tell our own stories.'

It was after midnight when we returned to the hotel, but the sidewalks were still full of people. Here and there were small groups of young people. They were listening to CD players and talking. Some were dancing on the sidewalks. I have the feeling that all those lights and sounds are going to stay with me for a long time.

TEXT 2

EXERCISE 12

Say if these sentences are true or false. Correct them if they are false.

1. When Daniel wrote his e-mail, he made some mistakes in his English.
2. Daniel and his aunt and cousins are going to visit some TV studios in the Chrysler Building.
3. Yesterday evening the three kids went out to a club with Mrs Miller.
4. A policeman told them the way.
5. New York is a very lively city, even at night.
6. Americans are allowed to drink alcohol at a younger age than Germans are.
7. Hip-hop music started in New York City.
8. Robert and Jasmine have rapped in front of audiences.
9. Hip hop is just a kind of music, and no one takes it seriously.
10. Daniel will not easily forget the scenes he saw on the streets of the city that evening.

EXERCISE 13

Complete the conversations. Use a form of *have to*, *be able to* or *be allowed to*.

➡ *Mrs Miller*   Did you lose your way?
  Sarah   Yes, but I had a map. I was able to find my way back to the hotel.

1. *Anna*   How did you get back without any money?
   Daniel   I simply … walk. There was no other way.
2. *Sarah*   Where can we have a picnic?
   Mrs Miller   We can have it here. I'm sure people … sit on the grass.
3. *Desk clerk*   Are you going to a show?
   Sarah   Yes, luckily this morning Anna and I … get tickets for '42nd Street'.
4. *Mrs Miller*   These guitars seem very expensive.
   Daniel   Yes, but they're good. If I save a bit more money, I … buy one soon.
5. *Mrs Miller*   If we go this way, we'll go past the entrance to the Chrysler Building.
   Anna   Do you think we … go inside?
6. *Anna*   I won't have time to clean my room today.
   Mrs Miller   Well, you … do it tomorrow because it looks a real mess.
7. *Sarah*   Your parents had a party Saturday, didn't they?
   Carol   That's right. Luckily I … stay up till after midnight.
8. *Daniel*   Isn't your boyfriend coming with us tonight?
   Anna   No, he can't come. He … do some work on his project.

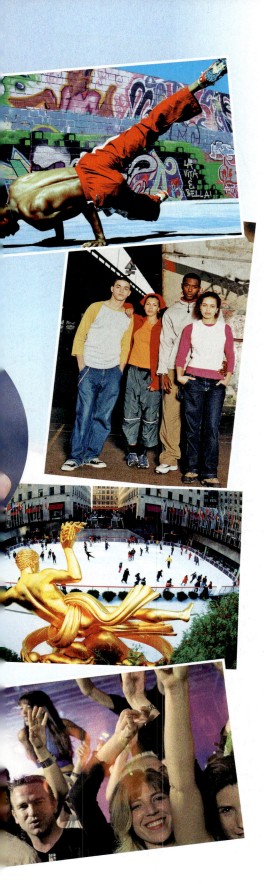

Unit 1 TEXT 2

EXERCISE 14

Complete the sentences. Look at each verb in italics and put in a noun from the same word family. Sometimes the noun has a special ending, and sometimes the noun and the verb are the same word.

➤ The cars *sound* a long way away when you're up here on the top of the building. You can hardly hear the sound of the traffic. (The noun is the same word.)
➤ His teacher *suggested* a report about the trip. But Daniel wasn't sure about this suggestion. (The noun has the ending *ion*.)

1 'Let's just *walk* a few blocks,' said Sarah. So they went for a … .
2 Daniel didn't *stay* very long in the US. So he tried to do as much as he could during his … .
3 In the vacation we're *free* to do what we like. We really enjoy our … .
4 Don't you *feel* excited? I always get this … when I come to New York.
5 I like to *visit* the city, but a … of three or four days is enough for me.
6 I'd love to *live* in Manhattan and have a really exciting … .

EXERCISE 15

Sometimes Americans use different words than the British, and sometimes they spell words differently.

We'll be on holiday. He stood on the pavement. I posted the letter. What colour is it? We watched a TV programme. It's a big tourist centre.	We'll be on vacation. He stood on the sidewalk. I mailed the letter. What color is it? We watched a TV program. It's a big tourist center.

How are these words different in America?

1 They stopped to get some *petrol*.
2 That's my *favourite film*.
3 We're going to the *theatre*.
4 There's a *marvellous* view from the top.
5 There were lots of *lorries* on the *main road*.
6 We *travelled* on the *underground*.
7 We live in a *flat*.

For more details about American English, look at pages 114-115.

EXERCISE 16

Practice this telephone conversation with a partner.

Lisa Hello?
Ryan Hi, Amanda. It's me, Ryan.
Lisa Oh, hi!
Ryan I'm going to show you and your friend some of the sights tomorrow morning.
Lisa That's great. Where should we meet?
Ryan What about the entrance to the Empire State Building?
Lisa OK.
Ryan What time?
Lisa Well, we'll have to take the subway from Brooklyn. Ten o'clock?
Ryan Fine. Ten o'clock at the Empire State Building.
Lisa We'll see you then.

Now you arrange to meet someone. Put in some different phrases and create your own conversation.

tomorrow: Monday, Tuesday, etc
the Empire State Building: the Guggenheim Museum, Radio City in Rockefeller Center, etc
Brooklyn: Queens, 96th Street, etc
ten o'clock: nine thirty, ten fifteen, etc

ACTIVITIES 2

HIP HOP – OUR PHAT WAY OF LIFE

HISTORY

Hip hop and rap started in the ghettos of the South Bronx, New York thirty years ago. People there are poor, but hip hop gave them the freedom to express themselves. Many rappers got into trouble with the police because they stole money or expensive clothes, took drugs, … . Today, the music, slang and fashion of the African Americans and Hispanics have become popular all over the world.

MUSIC

Rap music has a strong beat. The rapper speaks in time with the beat and uses rhymes to tell us what life in the ghetto is like, how to get away from it and how to live on when friends die from drugs or in a shooting.

axe ask
bama someone from the country (for example Alabama)
b-boying break-dancing
BG baby gangster
Djing cutting and scratching at the (record) turntables
MCing (*also:* emceeing) rapping
phat great, fantastic (originally: physically attractive)
226 the police code for drugs

BREAK-DANCING

The dancing has to match the music and words of the rap songs. The body language and crazy movements need courage and years of practice. A lot of time is what most of the young break-dancers have because many of them don't have a job. Break-dancers have to be fit enough to do dangerous jumps like the spectacular butterfly along with other quick steps and movements.

FASHION/SHOES

Poor young people in the ghettos always had to wear the over-sized pants that once belonged to their older brothers – and now these phatman-pants have become a symbol for hip hop. They wear them without belts and they wear shoes without laces to show that they think of their friends in prison who have to leave belts and laces at the prison entrance to make sure that they can't kill themselves.

→ **page 159**

Hey, G, looking for some dead presidents? – What? Ya don't understand? Where tha hell R U from? Oh, errm … , sorry, I thought U're a BG and want to steal some dollars, and there's dead presidents on all the dollars. Ya know, once a bama axed me for some 226, you see, but I said no. So what? I live hip hop without drugs. It's our movement, it's my way of life. Yuk, just call me Eazy-D. I can tell ya more about hip hop, things ya won't believe. Hip hop has 4 phat elements: DJing, MCing, b-boying and graffiti art.

GRAFFITI WRITING

At first graffiti was sprayed on trains and walls at night. This was against the law, of course. The first graffiti artists had to put up with a lot of trouble before they were allowed to show their works to an audience. Today, many people like a great work of graffiti better than the grey wall it hides. But to many artists it only counts as real graffiti if you write and draw on walls in public places where it's not allowed.

OVER TO YOU

Do a hip-hop music project in class. Each group of four students finds out more about a group or a singer. You have ten minutes to tell in class about them, to play their music and show what kind of clothes they wear. You can also give a demonstration of their singing and dancing – if you want to.

seventeen **17**

Unit 1   **COMMUNICATION**

The international spelling alphabet

Desk clerk   Good morning. May I help you?
Mr Klasnov   I'd like to book a room for two nights, please. April 17 and 18.
Desk clerk   A single room or a double room?
Mr Klasnov   A single room, please.
Desk clerk   And your name, please?
Mr K.   It's Klasnov.
Clerk   How do you spell that, please?
Mr K.   K as in Kilo, L as in Lima, A as in Alpha, S as in Sierra, N as in November, O as in Oscar, and V as in Victor.
Clerk   Thank you, sir.

EXERCISE 17

Now you book a room for one night next week. Practice the conversation with a partner, but give your own name. Use the spelling alphabet to spell your name.

A ➤ Alpha	E ➤ Echo	I ➤ India	M ➤ Mike	Q ➤ Quebec	U ➤ Uniform	X ➤ X-ray
B ➤ Bravo	F ➤ Foxtrot	J ➤ Juliet	N ➤ November	R ➤ Romeo	V ➤ Victor	Y ➤ Yankee
C ➤ Charlie	G ➤ Golf	K ➤ Kilo	O ➤ Oscar	S ➤ Sierra	W ➤ Whiskey	Z ➤ Zulu
D ➤ Delta	H ➤ Hotel	L ➤ Lima	P ➤ Papa	T ➤ Tango		

TEST YOUR ENGLISH

Ellis Island

Not far from the Statue of Liberty is a small island called Ellis Island. It was once an immigration station,
5 and today it's a museum. It tells the story of the greatest movement of people that the world has ever known.

About 150 years ago, most of
10 the immigrants to the US came from Britain, Ireland, Germany and Scandinavia. Then in the years around 1900, a huge number of immigrants –
15 about a million each year – arrived in the US from southern and eastern Europe. Most came because they wanted to leave behind the hard
20 times they were living through in their own countries. Some wanted more freedom to have their own opinions or to follow their own religion. Many of
25 them were Jewish. A third of Europe's Jews went to the US, most of them to New York.

Ellis Island was for third-class passengers, those who didn't
30 have much money. After two weeks in dark and crowded conditions near the bottom of the ship, they were glad to reach New York.

35 The immigration building was very crowded, with sometimes as many as 15,000 people there in one day. It usually took between three and five hours
40 because everyone had to wait in line. Doctors examined the immigrants to see if they had any serious diseases, and immigration officers asked
45 them questions to make sure they should be allowed to enter the country. One person in fifty was not allowed to enter and had to return home.

50 Most of the people who came through Ellis Island were poor country people who spoke little or no English. They saw the US as a land of
55 opportunity, where life was much better than in Europe. Some of the new immigrants soon returned home because they didn't like life in the
60 crowded slums. But many stayed and made a new life for their families. Today 40% of Americans can look back to a family member who landed on
65 Ellis Island.

18   eighteen

TEST YOUR ENGLISH

1 Complete each sentence with a single word. The information you need is in the text.

1 Ellis Island is only a ... distance from the Statue of Liberty.
2 Around 1900 the number of ... to the US was greater than ever before.
3 People wanted to live in a country where they ... say and do what they liked.
4 The ships were ... of people from all over Europe.
5 On Ellis Island people had to wait for several ... .
6 They had to give the right ... to the immigration officers' questions.
7 Most of the passengers were country people who knew little about life in a big ... .

2 An immigration officer is asking a German woman some questions. Put in the interpreter's words.

Officer	Where have you come from?
Interpreter	Woher ... ?
Woman	Aus Weiden. Wir sind ab Bremen mit dem Schiff gefahren.
Interpreter	She has come ...
Officer	How many children do you have?
Interpreter	... ?
Woman	Drei Jungs.
Interpreter	...
Officer	Is your husband already here?
Interpreter	... ?
Woman	Ja, er ist seit sechs Monaten hier, und er hat Arbeit.
Interpreter	...
Officer	How much money do you have with you?
Interpreter	...
Woman	Zwanzig Dollar. Und mein Mann hat auch Geld.
Interpreter	...
Officer	Have you ever been to prison?
Interpreter	...
Woman	Was? Natürlich nicht!
Interpreter	...

Dear Stefan,

Hi, my name is Brian Lesemann. I don't know ... you can help me. I ... (try) to find out about my family's ... . My great-great-grandfather was ... in Bamberg, Germany in 1839. His name was Wolfgang Lesemann. He ... (sail) to the United ... from Hamburg on a ship ... the 'Bavaria'. The ship ... in New York City August 24, 1871. Wolfgang went ... live in Pittsburgh, Pennsylvania, where he ... in a glass factory.
A few years later he ... (marry) Margaret Schulz. She came from Wiesbaden. They had eight children. I ... like to find out something about them if I can. Are you interested ... the Lesemann family history? Do you have any information ... might help me?

Yours truly,

Brian Lesemann

3 Brian Lesemann lives in the US. He is writing to someone called Stefan Lesemann in Germany. He wants to find out if Stefan is a relative and if he knows anything about the history of the family. Complete Brian's letter. Put in the missing words or the correct form of the words in brackets.

4 Listen to the interview. Someone is asking a young woman called Angela Delgado about her family and her great-grandfather's voyage to America. As you listen, note down the following information.

1 the first name of Angela's great-grandfather
2 his age when he first arrived in America
3 what part of Italy he came from
4 two things that people did during the voyage to America
5 how many sisters Angela's great-grandfather had
6 what Angela did when she found out she had relatives in Italy
7 if Angela feels that she is Italian, Irish or American

nineteen 19

Unit 1   READING   **Public Enemy Number One**

America's first Public Enemy Number One was a bank robber called John Dillinger. The idea of a Public Enemy came from J. Edgar Hoover, head of the Federal Bureau of Investigation (FBI). But the public didn't see Dillinger as an enemy; they saw him as a hero.

5 John Dillinger was born in Indiana in 1903. His father was a farmer. At the age of 21 John tried to mug the owner of a grocery store. The police arrested him and he went to jail for nine years. While he was there he formed a gang and learned a lot about the best way to rob banks.

10 Dillinger came out of jail in May 1933, and a month later he robbed his first bank. He also smuggled some weapons into the jail so that his gang could shoot their way out. In January 1934 the gang were robbing the First National Bank in East Chicago when the alarm rang. As Dillinger was getting away, he shot a policeman dead.

15 The 1930s were hard times for most Americans. Millions of people had no work. Farmers borrowed money from the banks and couldn't pay it back, so the banks took the farms and threw the families out of their homes. The banks were not popular. Dillinger robbed banks, and in the eyes of the public he was the good guy. He was
20 also handsome and charming, so they forgot that he was a killer.

After Dillinger killed a policeman, he tried to get away to Mexico, but the police caught him. In jail he made a fake 'gun' from a piece of wood and fooled his guards with it. He walked out of the jail and around the corner and stole the sheriff's car. Most of the old gang were now dead or in jail, so Dillinger formed a new gang with the killer 'Baby Face' Nelson. In April 1934 they
25 robbed banks in South Dakota and Iowa.

Dillinger had a girlfriend called Billie Frechette, and he took her home to meet his family. While they ate a meal, Hoover's FBI agents surrounded the house. But John's nephew fooled the FBI. He hid his face as he drove away from the house. The FBI thought it was Dillinger, and they went
30 after the wrong car. The next day the FBI arrested Billie in Chicago, and she got two years. John never saw her again.

A few days later the FBI again surrounded the gang at an inn in Wisconsin. When three men left in a car, the FBI agents shot them, but they were the wrong men. The gang got away through a back window. Hoover was furious, but most people thought it was all a big joke. The newspapers
35 and magazines were full of stories about how clever Dillinger was and how stupid the FBI was.

In June 1934, Dillinger became the FBI's Public Enemy Number One. The FBI was looking everywhere for him. They didn't even know if he was still in the country. Actually he was in Chicago with two girlfriends, Polly Hamilton and Anna Sage. But Anna was no friend. She went to the FBI, and they gave her money for information about Dillinger. On July 22 he took
40 Polly and Anna to see a movie at the Biograph Theater in downtown Chicago. The FBI didn't know if they would recognize Dillinger, so Anna agreed to wear a red dress.

The movie was about a gangster who went to the electric chair. Dillinger's last words were, 'Wasn't that a
45 good movie?' He left the theater with the two women, Anna in her red dress. When an FBI agent behind him said, 'We've got you,' Dillinger ran away. Shots rang out, and he was dead when he hit the ground.

Dillinger in early 1934

UNIT 2
THE AMERICAN WAY OF LIFE

Columbus Day

Mardi Gras

Thanksgiving

Independence Day

14

WORDS AND PICTURES

Americans love their special days and holidays. They celebrate the New Year, Easter and Christmas, but they have their own holidays, too. A holiday is a
5 time to celebrate and have fun. And sometimes it's a time to feel proud.

Independence Day is the country's birthday, July 4. It's a big day in the American calendar. There are flags
10 everywhere. It's a day for a family picnic and for a firework display in the park.

Columbus Day is the second Monday in October. Although he didn't really
15 'discover America', Christopher Columbus is a big hero in the US. He is especially popular with Italian Americans, and there are big parades in New York.

20 Thanksgiving, the fourth Thursday in November, is a bit like Christmas. The family has a big meal with turkey. It celebrates the time when the early European settlers thanked God that
25 some of them survived their first winter in the New World.

There are special days for the whole population and special days for different parts of the US and for
30 different groups of people. On March 17, St Patrick's Day, Irish-Americans have their big day. There are parades in New York and Chicago, and people wear green clothes.
35 In New Orleans, Mardi Gras is a special day, the last day of carnival week. There are parades, music, wonderful costumes and dancing in the streets. And later in the year,
40 German Americans in the Midwest celebrate the Oktoberfest.

twenty-one **21**

Unit 2   **INTRODUCTION 1**

  SITUATION 1

15

Jennifer Hansen is 16, and she lives with her parents in Tillamook, Oregon, on the west coast of America. Tillamook is a small town with a population of only 4,000. There are more cows than people, and the place is famous for its cheese. People go to Tillamook for 'cheese, trees and ocean breeze'. It's a long way from the skyscrapers of Manhattan.

At the Tillamook Cheese Visitor Center, you can see how cheese is made. Free samples of the famous cheese are offered to visitors. Milk products like cheese, butter and yogurt are sold in the store. There's also an ice-cream counter with lots of different kinds of yummy ice-cream. On a typical summer day, 4,000 ice-creams are served here. Altogether almost a million people visit Tillamook's cheese factory every year.

EXERCISE 1

Look at the pictures and tell the story of cheese from the cow to the supermarket.

The passive voice	→ page 103-104
Active	Passive
They **make** cheese.	Cheese **is made**.
The company **sells** milk products.	Milk products **are sold**.

▸ Milking the cows on the farm

1 Delivering the milk to the factory

2 Making the cheese in the factory

3 Cutting large blocks of cheese

4 Keeping the blocks cool for 60 days

5 Tasting a sample

6 Cutting and packing smaller pieces

7 Delivering the cheese to the store

8 Putting the cheese on the shelf

▸ The cows **are milked** on the farm. After that the milk ... . Then the cheese ... . Then the ...

22   twenty-two

INTRODUCTION 1

SITUATION 2

16 Jennifer has just met her friend Susan.

Jennifer Did you hear about Mrs Howard?
Susan No. What about her?
Jennifer She was in an accident this morning. Her car was hit by a bus and she was taken to hospital.
Susan Oh no!
Jennifer Two other people were injured in the accident.
Susan Was Mrs Howard badly hurt?
Jennifer They say she's going to be OK. But she won't be back in school for a few days.
Susan I've got biology with her in the last period.
Jennifer She takes us for physics. The class was taught by Mr Quinn this morning.

The by-agent → page 105

Active	Passive
An ambulance **took** her to hospital.	She **was taken** to hospital.
The crash **injured** two other people.	Two other people **were injured**.
	Passive with by
A bus **hit** her car.	Her car **was hit by** a bus.
Mr Quinn **taught** the class.	The class **was taught by** Mr Quinn.

EXERCISE 2

Read this paragraph about the internet.

Every day many millions of people go on the internet. It is used by all kinds of people for all kinds of purposes. People sit for hours in front of their computers. Information is read, downloaded and printed. Millions do their shopping on the internet. Things are bought and sold every second of the day and night. Huge numbers of e-mails are sent around the world. People enter chat rooms and talk to other people with computers. Important matters are discussed – and some not so important ones.

It is the year 3000. Someone is writing a magazine article about the internet. Complete the paragraph.
A thousand years ago something called the internet was very popular. Many millions of people went on the internet. It was …

EXERCISE 3

What can you remember? Make sentences from the table. Use the passive.

Hadrian's Wall (build)		black people in Harlem.
The poor young man in 'Titanic' (play)		the French.
The old missions in California (build)		Guy Fawkes.
The Mary Rose (sink)	by	Leonardo DiCaprio.
'Wannabe' (sing)		the Romans.
Harold of England and his men (defeat)		the Spanish.
Hip hop (start)		the Spice Girls.
Some gunpowder (hide) in a cellar		William of Normandy.

➥ Hadrian's Wall was built by the Romans.

twenty-three 23

Unit 2 **TEXT 1**

Jennifer's year

Jennifer Hansen goes to a high school in Tillamook, Oregon. She's got a new pen pal called Katja. Katja lives in Germany. Jennifer is sending her an e-mail with some photos.

Dear Katja,

Thank you for the nice e-mail you sent me. I'm glad you want to be my pen pal.

You asked about my school. Well, there are just three more days left before the summer vacation, so I have a whole year to talk about.

The name of my school is Tillamook High School. Everyone in Tillamook goes to the same school. It's a four year school, and I'm a junior, that's the third year. Next year I'll be a senior, and then I'll graduate. After that I'll go to college.

My schedule is the same every day. I'm taking physics, biology, English, French, US history, math and annual production. (I'm afraid German isn't taught at our school.) I think most of the classes are like your classes except annual production. This class puts together the yearbook, a book that has everyone's picture in it and details about the things we've done in the last school year.

Each class period is 55 minutes long, with five minutes between to get to your next class. We also have 30 minutes for lunch. We can eat lunch at school in the cafeteria, or we can leave and eat somewhere else. Once a week my friends and I go out to a fast food place. The rest of the time I eat at my house.

There are a lot of different activities that I've taken part in this year. I like sports. Even before classes started, I was practicing volleyball. After volleyball season, it was basketball. I play tennis, too.

You've probably heard about cheerleaders. My friend Susan is one. At football games, the cheerleaders sing songs and lead the cheering. It's taken very seriously.

There were many other activities. Each year our school puts on a musical, and this time it was 'West Side Story'. I got a small part. It meant a lot of practice, but I loved it.

For ten days in February we had a big drive, and the money was given to a children's hospital. I washed cars and helped to put on a boxing show. We worked hard for every dollar and cent. Our class made $27,000. The seniors made the most with $35,000, and we were in second place. Altogether a total of more than $103,000 was collected by the students. Not bad for a town of 4,000 people.

I went to some good dances. I really enjoyed the Winter Formal this year. I was asked by a guy who plays on the football team. He's called Carlos. We went to a nice restaurant and had seafood. Then it was on to the dance. The theme was 'Winter in the Park'. The hall was beautifully decorated. There were trees with snow on them and little white lights. The DJ played great music. It was a wonderful dance.

In November I was 16. I passed my driving test, and now I have my license. I can borrow the car — which is great.

As you can see, it's been a busy year for me. Now I have to think about which college I want to go to after I graduate next year.

I hope you can download the photos. Write soon.

Love, Jennifer

TEXT 1

EXERCISE 4

Choose the correct answer and find the words in the text which show that it is right.

➡ The school year
  a) has just begun b) is almost over.
  The answer is **b**.
  There are just three more days left before the summer vacation.
1 Jennifer is in
  a) her junior year b) her senior year.
2 Jennifer's day always starts with
  a) the same class b) a different class.
3 She usually has her lunch
  a) in the cafeteria b) at a fast food place
  c) at home.
4 At the beginning of the school year Jennifer played a lot of
  a) volleyball b) basketball c) tennis.
5 She also
  a) had a part in the school musical
  b) wrote articles for the school newspaper.
6 The purpose of the drive was to
  a) clean the school
  b) learn about money
  c) help children who are ill.
7 Jennifer and Carlos had a meal
  a) before the dance b) after the dance.
8 Jennifer a) is learning to drive
  b) can already drive.

EXERCISE 5

Explain these words from Jennifer's e-mail.

1 a pen pal   6   annual production
2 a junior   7   a cheerleader
3 a senior   8   a drive
4 college   9   the Winter Formal
5 a schedule   10   a driving test

EXERCISE 6

Imagine that Jennifer has sent the e-mail to you. Write an e-mail to send back to her. Tell her about your school and how it is different from an American high school. Include information about your class, the subjects you do, your schedule, where you have lunch, and so on. You can also write about things you do outside school.

twenty-five **25**

Unit 2 **TEXT 1**

EXERCISE 7

Put each verb into the simple past. Decide if the verb has to be active or passive.

At the beginning of the 19th century the United States **had** (have) a great opportunity to move into the land to the west. An expedition **was organized** (organize) to find out about the area. The expedition … (lead) by Meriwether Lewis and William Clark.

On 4 May 1804 Lewis and Clark … (leave) St Louis for their 7,000-mile expedition. The 45 members of the expedition … (travel) in three boats. They … (help) by an Indian guide. In the summer of 1805 they … (cross) the Rocky Mountains on foot, and in November they … (reach) the Pacific Ocean on the coast of what is now the state of Oregon.

Luckily they … (not attack) by Indians. Once Lewis … (hit) in the leg when a member of the expedition … (fire) a gun, but that was an accident.

Everything that Lewis and Clark … (see) on the expedition … (describe) in detail in their diaries. They … (discover) 122 animals that white people … (not know) about before. The group … (return) to St Louis in 1806, where they … (welcome) by people who … (think) they must be long dead.

EXERCISE 8

18+19

Listening

Allison wants to see a movie. She's telling her boyfriend Jordan about it. Listen to Part 1 of their conversation. Then make Jordan's diary for next week. Copy the diary page with the days of the week. Write the activities on a piece of paper and cut out each activity. Listen to Part 1 again and put the pieces of paper in the right place on the diary.

Now listen to Part 2. Put 'Movie with Allison' in the right place and take away the activity that Jordan will miss.

EXERCISE 9

Work with a partner. One of you should look at this page, and the other should look at page 94.

Now arrange a game of tennis this weekend with your partner. Begin like this:

You How about a game of tennis this weekend?
Partner Good idea.
You How about Friday evening?
Partner Sorry, I can't on Friday. I'm going …

ACTIVITIES 1

1 SQUANTO

The Wampanoag Indians saw the animals as their brothers and the forest as their mother. When they killed a buffalo, they always left some meat to help the smaller animals to survive. The first settlers from Europe, the Pilgrims, had to go through a hard winter. Half of them died, because they didn't know how to grow food on the new land. They were able to survive only because they met a Wampanoag called Squanto. He had learned the English language from other visitors – and he decided to help those poor people. He stayed with them for a few months, brought them food, built houses and taught them how to grow vegetables.

In the fall of 1621, the Pilgrims invited the Wampanoag people to their first harvest festival. For three days they celebrated Thanksgiving with a big meal. They had wild turkey, pumpkin, corn – the most important food the Indians had – and cranberries. Did you know that many common words like tomato, pumpkin, banana and potato have an Indian origin? Try to find some more.

Today, however, you can't find many Wampanoag people in Massachusetts any more. This is an extract from a Thanksgiving speech by a Wampanoag called Frank James:

Today is a time for celebration for you – a time of looking back to the first days of white people in America. But it is not a time for celebration for me. It is with a heavy heart that I look back upon what happened to my people. When the Pilgrims arrived, we, the Wampanoags, welcomed them with open arms, little knowing that it was the beginning of the end, that we and other Indians living near the settlers would be killed by their guns or die from diseases that we caught from them. Let us always remember, the Indian is and was just as human as a white person.

→ page 159

2 OVER TO YOU

Find out more about harvest festivals in other countries, for example in China and Africa.

3 BLUEBERRY PANCAKES

Have you ever had pancakes for breakfast? Millions of Americans wake up to blueberry pancakes …

This is what you need

50 g of butter	50 g of sour cream (10% fat)
2 eggs	
250 ml of milk	500 g of fresh or frozen blueberries
250 g of flour	
salt, maple syrup	

- Heat the butter in a pan and let it cool down again.
- Mix the eggs, butter, milk, flour, sour cream and a little salt in a bowl.
- Leave the batter for about an hour.
- Wash the blueberries.
- Heat some butter in the pan, add some batter and make flat pancakes. Spread some blueberries on them. Turn them over as soon as one side is golden.
- Go on in this way.

Serve them with maple syrup. Enjoy!

twenty-seven 27

Unit 2   INTRODUCTION 2

SITUATION 3
21 Sports are big in the US. They are part of the American way of life. Sports stars are paid huge amounts of money and treated like heroes. Football, baseball and basketball are all popular. Football is the game that people outside the US call American football. The game that the rest of the world calls football is called soccer in the US.

Every high school and college has its sports teams. There's everything from girls' soccer to men's volleyball. Inter-school games are big events, and they're given a lot of attention in local newspapers.

EXERCISE 10

Brandon Bone is a big basketball star. He lives in Boston and plays for the East Coast Kings. He's very rich. Read the information about him and put the verbs into the passive.

Man gab mir eine Karte.
I was given a ticket.

→ page 105

Brandon Bone is the most famous and the richest basketball player in the world. He is paid (pay) a lot of money. The other players on the team ... (pay) a lot, too, but Brandon gets the most. He ... (give) a new car every year. And all the players ... (give) free food by a big supermarket every week. Last year Brandon ... (offer) ten million dollars to move to another club, but he didn't take it. Now he ... (pay) an extra ten thousand dollars each time he throws a basket. Earlier this year he ... (pay) two million dollars to wear a certain kind of sports shoe. But bad things have happened to Brandon, too. Once he ... (send) a letter bomb. After that he ... (give) two security guards by his club. One or the other is with him the whole time.

SITUATION 4
22
Melissa	Have you seen the new soccer field?
Rachel	No, I didn't know there was one.
Melissa	It's next to the school. It's just been built. Why don't you come and play – join the club?
Rachel	How good is the team?
Melissa	Well, we've been beaten quite easily in our first two games, so we need some new players.

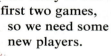

One of my pompoms has been stolen.

→ page 104

28   twenty-eight

INTRODUCTION 2

EXERCISE 11

These are all headlines from newspapers. Write them as full sentences. Use the passive of the present perfect.

- **New airport built**
- Truck driver sent to prison
- Grizzly bears seen near apartment block
- Man's body discovered in river
- President invited to visit Germany
- MONEY COLLECTED BY COLLEGE STUDENTS
- Four killed in road accident

» A new airport has been built.

SITUATION 5

POOL DATES

The swimming pool will open on May 30 and will close on Sept. 1. Opening hours will be from 1 P.M. to 6 P.M. The cost of a daily ticket will be increased to $3 for those 13 and over and $2 for children aged 12 and under. Family season tickets are $75, and individual season tickets are $30. These tickets can be bought at the pool during daily opening hours. Children aged 12 and under must be looked after by an adult.

The passive with modals → page 104

Active	Passive
We will clean the pool.	The pool will be cleaned.
You can buy tickets now.	Tickets can be bought now.
Someone must finish the job.	The job must be finished.
We should decorate the hall.	The hall should be decorated.

EXERCISE 12

Look at these actions.

touch   throw   catch   bounce   kick   hold   hit

Now read this paragraph.

In (American) football the ball can be thrown or kicked. It can be thrown backwards or forwards. A player can also run with the ball. The aim is to score a touchdown or to kick a goal. When a player is holding the ball, players on the other team are allowed to tackle him and throw him to the ground. Football is a violent game, and the right equipment should be worn.

Now complete this paragraph about soccer.

In soccer the ball is usually ... with the foot. It can't ... . The goalkeeper is the only ... who is allowed ... . When a player has the ball, he or she can ... , but ... pulled down. The aim is to ... .

EXERCISE 13

Find out about the rules of basketball. What's the aim of the game? Can the ball be held, thrown, bounced or kicked? Explain some of the more important rules to your classmates.

Choose another sport you like and tell your classmates the rules in about 80 words.

twenty-nine 29

Unit 2   TEXT 2

The AMERICAN SUPER BOWL
24

Football is America's most popular game, and the most important event in the American football season is the Super Bowl – the national professional football
⁵ championship game. Every year the Super Bowl is the most popular program on television. During the game, few cars are on the streets and highways, few telephone calls are made, and everything stops for the day. 'Super Bowl
¹⁰ Sunday' is treated like a national holiday.

At the end of each football season the ten top teams play in a series of games called play-offs. When all the play-offs have been played, the two winners then play one final
¹⁵ game to decide the national championship – the Super Bowl. This game takes place in January, and the host city changes every year. For example, it might be Miami, Los Angeles or New Orleans.

²⁰ However, the Super Bowl isn't just a football game. There are spectacular shows the night before and even at half time of the game. Hollywood directors create song, dance and fireworks programs that
²⁵ have some of the most famous entertainment superstars in them.

In the week before the game, the tension builds up. All over the US you can hear conversations like this.
'I guess the Super Bowl is going to be a pretty close game.'
³⁰ 'I think the Giants are going to win.'
'Are you crazy? The Ravens have got a much better team. And they play as a team. They're
³⁵ confident, and they're strong in defense. They didn't give away too many points in the play-offs. I guess their defense is one of the greatest in the
⁴⁰ history of the game.'
'Well, we'll see what happens.'
'Have you been invited to our Super Bowl party, Jeff?'
'No, I didn't know about a party.'
'Well, why don't you come over on Sunday? We're having
⁴⁵ about twenty people over to watch the game on TV.'
'OK, I'd like to be there. Thanks, Bob. See you Sunday.'

30   thirty

TEXT 2

The Super Bowl is a big television event. The whole game can be seen live on TV. It is watched by about half the population of the US and worldwide by about 750 million
5 people. The game makes a lot of money for the television networks because they are paid a lot of money for commercials. If you want to put a commercial on the Super Bowl program, it will cost you $2,600,000 for each
10 minute. Because of the huge cost, most commercials are short – about 15 seconds. But there are lots of them. If you're watching the game, you'll see over a hundred commercials.

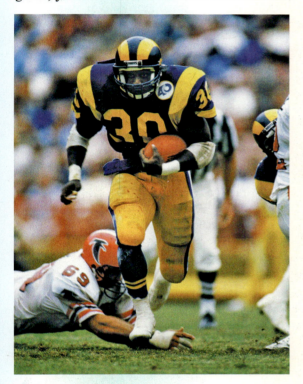

The Super Bowl has developed into the
15 ultimate sport and media event and the players are treated like heroes. Some people say that the idea of sport has been lost among
20 all the advertising, entertainment and parties. But no one can deny that it has become a big day in
25 the American calendar.

EXERCISE 14

Each of these headings goes with a paragraph in the text. Put them all in the right order.

a) Does the event have anything to do with sport?
b) Everyone is talking about the Super Bowl.
c) It's not only football but also entertainment.
d) Television and money are an important part of the Super Bowl.
e) The Super Bowl is a huge event for Americans.
f) Two teams meet at the end of the season.

EXERCISE 15

Answer these questions in one or two sentences.

1 How popular is American football in Europe? Is it on television? Are there any clubs in Europe?
2 What is your favorite sport? Where do you play or watch it? Is it played worldwide?

EXERCISE 16

Complete the sentences. Put in the correct form of *get, make, put* or *take*.

➤ I **took** these photos of the game.
1 We're … ready for our Super Bowl party.
2 The game is starting soon, so I'll … the TV on.
3 I must just … a phone call before the program starts.
4 At half time of the game they … on a wonderful song and dance show.
5 If you want to be in the team, you'll have to … fit first.
6 Tom had a chance to score, but he … a complete mess of it.
7 You … this game too seriously, you know.
8 The game … place in a violent storm.
9 Are you … part in the parade next weekend?
10 It … us hours to … the long journey home after the game last week.

Now translate the sentences into German. The verbs *get, put, take* and *make* have many different meanings, so be careful how you translate them. If you need to, look in a dictionary and find the meaning of the whole phrase.

➤ take a photo = *ein Foto machen*
   Ich habe diese Fotos vom Spiel gemacht.

If you can't find a phrase like *take a photo* under *take*, then you might find it under *photo*.

thirty-one 31

Unit 2 TEXT 2

EXERCISE 17

Add passive sentences using the information in brackets. Look at these two examples.

➤ The parade will be a big event. **It will be shown on television.**
  (They will show it on television.)
➤ Jennifer takes biology. **The class is taught by Mrs Long.**
  (Mrs Long teaches the class.)
1 This is wonderful cheese. … . (They make the cheese in Tillamook.)
2 Don't throw those bottles away. … . (We can recycle them.)
3 The college has a ghost. … . (Several students have seen the ghost.)
4 Independence Day is America's birthday. … . (People celebrate it on July 4.)
5 Our classroom looks much nicer now. … . (They have decorated it.)
6 Our neighbor is very rich. He writes pop songs. … . (They pay him huge amounts of money.)
7 We'll need some new costumes for the musical. … . (The Drama Club members and their parents will make them.)
8 At the big game there was a lot of cheering. … . (The cheerleaders from our school led it.)

EXERCISE 18

Write the story of what happened to Erica.

You can begin like this: *Erica and her classmates traveled to …*
What do you think happened after the accident? How badly was Erica hurt?
Think of an ending and complete the story in your own words.

ACTIVITIES 2

1 MEMBERS OF YOUR FAMILY IN THE STATES

Are you interested in your family history? Have you ever wondered if you have relatives in the US? You might have a great-great-grandfather or grandmother who left Germany, Russia or Poland a hundred years ago to make a new life as an immigrant there. The internet can help you to find out more. Maybe you'll find new pen pals with the same family name or maybe even members of your own family. Try different spellings of your surname, for example: Oberhellmann ➜ Oberhelman. On some websites you find the e-mail addresses of people who are looking for European relatives.
Why don't you send them an e-mail to ask if they know anything about the origins of their family?
Tell your class what you have found out: In which states do people with your surname live? How many of them answered your e-mails?

- Start your e-mail politely.
- Tell them who you are.
- Add where you've found their e-mail address.
- Give them information on your family history (any relatives who went to the US?).
- Explain any other useful details.
- Ask the family what they know about any relatives in Europe.
- Ask them to e-mail back.
- Find a friendly ending.

2 NEW FRIENDS IN THE STATES

Find new e-mail pen pals in the US. Ask your teacher for websites with links to American high schools. You can have a look at photos and articles from different schools before you decide on a partner school for your e-mails. Send an e-mail to the school and ask if a student or a class is interested in writing back. You can use these sentences.

Dear Sir or Madam
My name is *** and I'm writing to you because ***. I go to *** Realschule in ***, that's in Bavaria/Germany. My home town is a special place because ***. I'm *** old and my hobbies are *** and ***. My favourite bands are *** and ***. I also like ***. I'm looking for an American e-mail partner. He/she should *** and ***. Can you help me? Maybe one of your pupils is interested in ***.

➜ page 159

Sign in Fredericksburg, Texas

3 US CITIES WITH GERMAN NAMES

Search maps and the internet for German place names in the US. For example, you can find Frankenmuth, Berlin, Carlsbad, Frankfort, Bismarck, ... and many more. In which US state can you find a lot of German place names? Find out more about these cities and villages. Do they still have German traditions and celebrate German holidays for example? Somebody might be interested in answering your e-mail. Can you find your home town in the US?

thirty-three 33

Unit 2 **COMMUNICATION**

○ 25

When you don't understand

Sarah A lot of Hispanic people live in this area.
Daniel Sorry. What does 'Hispanic' mean?
Sarah Oh, people from countries where they speak Spanish. You know, Cuba or Puerto Rico or South America.
Daniel Oh, I see. Yes, there are a lot of signs in Spanish, aren't there?

Here are some ways of asking about the meaning of a word.

- Sorry. What's 'annual production'?
- What exactly are 'nachos'?
- What does 'breeze' mean?
- Sorry, but could you explain what 'Mardi Gras' means, please?

EXERCISE 19

Work with a partner and practice asking about and explaining the meaning of each word in italics. Start your conversations with these sentences.

➡ I wouldn't like to live in a *slum*.
Sorry. What's a 'slum'?
Well, if you live in a slum, you live in a part of town where the conditions are very bad.
1 Is there an *elevator* in the building?
2 We'll stay in Manhattan. We won't have time to visit the other *boroughs*.
3 I'm traveling home for *Thanksgiving*.
4 My brother plays baseball. He's a *pitcher*.

TEST YOUR ENGLISH

Technology? No, thanks!

Americans have always been good at inventing things. The telephone, the electric light, the camera, the elevator and many other useful things were
5 invented in the US. Americans are also good at developing new products and making and selling them. Even though the automobile was invented in Germany, they were first made in
10 large numbers in the US. Even though the computer was invented in Britain, today it is the US that leads the world in computers and computer software. But not everyone in the US is happy
15 with new inventions. The Amish people refuse to use them.

The Amish first came to America from Europe 300 years ago because they wanted freedom to follow their
20 religion. They settled in Pennsylvania, the Midwest and Canada. In Pennsylvania they are called the Pennsylvania Dutch, but this really means German (*deutsch*).

25 The Amish lead simple lives. They wear black clothes and no jewelry. They are good farmers, but they refuse to use modern machines. They use horses but not cars. They do not use telephones or electric lights. Some Amish people refuse to send their children to high school.

30 The Amish have become a big tourist attraction, and every year millions of people visit Lancaster County, Pennsylvania, where many Amish people live. The area now has lots of hotels, restaurants, gas stations,
35 souvenir shops and long lines of traffic.

Because of all this tourist activity, some of the Amish have moved to other states
40 where they might be left alone to follow their own way of life.

34 thirty-four

TEST YOUR ENGLISH

1 Name these things. They are all mentioned in the text.

1. four things that were invented in the US
2. two things that were invented in Europe
3. three places where the Amish settled
4. three useful things that the Amish refuse to use
5. four kinds of buildings that tourists might use in Lancaster County

2 Look at these explanations and find the words in the text.

1. something that is made and sold
2. be ahead of everyone else
3. say that you won't do something
4. go and live in a place
5. things you wear
6. something that people want to visit
7. something that will always remind you of your visit

3 Translate this information into German.

Lancaster County

Lancaster County is still a beautiful place, even though in some parts hotels and restaurants have been built for the many visitors. It is good farming country, and there are quiet country roads to drive or cycle along. If you see any Amish people, remember not to take their photo because this goes against their religion. If you want to learn more about them, you should visit the People's Place in Intercourse, 11 miles east of Lancaster City.

4 Complete this paragraph about the movie *Witness*. Put in the missing words or the correct form of the words in brackets.

There's a movie called 'Witness' … has some Amish characters in it. They are Rachel, a widow, and her ten-year-old son Samuel. Rachel and Samuel are traveling to Baltimore … visit some friends, and they have to … trains in Philadelphia. When Samuel … visiting the bathroom there, he witnesses a terrible murder. John Book is the detective who has to … the killer. The detective … (play) by Harrison Ford. He asks Samuel some … about the murder. Samuel sees a photo … the killer on a poster. The killer is a detective … job is to arrest people who sell drugs. John finds … that a number of corrupt detectives are … (secret / help) people in the drugs trade. These corrupt policemen try … kill John, and he is afraid they want to kill Samuel too. He takes Rachel and Samuel back to the Amish country where they will be … . Here John learns a lot … the world of the Amish. He starts to fall … love with Rachel.

5 Listen to the interview with Annie Stoltzfus. She comes from an Amish family, but she no longer lives in the Amish community. Answer the questions.

Part 1 (26)

1. How old was Annie when she left Lancaster County?
2. What was her job before she left?
3. Where does she live now?
4. What two things does Annie mention that the Amish are not allowed to use?
5. How did Annie feel before she left the Amish community?
   a) alone b) free c) happy d) shut in

Part 2 (27)

6. What work does Annie do now?
7. What does she do in her free time?
8. What is the good thing about the Amish way of life, in Annie's opinion?
   a) You always have a job.
   b) You are a member of a real community.
   c) There is no crime.

Unit 2   READING   **Which way now?**

I drove and drove, through flat farming country and little towns with no sign of life: Hull, Pittsfield, Barry, Oxville. On my map Springfield, Illinois, was about two inches to the right of Hannibal, Missouri, but it seemed to take hours to get there. That's because it really took hours to get there. In America, states are the size of countries. Illinois is almost twice as big as Austria, four
5 times the size of Switzerland. There is so much empty space between towns. You go through a little place and the café looks crowded, so you think, 'Oh, I'll wait till I get to Fuddville before I stop for coffee,' because it's only just down the road, and then you get out on the highway and a sign says FUDDVILLE 102 MILES. And you realize that this is a very different kind of geography.

When you leave the main roads, it becomes difficult to find your way around. Near Jacksonville
10 I missed a left turn for Springfield and had to go miles out of my way to get back to where I wanted to be. This happens a lot in America. Often on country roads you will come to a crossroads without any signposts and then have to drive twenty miles or more not sure where you are. And then suddenly you go round a bend and you're at an eight-lane intersection with fourteen traffic lights and a large number of signs, all with arrows that are pointing in different directions.

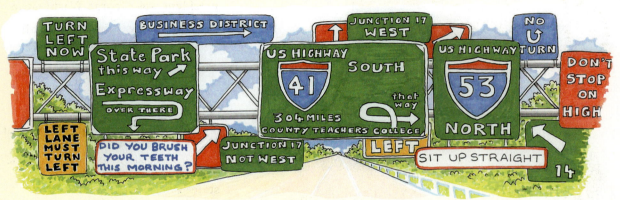

15 Just as you realize that you should be three lanes to the left, the lights change and you are taken away with the traffic like a cork on a fast river. This kind of thing happened to my father all the time. Every time dad went through a really big and important intersection, he came out of it somewhere he didn't want to be – a black hole of one-way streets or an expressway into the desert. Something my father often did was to lose the way when we could actually see the place we were
20 going to. Every time he arrived at an amusement park or tourist attraction, he first came to it from several directions. My sister and brother and I could always see it on the other side of the freeway. 'There it is! There it is!' we cried. Then after a minute we saw it from another direction on the other side of a factory. And then across a river. And then on the other side of the freeway again. Sometimes all that came between us and our goal was a high chain-link fence. On the other
25 side you could see happy families who were parking their cars and getting ready for a wonderful day. 'How did they get in there?' my dad cried. 'Why can't the city put up some signs, for Christ's sake? It's no wonder you can't find your way into the place,' he added. He forgot that 18,000 other people, some of them not especially clever, were already on the right side of the fence.

(adapted from Bill Bryson *The Lost Continent*)

Bill Bryson was born in Des Moines, Iowa in 1951. *The Lost Continent* was his first book. Bryson wanted to
30 find the typical small American town that he remembered from the movies he watched as a boy. He drove 14,000 miles, saw lots of gas stations and fast food places, but had little chance of finding that small town he was looking for. However, he wrote a wonderfully funny report on his journey.
Bryson lived in England for almost twenty years, and then in 1996 he moved back to America with his English wife and four children. *The Lost Continent* was followed by other travel books and by books on the
35 English language. Bill Bryson is hugely popular in Britain.

UNIT 3
LOOKING BACK

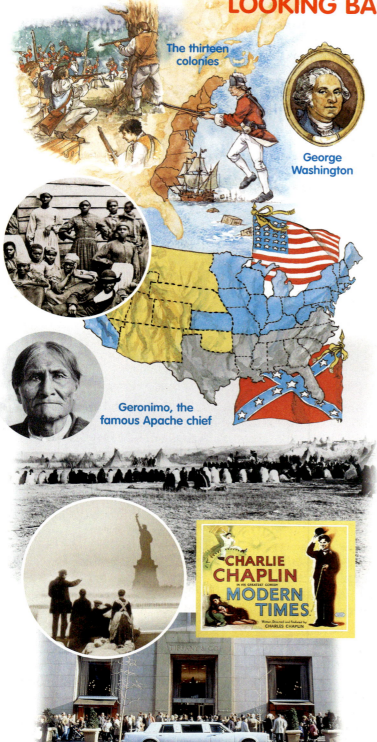

The thirteen colonies

George Washington

Geronimo, the famous Apache chief

WORDS AND PICTURES

In 1775 there were thirteen British colonies along the east coast of North America. In that year the war with Britain began that led to their independence. The colonies won the war and became the United States of America. The first president was George Washington.

The Americans believed that 'all men are created equal', but only rich white men had the right to vote. Black people had to work as slaves on the plantations of the South.

The Civil War (1861-65) was fought over the question of slavery. The North wanted to abolish it, but the South didn't agree. The southern states tried to break away. They were defeated by the North under President Abraham Lincoln, and slavery was abolished.

The Native Americans weren't equal either. They lost their land as the settlers moved west in the 19th century. Soon the United States went from coast to coast. Millions of immigrants came from Europe to America, where they hoped for a better life. They saw America as a land of opportunity. It had tall skyscrapers and wide open spaces.

The 20th century was the American century. Hollywood became the center of the movie industry. American products were sold all over the world. The United States landed a man on the moon. Most Americans had a high standard of living and were able to enjoy the good life.

thirty-seven 37

Unit 3   **INTRODUCTION 1**

● **SITUATION 1**

29

In the autumn of 1620 a group of more than a hundred people sailed from England to North America in their ship the Mayflower. These
5 people were called the Pilgrims. When they landed in December, they had been at sea for six weeks. They had decided to make the long voyage because they wanted to follow
10 their own religion and to have a better life in the New World. At first they had a hard time, but they were helped by the Indians, and the colony survived. After they had gotten through the first year, the Pilgrims started the
15 tradition of the Thanksgiving dinner.

The Pilgrims are the most famous of the early colonists. They landed near Plymouth Rock in Massachusetts, a place which is now visited by thousands of tourists every year.

20 But the Pilgrims were not the first colonists. There had been a British colony in Virginia since 1607. The Spanish had already settled in Florida and
25 New Mexico, where they had built missions. The French had arrived in Florida even earlier and had explored the Great Lakes region. The Pilgrims weren't even the first Europeans in Massachusetts. In the time before the Pilgrims
30 arrived, fishing boats from Europe often landed on the coast.

The simple past means a time in the past.

Simple past	Past perfect
I felt really tired last night. I had walked a long way.
When the girls came out of the store, they had spent all their money.
We finally reached the top of the statue after we had climbed 354 steps.

→ page 107

The past perfect means a time before that.

EXERCISE 1

Use the correct form of the verbs. Each time there is one verb in the simple past and one in the past perfect. Use the past perfect for what came first.

➡ The Pilgrims decided to leave England because their religion had created problems for them.
➡ Just over a hundred people had joined the group when the ship finally left England on 16 September.
1 The Pilgrims (sail) in the Mayflower, a ship which previously (carry) wine from France to England.
2 The Pilgrims (land) on the coast of North America in December 1620. Their voyage (be) long and difficult.
3 They (not be) the first colonists because the Spanish (settle) in Florida over 50 years before.
4 The Pilgrims (bring) the wrong kind of equipment with them, so they (find) it difficult to survive as farmers.
5 A couple of the Indians (learn) English from earlier visitors, so they (be) able to talk to the Pilgrims.
6 After a few months things (look) bad for the colonists. Half of them (die).
7 The others (eat) a Thanksgiving dinner to thank God that they (survive).
8 They (invite) the Indians who (help) them in the early days.
9 In 1957 a ship called Mayflower II (sail) from England to America, just like the first Mayflower (do) over three centuries before.

38   thirty-eight

INTRODUCTION 1

SITUATION 2

30

Kevin Where were you yesterday, Amber?
Amber Oh, my Aunt Laura and my cousin Megan are staying with us, and we drove to Williamsburg and looked around there.
Kevin Did you have a good time?
Amber Well, it was OK, but I'd been there twice before. Megan enjoyed it because she hadn't seen it before. But we were all pretty tired after that. We'd been to Richmond in the morning.

Kevin That sounds like a long day.
Amber And my dad got mad with my mom.
Kevin Why? What had she done?
Amber Nothing serious. She took a wrong turn and we went a few miles the wrong way. She said my dad wasn't reading the map right. They had a big fight.

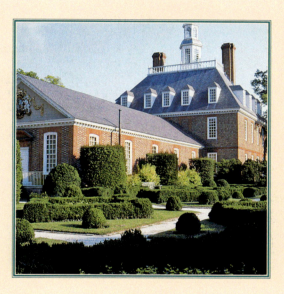

Williamsburg was settled in 1633. It became the capital and largest city of Virginia, but after the state government had moved to Richmond in 1780, Williamsburg became less important. Today you can look around the beautiful old buildings. You can also visit lots of gift shops.

EXERCISE 2

Complete the conversation. Put the verbs in the past perfect. Use a short form (*'d* or *hadn't*) in the statements where possible.

> **The past perfect** → page 106-107
>
> | | |
> |---|---|
> | | **Megan had heard** about Williamsburg before. |
> | **Short form** | **She'd learned** about it in her American history class. |
> | **Negative** | But she **hadn't visited** it before. |
> | **Question** | How many times **had Amber been** there? |

▶ *Jessica* I finally found that computer disk.
   Nicole Oh, good. What **had** you **done** (do) with it?
   Jessica **I'd put** (put) it in my purse.

1 *Natasha* I saw Justin last week. He … (just / be) on vacation with his family.
  Matthew Oh, where … (they / be)?
  Natasha They spent two weeks in Hawaii. He said they … (really / enjoy) it.

2 *Joseph* Did you get wet in all that rain yesterday?
  Brandon Yes, I did. I … (not / take) my umbrella with me. I … (leave) it at home.

3 *Katie* What did you two decide to do in the end? Go to the zoo?
  Adam Yes, we did. But we were too early. It … (not / open) when we got there. It doesn't open till eleven o'clock.
  Danielle It was my fault. I … (not / check) the opening times.

4 *Antonio* I was worried when Jennifer was so late. I waited ages for her.
  Natasha … (something / happen) to her?
  Antonio Her car … (break) down. I was worried that maybe she … (have) an accident.

thirty-nine 39

Unit 3 **TEXT 1**

Pocahontas

One day in April in the
year 1607, three ships
arrived at the mouth of
a river on the east coast
5 of Virginia in North
America. They carried
105 men, all those
who had survived the
five-month voyage from
10 England. (39 had died
on the way.) They called
the river the James River,
after their king, James I. They sailed up the
river and looked for a place where they could
15 start a colony. They chose an island in the
river. They called it – can you guess? –
Jamestown. It wasn't a very healthy place
because the water was bad. Less than half
of the settlers survived the first year.

20 When Europeans first sailed to America,
they did not find an empty continent. Native
Americans were already living there in
hundreds of different tribes. Christopher
Columbus called them 'Indians' when he
25 arrived in the New World in 1492, because
he thought he was in India. The 'Indians'
had actually entered America from Asia
maybe 30,000 years before, when there was a
land bridge between the two continents. So
30 the word 'Indians' wasn't really so silly.

The region that the English called Virginia
was the home of several Indian tribes. They
lived in villages, hunted deer and fished, and
they grew vegetables. Their chief was called
35 Powhatan. He had lots of wives and children,
but his favorite daughter was Pocahontas.
She was interested in the white people and
often visited them. At first the Indians were
friendly and traded with the whites.

40 The settlers weren't very good farmers, so
they needed food from the Indians. Soon
John Smith became leader of the colony. He
was a tough man who had enjoyed a life of
adventure. He learned the Indians' language
45 and found out about their way of life and
how they got food. It was thanks to him that
the colony survived the early years.

The 28-year-old Smith was a short man with a
beard. He and Pocahontas didn't look like the
50 characters in the Disney cartoon. But it seems
she liked him. The story goes that some Indians
captured Smith and decided to kill him. They
didn't like the way he was taking control of the
area. They were just getting ready to hit him on
55 the head when Pocahontas ran forward and laid
her head on his. Chief Powhatan then decided
that Smith could live. It's a popular story, but
we don't know if it's really true or not.

John Smith was hurt in an accident with some
60 gunpowder and went back to England.
Pocahontas was captured and taken to
Jamestown. She fell in love with a tobacco
farmer called John Rolfe, and they married in
1614. The marriage helped to bring peace
65 between the settlers and the Indians.

In 1616 Rolfe and his wife and their son Thomas
sailed to England, where Pocahontas was a big
sensation. The couple even met King James.
But before they could start the journey back to
70 Virginia, Pocahontas became ill and died
suddenly. She was only 22.

A year later Chief Powhatan died too. The
Indians then decided that the settlers were
taking too much of their land, and they attacked
75 and killed some of them. But they couldn't easily
fight against people with guns. Soon the Indian
population of the region had fallen from about
9,000 to 1,000. It wasn't just the guns – the
Europeans brought new diseases, too. Over the
80 next 300 years the Native Americans lost their
land and most of their people as the Europeans
moved west across the continent.

40 forty

TEXT 1

About two million Native Americans live in the US today. What do they think about this story that the white people like so much? Little Green Rising is a 12-year-old Cherokee from Alabama. 'I got a Pocahontas book for my birthday,' she says. 'I said thank you and tried not to hurt my friend's feelings. I see Pocahontas dolls, clothes, shoes and much more. I don't like any of this. It is so stupid.' Her brother, Majik Star Rising, agrees. 'In real life Pocahontas met Smith at the age of ten. In the movie she was a woman with good long hair (but not as good as my mom's). And I don't like Pocahontas purses. At one time they made purses out of Indians' skins, so this is really offensive.'

EXERCISE 3

Read these statements and then say if they are true or false. If a statement is true, find the words in the text which show that it is true. If a statement is false, you should correct it or explain why it is false.

1. Jamestown was the perfect place for a colony.
2. People were already living in Virginia when the colonists arrived.
3. When the whites landed, the Indians started a war with them.
4. John Smith could talk to the Indians.
5. Things happened exactly as in the Disney cartoon.
6. They say that Pocahontas saved John Smith's life.
7. Pocahontas married a tobacco farmer, went to England and met the King.
8. The Indians couldn't defeat the settlers because the settlers had guns.
9. Native Americans like the Pocahontas story.

EXERCISE 4

Can you tell the story? Complete the sentences which say what happened. Then decide what people are saying. Use the notes.

1 call / King James
2 good idea / Jamestown
3 daughter / chief / Pocahontas
4 John Smith / leader
5 love / marry
6 yes / and maybe / peace
7 John Rolfe / wife / Virginia
8 good voyage

In 1607 about a hundred settlers …

Pocahontas and John Smith …

In 1614 Pocahontas …

In England, the couple went to London and …

forty-one 41

Unit 3 **TEXT 1**

EXERCISE 5

Look at the explanation and give the word. All the words are in Text 1.

➡ where the land meets the sea: coast
1 a journey on the sea
2 a group of people with a chief
3 to run or ride after an animal and kill it
4 kinds of food such as potatoes or beans
5 to buy and sell things
6 something exciting that happens to you
7 the number of people who live in a place
8 a children's toy which is a model of a person

EXERCISE 6

Put each verb into the correct form. Use the simple present, the simple past, the past progressive or the past perfect. Some of the verbs have to be passive.

➡ The Indians **had been** in America for many thousands of years when Europeans first **came** there.
1 At the end of Jamestown's first year the colony (be) in trouble. More than half of the settlers (die).
2 The white settlers in the colonies (help) by the Indians, and so they (be) able to survive.
3 When John Smith first (meet) Pocahontas, she (be) about ten years old.
4 The story of Pocahontas (know and love) by most Americans today.
5 Even today no one (know) if Pocahontas really (save) John Smith's life or not.
6 Rolfe and his wife (get) ready for the voyage back to America when she suddenly (fall) ill.
7 Soon there (be) war between the settlers and the Indians. Powhatan (die) some time before. The whites (be) sorry because he (be) a good friend to them.

 ### EXERCISE 7

32+33 **Listening**

The Comanche Indians hunted buffalo on the prairie, but the government wanted to put the Comanches in a reservation. The Comanches fought against the army but were finally defeated in 1875. Listen to the words of Ten Bears, an old Comanche chief, to the white people. What he says is in two parts.

Part 1 (32)

What explanation does Ten Bears give of how the fighting started?

a) The soldiers attacked the Comanches at night.
b) The soldiers attacked the Comanches during that day.
c) The Comanches attacked the soldiers first.

Part 2 (33)

Two of these statements are true and two are false. Find the true statements.

a) The Comanches felt happy and free on the prairie.
b) Ten Bears would like to live in a nice house.
c) He feels hopeful about the future.
d) The President once said that the Comanches could stay on the prairie.

ACTIVITIES 1

1 NATIVE AMERICANS: HOW THEY WROTE

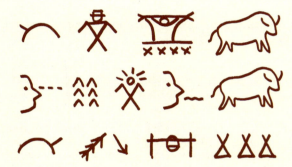

Can you understand this message from Fights With Her Teachers? She was a Navajo girl who wrote down signs for her Apache friend Little Buffalo. Write down her message in complete English sentences.

→ page 159

Indian pictionary

morning — trail of a horse
white man — wise Indian
look for — peace

Invent a sign for these words:
rain / gun / buffalo skin / lake / friendly / dangerous / tall tree / shooting / stone / axe / cowboy.
What was Little Buffalo's answer? Write down his answer in 'Indian' signs. If you want you can use some of your own signs.

2 WHERE THEY LIVED

Many American rivers, cities and states have names with a Native American origin.

From many names we learn that water was quite important, like Oregon ('beautiful water') or Minnesota ('sky-coloured water'). Other names tell us more about the landscape, like Massachusetts ('place of the big hill') or Kentucky ('hunting ground').

Try to find out from the internet what the names Arizona, Dakota, Oklahoma and Kansas mean.

Can you find more names of rivers and cities with Native American origins? Use a map.

Which Native American name would you give to your home town and your country?

3 THE DREAM CATCHER

Native American children love these dream catchers because they catch all the bad dreams and let some nice dreams fall down on your pillow. The idea comes from old stories.

**This is what you need:
a flexible twig about 30 centimeters long • thin wire
• some red or blue twine •
wooden beads • feathers**

Make a hoop from the twig and fix the ends together with thin wire. Now tie the twine to one side of the hoop. Put two or three beads onto the twine and put the twine around the opposite side of the hoop (see picture). Keep going with more beads until your dream catcher looks interesting. Finally tie three or more pieces of twine with beads and feathers to the bottom side of the hoop and hang your dream catcher near your bed. Sweet dreams!

forty-three 43

Unit 3   **INTRODUCTION 2**

 SITUATION 3

34
Ryan   Oh, is this our homework on slavery you're doing? Can I see?
Tiffany Sure.
Ryan   'Africans were first brought to America as slaves in the 17th century. The Europeans found that they couldn't do all the work themselves. They needed slaves on the plantations in the South. Africans were bought and sold like animals, and they had to work hard for long hours. They had no rights. If they tried to escape they were punished, sometimes killed. There was a slave revolt in Virginia in 1831. It was led by a man called Nat Turner. Slaves killed about fifty white people before they were captured. Turner himself and eighteen others were hanged.' Hey, did you write this yourself?
Tiffany Sure I wrote it myself. Actually, I printed it out from the internet.

Emphatic / reflexive pronouns

They couldn't do all the work **themselves**.

Turner **himself** was hanged.

I - myself
you - yourself
the King - himself
Pocahontas - herself
the house - itself
we - ourselves
you - yourselves
they - themselves

➔ page 108-109

EXERCISE 8

Express the idea with an emphatic pronoun. Instead of the words in italics, use *myself*, *yourself*, etc.

➡ *Nicole*   Tiffany is pretty clever. She fixed the computer. *No one helped her.* She fixed the computer **herself**.
1 *Michael*   Do you know what I did? I cooked a meal for the whole family *without any help*.
2 *Robert*   Guess what. J.K. Rowling *(not someone in a bookstore)* gave me this Harry Potter book.
3 *Megan*   Yes, I've heard the story. You told me. *No one else did.*
4 *Mr Brown* We had a great holiday. We arranged it all *without a travel company*.
5 *Michelle* I rang the company today. The manager *(and not one of the people who work for him)* answered the phone.
6 *Justin*   We enjoyed the trip to 3 Com Park. But the game *(what we'd actually gone there to see)* wasn't very exciting.

 SITUATION 4

35
Tiffany I've found something about the Underground Railroad too. Listen. 'Some slaves won freedom for themselves on the Underground Railroad, a secret organization that was run mainly by black people. They helped slaves who escaped and traveled to the northern states or to Canada, where there was no slavery. The slaves traveled on foot at night, and during the day they hid in safe places, stations on the railroad. A station might be a farm building or someone's house. There were also guides who helped the slaves on their way.'
Ryan   And what about that woman, Harriet someone?
Tiffany There's something about her too. Yes, here it is. 'About 50,000 slaves escaped on the Underground Railroad. The most famous was Harriet Tubman. After she had escaped from slavery in Maryland, she returned secretly to the South 19 times to lead 300 other slaves to freedom. She put herself in great danger, but she was never caught.'
Ryan   This is good. Now we'll be able to do our homework in about ten minutes. So we can go out tonight and enjoy ourselves.

Harriet Tubman

A 'station' in Ohio

INTRODUCTION 2

EXERCISE 9

Complete each conversation. Put in a reflexive pronoun.

➡ *Joseph*   I feel tired.
   Kevin   You ought to stop watching TV all night.
              You'll make yourself ill if you do that.
1 *Lisa*   How was your trip to Williamsburg?
  Amber   OK. We enjoyed … .
2 *Tiffany* How do you like the new boy?
  Natasha He's very strange. He's talking to … .
3 *Ryan*   You haven't switched off the computer.
  Tiffany It's OK. It'll switch … off in a few minutes.
4 *Brandon* Those guys on the football team think they're really important, don't they?
  Tina   Yes, they have a pretty high opinion of … .
5 *Teacher* How did Pocahontas save John Smith's life?
  Lisa   The Indians were getting ready to hit him on the head when she threw … on him.
6 *Katie*   Isn't Natasha's dress awful?
  Nicole   Don't tell her, but I think it's a big mistake. I can't imagine … wearing a dress like that.

SITUATION 5

Ryan There's something about the Civil War on the screen here. 'North and South could not agree about slavery. By 1861 eleven southern states had declared themselves independent. The fighting began at Charleston, South Carolina. The two sides fought each other for four long years.'

The Civil War began here at Fort Sumter.

→ page 109

They're looking at each other.

They're looking at themselves in the mirror.

EXERCISE 10

Ryan has a twin brother called Kevin. Rewrite the information about them in a shorter way. Use *each other* or *themselves*.

➡ Ryan is helping Kevin with his homework, and Kevin is helping Ryan with his.
   Ryan and Kevin are helping each other with their homework.
➡ They both fell off their bikes. Ryan hurt himself, and Kevin did too.
   They both hurt themselves.
1 The twins are fifteen now. Ryan can look after himself, and the same goes for Kevin.
2 Ryan and Kevin went to the beach. Ryan took some photos of Kevin, and then Kevin took some of Ryan.
3 The twins have got a dog and a cat. The dog hates the cat, and the cat hates the dog.
4 Kevin has got a pen pal. He writes letters to her, and she writes back.
5 The twins' parents are at a barbecue tonight. Mom is enjoying herself, and dad is, too.

forty-five 45

Unit 3 TEXT 2

Front of the bus

At the end of the Civil War between North and South, slavery was abolished in the US. But that didn't mean that all the problems were over for the black population. Many of them couldn't find work. In the South, the whites wanted to keep black people 'in their place' – at the bottom. There was segregation in schools, hospitals, cinemas and swimming-pools. Black people who protested were sometimes lynched – usually hanged from a tree. These things went on into the 20th century. It was a hundred years after the end of the Civil War before black Americans finally won equal rights.

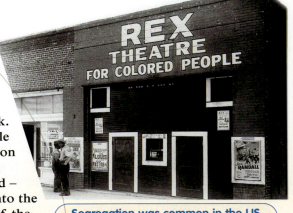

Segregation was common in the US for a long time in the 20th century.

An action by one individual helped start the civil rights movement. In the evening of December 1, 1955, a 42-year-old woman called Rosa Parks got on a bus in Montgomery, Alabama. In those days there were seats for whites at the front of the bus and seats for blacks at the back. Black people had to give up their seats if white people were standing. This is what happened to Mrs Parks that day.

When she got off from work that evening, she went to Court Square as usual to catch the Cleveland Avenue bus home. There was an empty seat in the black part of the bus and she took it. A man was sitting next to her and there were two women across the aisle.

The next stop was the Empire Theater, where some whites got on. They filled up the white seats, and one man had to stand. The driver, who had noticed the man, looked at the black people and told them to stand up. He said, 'Let me have those front seats.' Nobody moved. Then the driver spoke a second time. 'Are you going to let me have those seats?'

The man in the seat next to Mrs Parks stood up. She looked across the aisle and saw that the two women were also standing. But she didn't stand up.

In her book *My Story* she explains, 'People always say that I didn't give up my seat because I was tired, but that isn't true. I was … no more tired than I usually was at the end of a working day. … No, the only tired I was, was tired of giving in.'

The bus driver asked, 'Are you going to stand up?' When Rosa Parks refused, he said, 'Well, I'm going to call the police.' Then she said, 'You may do that.' These were the only words they said to each other. She didn't even know his name, James Blake, until they were in court together.

This photo of Rosa Parks on the bus was taken for the newspapers after she had been arrested.

When at last two policemen came, one of them asked Mrs Parks why she didn't stand up. 'Why do you all push us around?' she said. 'I don't know, but the law is the law and you're under arrest,' he said. He picked up her purse, the other her shopping bag and they took her to the squad car.

46 forty-six

Mrs Parks had gotten herself into trouble. She was fined $10, and she lost her job. But her action started something big – a bus boycott by the black community in Montgomery. The campaign was led by a man called Martin Luther King.

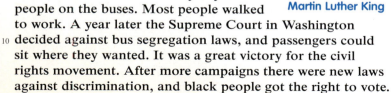

The Reverend Martin Luther King

For months there were hardly any black people on the buses. Most people walked to work. A year later the Supreme Court in Washington decided against bus segregation laws, and passengers could sit where they wanted. It was a great victory for the civil rights movement. After more campaigns there were new laws against discrimination, and black people got the right to vote.

Even today black Americans do not really have equal opportunities because they are more likely to be without a job or to live in poor housing. But they have come a long way since the time when they couldn't sit at the front of the bus.

TEXT 2

EXERCISE 11

Each of these headings below goes with a paragraph in the text about Rosa Parks. Put them all in the right order.

a) Black people finally won their civil rights.
b) Mrs Parks tells her story.
c) The end of slavery didn't mean the good life for black people.
d) The black population's journey is not yet over.
e) One woman's action started the civil rights movement.
f) Mrs Parks was fined, but the boycott began.

EXERCISE 12

These sentences are about Text 2. Some of them are about the important parts of the story, and some of them are about the details. Find the five important sentences. Then write them in the correct order to create a summary of the text.

- A woman called Rosa Parks was told by a bus driver that she should give up her seat to a white man.
- Even after the Civil War, there was discrimination against black Americans, and they did not have civil rights for another hundred years.
- One policeman picked up her purse, and the other picked up her shopping bag.
- Rosa Parks refused.
- She caught the bus in Court Square.
- Something happened in Montgomery, Alabama in 1955 which started the civil rights movement.
- The driver was a man called James Blake.
- This action led to a bus boycott by black people and to a movement which ended discrimination.

Civil rights demonstration against segregation.

Martin Luther King gives his 'I have a dream' speech in Washington, 1963.

forty-seven   **47**

Unit 3 **TEXT 2**

EXERCISE 13

The bus driver James Blake is in court. He is telling his story of what happened. Tell the story. You can begin like this.

On that day I was driving a bus to Cleveland Avenue. At the Empire Theater …

EXERCISE 14

Answer the questions.

1 Give two examples of how life after slavery was not as good as many black people had hoped.
2 What was the result of Mrs Parks's action for herself and for the black people of Montgomery?
3 Do you think Mrs Parks was right to say no to the bus driver? Give a reason for your answer.

Rosa Parks on her way to court.

EXERCISE 15

Rosa Parks became an important person in the civil rights movement.

Put in the missing words and complete the sentences. Each missing word is in the text.

1 Many people who had been slaves were … because there was no work for them.
2 Black people were not allowed to sit in the white … of the bus.
3 The policeman told Mrs Parks that she was under …
4 She had to appear in … , where she was fined $10.
5 The civil rights movement organized a big national … for black rights.
6 They wanted … rights for black people.
7 Some white people also … against segregation.
8 When new laws were brought in, it was a great … for the movement.
9 Segregation was finally … in the US.

EXERCISE 16

Look at this sentence and the German translation.

My brother didn't feel well.
Mein Bruder fühlte sich nicht wohl.

There are some English verbs which do not have a reflexive pronoun even though there is a pronoun in German (*feel* → *fühlte sich*). These verbs include *argue, change, imagine, remember, sit down* and *turn round*.

Translate the sentences 1–8 into English. Sometimes you need a reflexive pronoun and sometimes you don't.

1 *Seit jener Zeit hat sich vieles verändert.*
2 *Die Schwarzen haben mehr Rechte für sich gewonnen.*
3 *Mrs Parks setzte sich in den schwarzen Teil des Busses.*
4 *Der Busfahrer drehte sich um.*
5 *Könnt ihr euch die Szene vorstellen?*
6 *Mrs Parks wollte sich nicht mit dem Busfahrer streiten.*
7 *Sie hat sich in Schwierigkeiten gebracht.*
8 *Viele Menschen erinnern sich heute noch an Rosa Parks.*

48 forty-eight

ACTIVITIES 2

1 EBONY AND IVORY
BY PAUL McCARTNEY & STEVIE WONDER

SONG 38

Listen to the song. With a partner decide where these words go in the song: *people, bad, side, harmony, good, together, piano, same, survive, alive.*

→ page 159

CHORUS

*Ebony and Ivory
Live together in perfect *¹
Side by side on my *² keyboard
Oh Lord, why don't we?*

*We all know that *³ are the same wherever you go
There's good and *⁴ in everyone
We learn to live, we learn to give each other
What we need to survive *⁵ alive*

CHORUS

*Ebony, Ivory, living in perfect harmony
Ebony, Ivory, ooh*

*We all know that people are the *⁶ wherever you go
There's *⁷ and bad in everyone
We learn to live, we learn to give each other
What we need to *⁸
Together *⁹*

CHORUS

*Side by *¹⁰ on my piano keyboard
Oh Lord, why don't we?*

Ebony, Ivory, living in perfect harmony

Write the words of this song in your exercise book.

2 PROJECT WORK

In the 19th century, there were four million slaves in the United States. Which countries did they come from? What was their daily life like? Today about 36 million African Americans live in the US. What is their situation like today?

Work in groups of four students and try to find as much information as possible on one of the following topics. Present your results in class. You can play songs, show pictures, mention some famous speeches, put up posters, make a quiz, ...

Where did the slaves come from?
Draw a map of these countries, find out how many arrived in each year, where they were taken, ...

Reasons for slavery
Why did the United States buy slaves? Find out about their work, the conditions of work, prices, ...

The story of a slave
Search the internet for a real biography and interviews, or tell the story of a film on slavery, ...

Black music
Play some gospel and soul songs, find out about their origins, talk about their lyrics, ...

Martin Luther King and the Civil Rights Movement
Find out about the aims of King's movement, tell us when African Americans got civil rights, ...

Slavery today
Think of slavery in Europe and India today, think of children and women, find out where slavery still exists and give reasons, ...

Famous black people
Choose four black people of the past and/or present and tell us about their lives, ...

The situation of African-American people in the US today
What percentage are jobless? How much do African-American people earn? What can you find out about their education? ...

Unit 3   **COMMUNICATION**

Interviewing people

Interviewer   Mrs Parks, do you remember that day back in 1955 when you refused to give up your seat on the bus?
Mrs Parks   Of course I remember it. To me it's like yesterday.
Interviewer   Can you tell us why you said no?
Mrs Parks   White people always pushed us around. I'd had enough of it.
Interviewer   Do you think your action started the whole civil rights movement?
Mrs Parks   Well, lots of other people were already working for civil rights. I was just one of many who fought for freedom.

- Do you remember your first TV show?
- Can you tell us about your European tour?
- What do you think of Germany?
  Do you like it here?
- What/Who is your favorite team?
- Are you working on a movie at the moment?
- What are your plans for the future?

EXERCISE 17

Practice an interview with a partner. One of you is a chat show host and the other is a famous person such as Britney Spears, Michael Schumacher or Tom Cruise. First you should get ready for the interview. The host writes down the questions, and the guest thinks about the answers and takes notes. Then do the interview in front of your classmates. At the end the host should thank the guest for coming on the show.

TEST YOUR ENGLISH

The railroad

In the middle of the 19th century, it took months to travel by wagon from the East to California, and it was a difficult and dangerous journey. At that time the railroad
5 only went halfway across the country. The government decided that it should go coast to coast. In 1865 the Union Pacific Railroad began laying track westward across the prairie from Omaha, Nebraska. Many of the workmen were Irish immigrants.
10 They laid 1,086 miles of track in less than four years, even though they were sometimes attacked by Indians. The Indians were angry that the railroad was driving away the buffalo
15 that they needed for their food.

Near the end of the line there was always a small town of tents and wooden
20 buildings, with places where the workmen could spend their money on drink. When the railroad moved on, everyone went with it, and a new town was built
25 fifty miles further west.

At the same time another company, the Central Pacific Railroad, was working in the west. It was laying track eastward from Sacramento,
30 California, up into the mountains. The Central Pacific workmen also had to work in difficult conditions. They had to cut tunnels through the stone. The work was dangerous,
35 and hundreds of men were killed. The Central Pacific employed thousands of Chinese immigrants from San Francisco. When the company saw how well they worked,
40 it brought another two thousand men over from China.

50   fifty

TEST YOUR ENGLISH

Each company was given money and land for each mile of track it laid. On one day in April 1869 the Central Pacific laid ten miles of track in twelve hours. The tracks finally met at Promontory, Utah on May 10 1869. Now you could travel from east to west in only eight days, although the journey often took longer. It was dangerous too. Trains were attacked by Indians, and there were accidents
5 because some of the track wasn't very safe. But the railroad had brought east and west together.

1 The Union Pacific's chief engineer is called Grenville Dodge. He's answering a reporter's questions. Complete Mr Dodge's answers.

1 *Reporter* How many miles of track has the Union Pacific laid?
  Mr Dodge I can tell you exactly. We've laid … of track.
2 *Reporter* And when did you start the work?
  Mr Dodge About … years … .
3 *Reporter* And where did you find the workmen?
  Mr Dodge … of them … .
4 *Reporter* What was the biggest danger to your workmen?
  Mr Dodge The biggest danger? Well, sometimes … .
5 *Reporter* Why were the Indians so angry?
  Mr Dodge Because … .
6 *Reporter* Have you earned any money from the railroad yet?
  Mr Dodge Yes, the government … .
7 *Reporter* How long will it take now to travel from the east coast to the west?
  Mr Dodge …
8 *Reporter* What has this railroad done for our country, do you think?
  Mr Dodge …

2 You are reading this notice by the railroad track at Promontory. Can you translate it into German?

> HERE ON MAY 10 1869, THE LAST PIECE OF TRACK WAS LAID IN THE RAILROAD LINE WHICH FIRST CROSSED THE COUNTRY FROM COAST TO COAST. THIS EXCITING NEWS WAS WELCOMED ALL OVER THE COUNTRY, AND CHURCH BELLS WERE RUNG.
>
> FROM THE EAST THE UNION PACIFIC HAD LAID 1,086 MILES OF TRACK, AND FROM THE WEST THE CENTRAL PACIFIC HAD LAID 690 MILES. THE WHOLE PROJECT TOOK ONLY FOUR YEARS. DURING THAT TIME HUNDREDS OF WORKMEN LOST THEIR LIVES.

3 Complete this information about Buffalo Bill. Put in the missing words or the correct form of the words in brackets.

William Cody was … in Iowa in 1846. His father … (kill) when William was only 11, and so he had … look after the family. He … (can) already ride and shoot, and he … (become) a Pony Express rider. At the … of 17 he … (go) to Colorado to look … gold and then he … (fight) in the Civil War on the Union side. When the railroad … (come) west, William got a job … a buffalo hunter in Kansas. In 17 months he … (shoot) 4,280 buffalo.

William … (know) as 'Buffalo Bill'. There had … millions of buffalo before the white men arrived, but soon … weren't any left in Kansas. The West was … (change). Where the buffalo … (have/live), the settlers now had their … (cow) and their … (sheep). William … (work) for the army … a time and then he started his 'Wild West Show'. The old West … longer existed, but it survived in books and magazines and in movies … were seen … people all over the world.

4 Listen to the conversation. Someone is phoning Amtrak and asking about trains from New York City to Washington.
40 He wants to know:

- how long the journey takes
- if there is a train at about 8.30 or 9.00 A.M.
- which station it goes from
- the price of a one-way ticket
- the age at which you have to pay the full price
- if you need a reservation

Take notes as you listen. Write down only the most important pieces of information in a word or phrase. Do not try to copy whole sentences.

fifty-one 51

Unit 3   READING   **Ellen's diary**

The year is 1858. Ellen, Joseph and their children are traveling the Oregon Trail.

May 5
Here we are in Independence, Missouri, at the start of the Oregon Trail. There are hundreds of people here getting ready for the journey west! The five of us are all so excited! We've been thinking about the trip for a full year. My sister did the trip three years ago and told us how beautiful the river valleys of Oregon are and how good the farming is. The trail is 2,000 miles long, and with God's help we'll get to our destination by October.

May 13
We are in a train of 15 wagons. There are 76 people in our company. In a smaller group, I'd be afraid of attacks by Indians. We hired Major Brown to be our guide. We have been going 15 miles a day.

May 21
We are traveling along the prairie by a river called the Platte. We need to follow along as many rivers as we can because we need the water. I was sorry that we had to throw our iron stove out of the wagon, but it just weighed too much. The oxen couldn't pull it any more. Now every evening I cook over an open fire. It's difficult to find firewood, because the people on the trail before us cut all the trees along the river. I have to use buffalo chips.

June 5
Three days ago James, my youngest, was bitten by a rattlesnake while he was fetching buffalo chips. He has been very sick, and I am worried for his life. We have no doctor with our group, and I pray to God he will get better.

June 12
It is very hot! We have to stop our wagons in the afternoons and lie under them to rest. Almost every day there's a thunder shower around 3 P.M. I think about poor little James. He died of fever, and we had to bury him. Why did we ever come on this journey?

July 4
Independence Day! We are on our way up the Rocky Mountains. We climbed a big rock, and Joseph carved his name and ILLINOIS our home state into it. There are hundreds of names. They call this place Independence Rock. If you aren't here by July 4, you are traveling too slow and may get into a snowstorm when you reach the Cascade Mountains.

July 31
I have never been so hot in my life! We are traveling along the Snake River in Idaho. One of our oxen has died from the heat. This part of the trail has lots of broken wagons and dead animals. They're just lying in the sun. Will we ever get to Oregon?

August 15
We are at a place called The Dalles, ready to start over the Cascade Mountains. The road is very bad, they say, but it's the only way to get to the valley. We can see Mount Hood covered in snow, and it sure is pretty, but I hate to think that our road goes way up on the side of it.

September 3
We have reached Oregon! We're at my sister's farm. How beautiful it is! Joseph wants to get us a farm soon, so that we will be ready to plant crops next spring. The children are getting fat again on all the good food that Esther and her husband have given us. I think about our home in Illinois and how I will never see my friends again, and I think about my little one we lost along the way. We paid a price to get here, but I know God will make a good life for us.

52 fifty-two

UNIT 4
STARS AND STRIPES

Alaska

The American flag is the Stars and Stripes. There are fifty stars, one for each state. And there are thirteen red and white stripes. The stripes are for the states which were once British colonies and which formed the United States over 200 years ago.

41

WORDS AND PICTURES

The capital of the US is Washington DC. But it isn't part of any state. Do you know where it is? And there are two states which do not have a border with another US state. They are Alaska and Hawaii. Try to find them in an atlas.

Hawaii

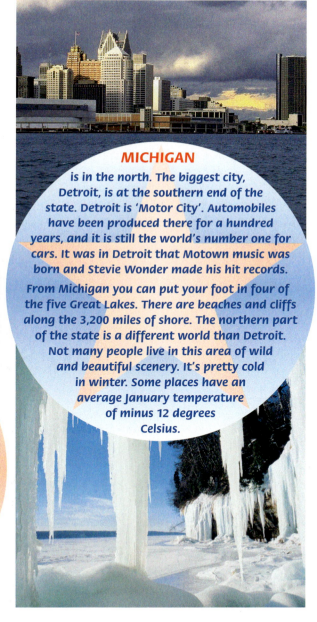

MICHIGAN is in the north. The biggest city, Detroit, is at the southern end of the state. Detroit is 'Motor City'. Automobiles have been produced there for a hundred years, and it is still the world's number one for cars. It was in Detroit that Motown music was born and Stevie Wonder made his hit records.

From Michigan you can put your foot in four of the five Great Lakes. There are beaches and cliffs along the 3,200 miles of shore. The northern part of the state is a different world than Detroit. Not many people live in this area of wild and beautiful scenery. It's pretty cold in winter. Some places have an average January temperature of minus 12 degrees Celsius.

TEXAS is the second biggest state (after Alaska). It's famous for its oil and its cowboys. Of the ten largest cities in the US, three are in Texas: Houston, Dallas and San Antonio. The state also has forests, deserts and mountains.

Texas was once part of Mexico. In San Antonio you can visit the Alamo, the famous mission where in 1836 almost 200 men lost their lives after they had defended the building for two weeks against a Mexican army of 4,000. Today Texas has a large Hispanic population, and in some places Spanish is the main language.

About 150 years ago many German families went to live in central Texas in places such as Fredericksburg.

fifty-three

Unit 4   **INTRODUCTION 1**

SITUATION 1

42

Andrew	Are we going on vacation this year, mom?
Mom	Well, I don't know. Your sister wants to go to Florida. She wants some sunshine.
Andrew	Joe's family went someplace in Utah. If we go there, we can ride on mountain bike trails. Joe says it's great.
Dad	What about a vacation job? You say you never have enough money. If you get a job, you can earn some.
Andrew	Oh, dad!
Mom	And what about summer camp? If you try it again, you might enjoy it this time.
Andrew	Are you kidding? You know I hate summer camp.
Mom	You said last year you liked the windsurfing.
Andrew	Yes, but the food was awful. If I go there again, I'll die.

Some young Americans at a summer camp

> **Sentences with if** → page 110
> If … simple present … , … will / can / etc. …
> If we take a taxi, it'll be quicker.
> If it doesn't rain, we can go to the beach.

If you think back to last year, you might remember this.

EXERCISE 1

Put the verbs in brackets into the correct form. Sometimes you need a modal verb such as *will, can, might* or *should*.

If you **want** (want) a great vacation, you**'ll get** (get) it in the United States. The country has everything. If you … (be) a city person, you … (find) lots to do in New York City, Chicago or San Francisco. You … (get) wonderful views if you … (climb) to the top of the Statue of Liberty in New York, or if you … (take) a cable car up San Francisco's Nob Hill. And if you … (be) interested in movies, you really … (visit) Hollywood. Or you … (take) a ride through your favorite movie if you … (go) to Universal Studios in Florida.

And you … (not have) any reason to complain if you … (like) the wide open spaces. There are lots of national parks in the US. If you … (visit) Yellowstone, you … (see) a bear. And if you … (visit) the Grand Canyon, you … (not forget) it in a hurry. If you … (choose) the US this year, you and your family … (have) the time of your lives.

EXERCISE 2

Write five sentences that tell Americans what they can do on vacation in Bavaria.

➡ If you like winter sports, you'll enjoy Garmisch-Partenkirchen.
1   … want to see … , … should … Rothenburg.

54   fifty-four

INTRODUCTION 1

SITUATION 2

43

The US is huge. It's almost three thousand miles from New York City to San Francisco, and there are four different time zones. If you were in San Francisco at ten o'clock in the evening and you phoned someone in New York, you would probably wake them up. It would be one o'clock in the morning where they were.

If you started walking across the country from coast to coast, you'd walk for a very long time. If you walked eight hours every day, it might take four months to reach your destination. You'd be pretty tired if you did that. And if you drove a car, you couldn't do it safely in much less than a week. No wonder Americans fly so much. Many US states are bigger than European countries.

Texas is bigger than Belgium, the Netherlands, Germany, Austria and Switzerland put together. If you picked up Bavaria, carried it across the Atlantic and put it down in the American West, no one would notice it was there.

Germany

Now look at this.

More sentences with if → page 110-111

If … simple past … , … would / could / might …

If **Anna** had **enough money**, she **would visit** Europe.
If **she** went **to Germany**, she **might see** Daniel.
If **Daniel** wasn't **at school**, he **could show** Anna **around**.

… would / could / might … if … simple past …

Anna would visit Europe if **she** had **enough money**.
She might see Daniel if **she** went **to Germany**.
Daniel could show Anna around if **he** wasn't **at school**.

EXERCISE 3

What would you do if you had a million dollars? Ask the other pupils what they would do. Your teacher will give you a questionnaire.

Buy a very expensive stereo?	✗
Travel around the world?	✗
Give some of your money to charity?	◼
Pay a record company to promote you?	◼

EXERCISE 4

What would you do in these situations?

▸ You miss the last bus home: walk home in the dark / ring your parents?
If I **missed** the last bus home, I **would call** my parents. I **wouldn't walk** home in the dark because it's dangerous.

1 A stranger offers you a ride in his car: get in the car / refuse?

2 You find a friend's phone in your bag: use it to make a few calls / give it back?

3 You buy a new watch, but it doesn't work: take it back to the shop / throw it away?

4 A man with a gun is running along the street: stop him / call the police?

5 You see a ghost in the middle of the night: try to hide / speak to the ghost?

6 In Yellowstone National Park you suddenly see a bear in front of you: lie down and keep still / run away / try to climb a tree?

fifty-five **55**

Unit 4 **TEXT 1**

FLORIDA VACATION

HAVE FUN IN THE SUN IN FLORIDA, AMERICA'S FAVORITE VACATION PLACE.

YOU'LL FIND ALLIGATORS AND SPACESHIPS, MICKEY MOUSE AND ORANGE TREES, BASEBALL, MOTOR RACING, TENNIS, GOLF … AND THOUSANDS OF MILES OF BEACHES FOR SWIMMING, WINDSURFING AND WATER-SKIING.

IT'S ALL IN THE SUNSHINE STATE, BETWEEN THE GULF OF MEXICO AND THE ATLANTIC. YOU COULDN'T THINK OF A BETTER PLACE IF YOU TRIED.

1 Enjoy a tour of the Kennedy Space Center, where rockets are launched. Walk through the 'rocket garden'. Experience the excitement of the Apollo 8 moon launch.

2 Walt Disney World near Orlando is the biggest theme park in the world. It's twice the size of Manhattan, so if you stayed there a week, you wouldn't get around all of it. Actually there are four parts: the Magic Kingdom (mainly for kids), the Epcot Center (science and technology), Disney-MGM Studios and Disney's Animal Kingdom.

3 Orlando has plenty of other attractions. At Sea World you can walk through a glass tunnel and get very close to a real shark. At Universal Orlando you can ride through a movie.

4 Ocean Drive, Miami Beach, is probably the trendiest place on earth. Models are sometimes photographed in front of its beautiful pink, blue and yellow buildings.

5 Take a boat trip or a bike trip in Everglades National Park. But don't feed the alligators. If you do, they might bite your arm off. Members of the Miccosukee tribe live in Everglades, and you can visit the Miccosukee Indian village.

6 Drive a hundred miles over 31 islands to Key West, where the writer Ernest Hemingway lived. Here people come to Mallory Square every evening to watch the beautiful sunset. And if you aren't interested in seeing the sunset, you can watch the clowns, jugglers and fire-eaters.

TEXT 1

FLORIDA FACTS

- 14 million people live in Florida. It has the fourth largest population of all the states.
- The name Florida comes from Spanish and means 'Land of the Flowers'.
- Florida is 430 miles long from north to south. It is about the same size as England.
- Florida has a big Latin American and Caribbean population. Half the people in Miami are Hispanic, mostly from Cuba. Many of them live in the Little Havana area of the city, where you're more likely to hear Spanish than English.
- In Florida there is a hurricane about once every two years, usually in August, September or October. In 1992 Hurricane Andrew killed 50 people, injured many more and left 250,000 homeless.
- In a year Florida produces 140 million crates of oranges and 3,600 million liters of orange juice.

EXERCISE 5

Here are some answers that a guide has given to tourists in Florida. What were the questions?

▶ It's a part of Kennedy Space Center where you can see some space rockets.
   What is the 'rocket garden'?
1 Oh, it's very big. They say it's twice as big as Manhattan.
2 Little kids? I think they would enjoy the Magic Kingdom most.
3 Yes, there are. There's Sea World, for example. And Universal Orlando.
4 It is famous for its fine buildings with their beautiful colors.
5 Because they're dangerous. They could kill you.
6 They're an Indian tribe in Everglades.
7 They go there to watch the wonderful sunsets.
8 It means 'Land of the Flowers'.
9 It's called that because so many Cubans live in that part of the city.
10 It killed 50.

EXERCISE 6

Find the members of the word family.

▶ sun   There's plenty of warm **sunshine** in Florida.
         That evening we watched a beautiful **sunset**.
         The weather was warm and **sunny**.
1 soft   The girls were playing … .
         The company makes computer … .
2 pop   Of all the states, California has the largest … .
         Orlando is a very … tourist destination.
3 photo I want to … the view from our hotel room.
         I must … these two pages.
4 water I'd like to do … . It looks fantastic.
         The tallest … in the US is in Yosemite National Park.
5 every I've packed … into one case.
         … is coming to my party.
         I can't find the disk. I've looked … for it.

fifty-seven 57

Unit 4 **TEXT 1**

EXERCISE 7

Read about some more places in Florida that you could visit.

Imagine you are staying in Orlando and you are deciding which of these places to visit on the last day of your vacation. Discuss this in groups. You can use phrases like these.

Let's ...
I'm not interested in ...
What about ... ?
... would be better than ...
I'd like to ...
... is too far.

St Augustine, in north-east Florida, is the oldest town in America. There is an old Spanish fort there.

At Daytona Beach on the Atlantic coast you can drive your car along the beach. And you can go to the speedway track and watch a race – cars, motorbikes or go-karts.

Wet 'n' Wild near Orlando is a water theme park. You can try water-skiing on your knees, and there are some exciting rides.

At Cypress Gardens near Orlando there are lots of beautiful flowers. And you can see a marvelous water-ski show on the lake.

Busch Gardens is a theme park and zoo near Tampa, on the Gulf Coast. It has the fastest roller coaster in Florida.

EXERCISE 8

Write sentences from the table.

If you're ill,	I could show you the way.
We could do the math homework	I'd visit the Grand Canyon.
We won't be able to go to the concert	I'll be in big trouble.
If I had a map,	if we all went on vacation together.
If I'm late for school again tomorrow,	if we don't get tickets.
We'll get wet	if we go out in this rain.
If I had the chance to go to America,	if we help each other.
It would be great	you should see a doctor.

➡ If you're ill, you should see a doctor.

Now complete the last two sentences in your own way.
If I had the chance to go to America, ...
It would be great ...

EXERCISE 9

 Listening

45+46 You are with a group of tourists in St Augustine, Florida. A guide is taking your group on a walking tour of the town.

Listen to what the guide is telling you. What she says is in two parts.

Part 1 (45)

Choose the right answer.

1 Why is St Augustine famous?
  a) It is the oldest town in America.
  b) It is where Columbus landed.
2 When was a colony first started there?
  a) in 1513 b) in 1565 c) in 1821
3 Which country did Florida belong to before it became part of the United States?
  a) Britain b) France c) Spain
4 What did Henry Flagler do?
  a) He gave money to colleges in Florida.
  b) He brought oil to Florida.
  c) He built a railroad to Florida.

Part 2 (46)

Answer the questions.

5 What building are the tourists going to look at after Flagler College?
6 What street are they going to walk along after that?
7 What two things in this street does the guide mention?
8 What happened in St Augustine in the year 1702?

58 fifty-eight

ACTIVITIES 1

Grizzly!

Last summer in Yellowstone National Park, Teresa, Mia, Juan and Eric from a high school near Los Angeles were looking forward to their camping trip in the country.

→ page 159

How do the four friends feel and what do you think they will do? What would you do? Find an ending and rewrite the story from Juan's or Mia's point of view.

fifty-nine 59

Unit 4 **INTRODUCTION 2**

SITUATION 3

48

Andrew and Kayla and their dad have just arrived in Detroit for a short visit.

Dad	What are you looking at?
Andrew	I'm just reading this information about the Henry Ford Museum.
Kayla	Where did you get that from?
Andrew	The desk clerk in the motel gave it to me this morning. The museum sounds interesting. There are all kinds of things there. You can see the car President Kennedy was riding in when he was shot.
Dad	Do we want to see that?
Kayla	Of course we do. How could we resist it?
Andrew	Come on, what are we waiting for?

HENRY FORD MUSEUM & GREENFIELD VILLAGE

The preposition goes at the end of the question.

What is he talking about? What's a preposition?

EXERCISE 10

What are you looking at?
Where can we get a bus from?

→ page 112

People don't always tell you everything you want to know. Try to get more information from them. Ask questions with a preposition at the end.

➡	Sarah	I went out with a friend.	You	Who did you go out with?
1	Andrew	I was just thinking about something.	You	
2	Robert	I'm waiting for someone.	You	
3	Melissa	My brothers were laughing at something.	You	
4	Nicole	Jennifer is talking to someone.	You	
5	Justin	I'm looking for something.	You	
6	Kayla	Andrew is worried about something.	You	
7	Ryan	At the party I talked to someone famous.	You	
8	Amber	You'll never guess where Jasmine comes from.	You	

60 sixty

INTRODUCTION 2

SITUATION 4

49

Andrew Who were you talking to on your cellphone?
Kayla Lindsey. She's very upset.
Andrew Why? What's happened? What has she done this time?
Kayla It's Ryan, her new boyfriend. He can't come to her party on Friday.
Andrew Oh, a big tragedy.
Kayla It's serious, Andrew.
Andrew OK, sorry.
Kayla And we're both invited to the party.
Andrew Oh! Who else is going? Who has she invited?
Kayla All the usual people. Your girlfriend will be there, don't worry.

Subject question
Who phoned you just now?
(Someone phoned you.)

What is making you nervous?
(Something is making you nervous.)

Object question
Who did you phone just now?
(You phoned someone.)

What are you making? A cake?
(You are making something.)

→ page 111-112

EXERCISE 11

Read this paragraph and then answer the questions.

It was the school dance. David and Jessica were dancing. Jessica thought David was wonderful. She couldn't take her eyes off him. He was explaining to her how the basketball team had won an exciting victory the day before. But at the same time he was secretly watching Sarah. She looked beautiful, he thought. Sarah was dancing with James. She was telling him about her job at a fast food place. But James wasn't feeling too good. He had a headache – he thought it was because of the loud music. He and Sarah went and sat down at the end of the room, and he took an aspirin that she had found in her purse. David had seen what was happening and was trying to get away from Jessica so that he could talk to Sarah.

1 Who was looking at David?
2 Who was David looking at?
3 Who was talking to Jessica?
4 Who was Sarah talking to?
5 What gave James a headache?
6 What did Sarah give James?

EXERCISE 12

Kayla has been away from home for a few days. She wants to know all the details of what has been happening. Ask the questions for her.

▶ (Someone hurt his leg in a football game.)
   Who hurt his leg in a football game?
▶ (Robert brought something interesting to school.)
   What did Robert bring to school?
1 (Megan is writing something for the yearbook.)
2 (Someone had an argument with Mike.)
3 (Something strange happened at the dance.)
4 (Katie danced with someone.)
5 (Adam got upset about something.)
6 (Someone is starting a heavy metal band.)
7 (Nicole has done something to her hair.)
8 (Ashley said something silly to her English teacher.)

sixty-one **61**

Unit 4 TEXT 2

🔊 Rattlesnake!

Jason Kline (18) and his friend Brian Johnson (17) live in Chicago. They both enjoy mountainbiking. In
5 America, when you say 'mountainbiking', you think of Utah and the many trails around the town of Moab in the eastern part of the state.
10 Last September for the first time Jason and Brian went to Utah on vacation. They flew to Salt Lake City, where they stayed a night. The next day they rented a car and drove almost three hundred miles to Moab.

15 Moab was a green oasis in a small valley. When they got out of the car, they felt the hot wind – the temperature was already over 35 degrees Celsius. Luckily their motel room had air conditioning, and there was a swimming pool.
20 Of course they had expected to find one or two stores where they could rent bikes. Actually they found dozens of stores where they could do just that. Several store owners gave them the same advice – they should spend a few days on short,
25 easy bike trips so they could get used to the hot climate before they tried the longer trails.

There were many dirt roads that led out into the desert of red-colored rock west of the town. For two days they rode the trails and drank plenty of
30 water. When they were ready for a longer trail, they drove to Canyonlands National Park about 20 miles away. They packed three liters of water each and expected to drink it all on their ride.

Their trail went along the Green River and
35 each turn led them to rock formations of towers and arches. For several miles they rode, with stops for water and to take photos. They got thirsty very quickly. It was very hot, and they were almost alone on the trail. When they
40 got close to the river, they could see the cool water. Who could resist it? 'What are we waiting for?' asked Jason, and they took off their shoes and jumped into a blue-green pool. 'This is wonderful,' said Brian.

45 An hour later, they were ready to go on. Brian got out of the river and walked over to where they had left their shirts and shoes. A stick had fallen on his shirt. The stick moved and began to hiss. A rattlesnake! Brian jumped back. He
50 fell into Jason who was just getting out onto the bank.
'Yaaaahhh,' was all Brian could say as he pushed Jason back into the water.
'What are you doing, man?' shouted Jason.
55 'What happened?'
'Snake! Rattler!' Brian yelled even louder. They looked at each another. 'Now what do we do?'
Jason scratched his head. 'Well, don't yell for help because if someone comes, the
60 snake might bite him,' Jason said.

62 sixty-two

TEXT 2

They were both talking more quietly now. They watched as the snake moved off the shirt and onto the sand and looked all around. Jason and Brian were now completely quiet and didn't move. The snake looked over to where they stood in the river.
5 'What is he looking at? Can he see us?' Brian whispered.
'Don't know,' Jason answered. He was trying not to move his lips. Slowly, the snake moved into the short grass away from the river. The young men waited a half hour before they got out of the river and then they put on their shirts and shoes in seconds and were
10 away on their bikes.

Back in Moab, they told the story to the manager of the motel. 'They only bite if you frighten them,' he said. 'What were you worried about? You guys weren't in any danger.'
'Not in any danger!' Brian said while they were eating dinner. 'Who is he kidding? Rattlesnakes are poisonous. What if it was inside my shirt instead of on top of it?'
15 Jason and Brian never saw another snake while they were in Utah, but they told the story over and over when they got back home.

EXERCISE 13

Put the words with the right pictures. Then put them all in the right order so that they tell the story.

1   They drank water, but they were soon very hot.
2   Then they put their clothes on quickly and rode away.
3   They stayed in the water until the snake had gone.
4   When they came out, there was a rattlesnake on Brian's shirt.
5   In the morning Jason and Brian started on the trail.
6   So they decided to swim in the Green River.

sixty-three **63**

TEXT 2

EXERCISE 14

Complete these sentences about the text.

1. Jason and Brian went to Utah because …
2. In Moab the weather …
3. They didn't go on a long trail on the first day because …
4. When they rode along by the Green River, they felt they just had to …
5. When Brian came out of the water, he saw …
6. The two young men stopped talking because …
7. When they got out of the river again, they left quickly because …
8. The manager of the motel didn't think …

EXERCISE 15

Jason and Brian told the story over and over when they got back to Chicago. How did Brian tell it? You can begin like this.

Something happened while we were mountainbiking in Utah. We were riding along by …

Then invent a story that will impress your American friends. Tell them what you did in a dangerous situation. Your story can be about a bear you met in Yellowstone National Park or an alligator in Everglades.

EXERCISE 16

Show the difference in meaning between each pair of words.

➡ hotel / motel   A hotel is a building where you pay to stay. A motel is a special kind of hotel for people who are traveling by car.

➡ vacation / holiday   In the US a vacation is the time you spend away from work or school, perhaps in a place where you can relax and have fun. A holiday is a special day for the whole country, when people don't go to work or to school.

1. rent / buy   2. desert / oasis   3. whisper / yell   4. pool / lake   5. trail / highway

EXERCISE 17

Work with a partner. One of you should look at this page, and the other should look at page 94.

You are a reporter, and you are going to interview Stevie Wonder. Use the notes to ask your partner questions.

- *He's blind. How long?*
- *Born where?*
- *Real name?*
- *Got his first record contract when he was how old?*
- *Someone wrote the songs on 'Where I'm coming from'. Who?*
- *First used electronic music - when?*
- *Someone played all the instruments. Who?*
- *Something happened in 1973. What?*
- *His next concert - when?*
- *Made a hit record with an English singer. Which one?*
- *Took part in a campaign to make Martin Luther King Day a national holiday. Why?*

You can begin the interview like this.

You   May I ask you, how long have you been blind?
Stevie   Oh, since I was born. That's a long time, you know.
You   And where … ?

Note down Stevie's answers. If he says something you don't understand, you should say *Pardon?* or *Could you spell that, please?*

ACTIVITIES 2

It's quiz time!

The United States is a huge country. There are many exciting attractions and beautiful sights. We've already learned many new things about the US. How much can you remember? Get into groups of four students and find the answers to these questions. Which group is the US expert?

→ page 159

1. Which river tumbles down the Niagara Falls?
2. Name ten states of the United States.
3. Which lady can't leave New York City?
4. Mr Strauss from Buttenheim near Bamberg in Bavaria created something famous to wear in 1853. What is it?
5. Name five US presidents.
6. Where does the American president live?
7. What's the first name of his wife / her husband?
8. Which river has created the Grand Canyon?
9. What color are American school buses?
10. Which city in Texas is the first word that was ever spoken on the moon?
11. Which street in Manhattan is the heart of the US money business?
12. Where in Texas was John F. Kennedy killed?
13. Which country gave the Statue of Liberty to the US in 1886?
14. Why are there thirteen stripes on the American flag? How many stars are there?
15. Which is the largest of the US states?
16. Which city is famous for jazz music?
17. Which US state starts and ends with an 'O'?
18. Which American city has got cable cars?
19. How long is the Mississippi? Guess how many kilometers!
20. What happened on July 4, 1776?
21. In which month do the Americans celebrate Thanksgiving?
22. Who doesn't survive Thanksgiving?
23. The first Pilgrims arrived on a ship called … .
24. What are the American words for: shop / tube / city centre?
25. Name three Native American tribes.

sixty-five

Unit 4

COMMUNICATION

51

Making a request

Biker Could you let me have some of your water, please? I've drunk all of mine.

Jason I'm sorry, we've hardly got enough for ourselves. But you'll be in Moab in a few minutes.

Biker OK.

Requests	• Can you help me, please?
	• Can I borrow your pen?
	• Could you write your address on this piece of paper?
	• Could I use your cellphone, please?
	• Do you think you could play your music a bit more quietly, please?
Agreeing	• Yes, OK. / Yes, all right.
	• Yes, of course. / Yes, sure.
Refusing	• I'm sorry, but I can't just now. I'm meeting my friend in a minute.
	• I'm afraid it doesn't belong to me, so I can't lend it to you.
	• Actually, I need it myself. Sorry.

EXERCISE 18

Make requests from these notes.

▶ could – come – with me – show – way
 Could you come with me and show me the way, please?

1 can – borrow – bike
2 think – could – video – movie – nine o'clock
3 could – give – lift – your car
4 can – put up – tent – me
5 could – use – computer
6 think – could – walk – faster
7 can – translate – story – German – me
8 could – lend – ten dollars – tomorrow

Then try to think of reasons to refuse the requests. Practice asking and refusing with a partner. Remember to be polite when you refuse, so use phrases like *I'm sorry* or *I'm afraid …*

▶ Could you come with me and show me the way, please?
▶ I'm afraid I don't really have time at the moment. I have to go to my piano lesson. Sorry.

TEST YOUR ENGLISH

The elephant's cousin

If you ever go to Florida, make sure you see a manatee. There are places where you can go and look at them. The manatee
5 lives in water. It's a strange animal. It's about ten feet long and gray-brown in color. It has a big heavy body with two flippers at the front and a tail,
10 and it has a small head with big fat lips. It moves quite slowly. It is sometimes called a 'sea cow', but actually it is a cousin of the elephant. It can live to an age of
15 60 years. Manatees are found on coasts and in rivers in parts of West Africa and America. They like warm weather. About 3,000 of them spend the winter
20 in Florida, and in summer they

travel up the coast, sometimes as far as Virginia. Manatees usually live in family groups. They feed on water plants.

25 They eat, rest and swim around. Every few minutes they come up to breathe. It sounds like a nice life, doesn't it? Manatees have no enemies
30 except humans. Alligators don't attack them because the manatees are too big. In some places manatees are hunted by humans for their meat, skin and
35 oil, although hunting them is against the law in the US. Manatees in Florida are sometimes killed or injured when they are hit by a boat or by a
40 boat's propeller. Something has now been done to protect the animals, and there are areas where boats aren't allowed and zones where they have to go
45 slowly. People are worried that one day there will be no manatees left in the world.

66 sixty-six

TEST YOUR ENGLISH

1 Correct the sentences.

1 A manatee is an animal that lives in trees.
2 It has a small body but a large head.
3 The manatee's nearest relative is the cow.
4 Manatees live only in America.
5 They eat plants that grow in fields.
6 Their greatest enemies are alligators.
7 There are two useful things that people want from manatees.
8 Manatees sometimes sink boats.
9 There are some places where swimmers have to go slowly.

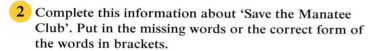

2 Complete this information about 'Save the Manatee Club'. Put in the missing words or the correct form of the words in brackets.

Save the Manatee Club, or SMC, … (start) in 1981 by a group of people … were worried that soon there might … be any manatees left. The aims of the … (organize) are to find … more about manatees, to teach people about them, to … after manatees that have … injured, and to take … in campaigns for new laws so that the animals … (can / protect). SMC gives boat … (own) advice on how they can stop … (injure) manatees. It also works … protect manatees in … (Centre) America and South America.

… the moment SMC has about 40,000 members. There is a website with information, and … you have a question about manatees, you can send an e-mail. SMC gets thousands … requests for information every month. On the website you can even buy gifts … as a manatee plate, a manatee cap or a book … manatees.

3 Look in the text and find the opposite of each word.

1 small   7 down
2 back   8 near
3 thin   9 work
4 quickly   10 many
5 die   11 friends
6 cool   12 nothing

4 Look at these explanations and find the word in the text.

1 having great weight
2 how old something is
3 take air into your body
4 what covers your body
5 badly hurt
6 keep someone safe from danger
7 a rule that says what the people of a country can and can't do

5 Whitney is telling her friends how she met a manatee. Listen to the conversation and then say which summary is the true one.

52

1 A manatee came to Whitney, and she scratched its back. But the manatee didn't like it, so it went away to play with some of its friends.
2 Whitney swam after a manatee and caught it. She scratched its back. The manatee seemed to like it, but it went away. When it came back, she scratched it under its flipper.
3 A manatee came to Whitney, and she scratched its back. The manatee seemed to like it, but it went away. When it came back, she scratched it under its flipper.
4 Whitney swam after a manatee and caught it. She scratched its back. But the manatee didn't like it, so it went away and didn't come back.

sixty-seven **67**

Unit 4 　 READING 　 **Blizzard**

Stefan opened his eyes. He was in bed in a strange room. Through the window he could see the gray sky. On the wall was a picture, and under the picture it said 'Blick auf Frankfurt am Main'. Was he at home in Frankfurt? Something had happened, but Stefan couldn't remember what it was. He felt tired. He closed his eyes.

5   When Stefan woke up again, it started to come back to him. He was driving. The road was very straight and flat. For miles around there were fields of snow, where in summer there had been corn. There wasn't much traffic. The road went on and on. The sky had been gray and heavy all day, and now it started to snow again.

10 The car Stefan was driving wasn't his – he'd rented it at the airport. He'd driven a long way, over the mountains. The night before he'd stayed at a hotel in Des Moines. Yes, Des Moines, Iowa! He was driving across Iowa, in the American Midwest. Stefan and his girlfriend Gabi had planned a trip around the States. But then at Christmas they'd had a big
15 fight, and Gabi had left him. So he'd come alone …

The door opened and a man came in. He was about sixty, tall and thin, with gray hair. 'Are you all right?' he asked. 'Yes,' said Stefan. 'But where am I?' 'You're not far from Millersburg, Iowa. I'm Jim Hartmann, and this is my wife Sylvia.' A woman had come into the room behind Jim.
20 'I'm Stefan Bauer. But what's happened?'

As Stefan asked the question, it all came back to him. He was on the road to the Amana Colonies, and he turned off the main highway. 'I might find a more interesting route,' he thought. But the scenery was the same. The snow was falling heavily now. Soon he was in a blizzard. Huge snowflakes fell on the windshield. It was getting dark, too. He drove very slowly through the snow.
25 He couldn't see very well, and he was completely lost. The snow was getting deeper, and finally the car stopped.

Stefan sat there for a few minutes. 'What should I do now? If I stay here, I might freeze to death,' he thought. 'Maybe I can find a farmhouse.' But there was no light anywhere.

When Stefan got out of the car, the wind hit him. The snow blew straight into his face. He fought
30 his way forward, but the snow was above his knees. He bent his head against the wind and tried to go on. He was starting to think he should go back when he fell. He fell down gently in the snow.

'Your car got stuck in the snow last night,' said Sylvia. 'There was a blizzard. We had a power cut.'
'Yes, I remember now.'
'Jim saw the car lights. Luckily he was able to bring you in on the
35 tractor.'
'You saved my life. I'm lucky to be alive. And you've looked after me and given me a bed. I'm very grateful.'
'What brought you here?' asked Jim.
'I got lost when I turned off the main highway. I was on my way to
40 the Amana Colonies. I'm German, you see.'
'My grandfather was German,' said Jim. 'He came to Iowa from Frankfurt.'
'I come from Frankfurt, too.'
'Oh, really? Maybe we can talk about that while you have something
45 to eat.'

'You'll like Amana,' said Sylvia later. 'It's a nice village with an old-world atmosphere. There's a museum all about the German settlers.'
'And good food,' said Jim. 'Good old-style German food.'

the Amana Colonies

68   sixty-eight

GUNS IN SCHOOL

EXTRA PAGES Unit 1

 53 These two reports are about a shooting incident at a high school in Santee, a town near San Diego, California.

→ page 159-160

Tuesday March 6, 2001

Shooting at Santana High School

Two years ago Andy Williams moved with his dad to Santee, California. He was a
5 small, thin boy from a broken home, and some of the other kids at Santana High School liked to bully him. When he couldn't do stunts on his skateboard, they laughed at him. One or two of the kids liked to hit Andy in the face. He never did anything back. Then someone stole his skateboard. Yesterday morning the 15-year-old student took one of his father's revolvers from the apartment where they lived, carried it to
10 school in his backpack and then fired at least thirty shots at students and teachers. He killed two students and wounded 13 other people, including a teacher and a security guard. The two who died were Randy Gordon (17) and Bryan Zuckor (14).

When they first heard the shots, most students thought it was fireworks, but then they started running. Alicia Zimmer, a student at the school, said that it happened as classes
15 were changing. 'I was probably about 10 feet away from a couple of the victims. It was in the middle of the hall. One victim, a boy, was lying on the floor with his face down. A girl was standing there with blood all over her arms. We heard more shots. It was terrible. Everybody was running. A lot of people were crying.' The police described it as a 'nightmare situation'.

sixty-nine 69

Unit 1 EXTRA PAGES

Are High Schools Safe?

The incident at Santee is the latest in a series of shootings in American high schools in the last few years. In April 1999, for example, two students in Littleton, Colorado killed 12 students and a teacher and wounded 23. Only a month later a 15-year-old boy fired at students at a high school in Conyers, Georgia and wounded six people. Other incidents caused the deaths of 106 school students in five years. The most shocking incident came in Flint, Michigan in February 2000 when a 6-year-old boy shot and killed a girl in his class.

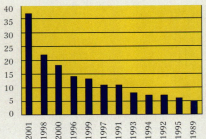
OCCURRENCIES PER YEAR

Statistically, US high schools are safe places for children. For every school which has had a shooting incident, there are ten thousand which haven't had one. But each incident is so terrible that it shocks the whole country. High school shootings are big news, and schools are doing their best to prevent them. At many schools now there are security cameras, and guards inspect schoolbags with metal detectors so that no guns get into the school. It's so easy to buy a gun – or steal one. Most adults own one, and there are probably about 200 million guns in the United States.

Some people think metal detectors are not the answer. Maybe instead we should just listen to what people say. Last weekend Andy Williams told at least twenty people about his plan to shoot people. Then he said it was just a joke. But he took his dad's gun and shot 15 people with it. Why did no one listen to him? Why can't we keep our ears open?

'The best metal detector is the student,' says Ronald Stephens of the National School Safety Center. In three quarters of all incidents, the person with the gun already talked openly about his plan. Students are starting to see that you aren't a snitch if you tell an adult about it. Last week in Twenty-nine Palms, California, 17-year-old Victoria Sudd told her mom about two boys who said they wanted to kill people. Her mom called the police, and they searched the boys' homes and found a gun and a 'death list' with the names of 16 students on it. To the other students Victoria is a hero, not a snitch.

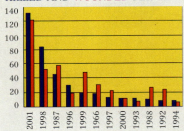
KILLED AND **WOUNDED** PER YEAR

Yesterday California Governor Gray Davis said people should become better at listening. 'We have to hear the signs of alarm or loneliness from kids. We have to make them feel part of the community so that these terrible incidents don't keep happening,' he said. The answer to the problem may lie in better gun controls and better school security, but it also lies in what we say and do when we're with other people – listening to them, making friends, not getting angry, solving problems without bullying or violence.

EXTRA PAGES Unit 1

EXERCISE 1

Write one or two sentences to explain who or what they are.

➡ Santee   Santee is a town near San Diego, California, where there was a shooting incident at a high school.

1 Andy Williams
2 Bryan Zuckor
3 Alicia Zimmer
4 Littleton
5 Flint
6 Ronald Stephens
7 Victoria Sudd
8 Gray Davis

EXERCISE 2

Answer the questions.

1 Why did Andy Williams decide to shoot people?
2 What did the police mean when they called the incident a 'nightmare situation'?
3 Why was the shooting in Michigan especially shocking?
4 Why didn't people believe Andy Williams when he told them about his plan?
5 Do you think Victoria was right to tell an adult about the two boys? Say why or why not.
6 What possible answers are there to the problem of violence in schools?

EXERCISE 3

After the shootings at Santee, reporters were asking the students some questions. Complete their answers.

➡ Reporters How old is Andy?
   Students   He's fifteen.
1 Reporters And how long has he lived in Santee?
   Students   About … .
2 Reporters Where does he live?
   Students   … with … in … .
3 Reporters Do you know where he got the gun?
   Students   I think … belongs … .
4 Reporters Why do you think he shot those people?
   Students   Well, some … him.
5 Reporters How did they bully him? What did they do?
   Students   They laughed … when … . Some … face. And someone … . I expect he felt … .

EXERCISE 4

Which verbs go with which group of objects? Use these verbs: *describe, fire, hear, prevent, search, solve*.

➡ *hear* a noise, a shot, the bell
1 … a shot, a gun, a weapon
2 … a scene, someone, an incident
3 … an accident, a crime, diseases
4 … my bag, a house, the internet
5 … a problem, a puzzle

Then write five sentences of your own. Use each verb with one of its objects.

➡ When I heard the noise, I looked out of the window.

EXERCISE 5

Look at what students told police and reporters after a shooting incident. Each sentence has a verb in the simple past and one in the past progressive. Put each verb into the correct form.

➡ *Michael*   The shooting started (start) while we were doing (do) math.
➡ *Megan*   As I was walking (walk) through the hall, I saw (see) a boy with a gun.
1 *Jessica*   I … (talk) to my friend when we … (hear) a shot.
2 *Chris*   While we … (wait) outside the classroom, suddenly there … (be) a noise like fireworks in the distance.
3 *Brittany* As I … (walk) along the path, someone … (fire) a shot at me.
4 *Matt*   My friend and I … (go) to lunch when we … (see) a boy on the floor with blood on his shirt.
5 *Anthony*   As I … (sit) at the computer, suddenly something … (hit) the window and … (break) it.
6 *Erica*   While a group of us … (stand) around on the grass, a boy suddenly … (take) out a gun.
7 *Danielle* As we … (go) to our classrooms, a security guard … (shout) at us to warn us.
8 *David*   I … (write) some notes on a piece of paper when someone … (start) firing a gun.

seventy-one 71

Smokejumpers

→ page 160

It might be a spectacular scene from a horror movie. Thick smoke is rising from a forest fire in Montana. The fire storm has already destroyed about 60 square miles of forest in only two hours. Its temperature has reached 870°F and it is moving forward over an area several miles wide. The winds take the clouds of smoke to a height of more than 30,000 feet.

Suddenly a small DC-3 plane appears. Right above the forest, ten people in yellow suits and big safety helmets jump out of the plane. Their parachutes open, and after about a minute in the smoke they land safely in a little clearing. Easier said than done, of course. They have arrived at their workplace, but they don't know how they're going to get home again. They are not magicians – they are firefighters. It's their job to fight the fire with the 65 pounds of equipment they carry on their backs. They're called smokejumpers, and they've been to hell and back.

Hell is daily life for about 400 smokejumpers in the US. It can take a few hours to stop a fire, or it can take weeks if the fire is spreading fast. Sometimes it seems an impossible job. Even when the smokejumpers think they have the fire under control, it may suddenly break out again when they aren't expecting it. And who is going to rescue the smokejumpers? Death is pretty close most of the time.

For forty-two years, smokejumping was a man's world. Then in 1981 Deanne Shulman became the first woman smokejumper, and others soon followed. Today one smokejumper in twenty is a woman. They have to pass the same tough physical tests as the men. Shelly Dunlap passed them at the age of 45. One of the things she did was to carry 110 pounds a distance of three miles in under 90 minutes.

Each year these terrible fires take the lives of almost a thousand people. Sometimes people start fires deliberately, but most of them are started by the summer storms that attack North America's huge forests. The smokejumpers try to stop the fire from spreading. Once it is stopped, it will die out. So they hurry to dig ditches, often several miles long, and stop the fire.
5 However, to save other parts of the forest, they often have to cut down trees. It feels terrible to destroy these beautiful trees – 90 feet high, seven feet thick and hundreds of years old – but it has to be done.

Sometimes smokejumpers work for more than 20
10 hours without any rest or sleep. They know they must put out the fire. Even at night they can't leave it. If they need to
15 sleep, they find a safe place which has already been destroyed by the fire. Then they lie down in their sleeping bags.
20 They're clearly a special kind of people.

Smokejumpers must not weigh more than 200 pounds because landing on hard ground is dangerous for their knees and
25 feet. Most go on jumping until they have to stop because of the pain. Some have done it for more than 20 years. They still like it better than an ordinary job. 'It's great fun,' they say. They like being in a close group
30 with its own private language. Sometimes a fire which has been burning for days will suddenly explode into a huge ball. The smokejumpers call the explosion 'Big Ernie'.

A famous smokejumper, Billy Martin,
35 jumped to his death in 1991. He once said: 'Our job is simply the best in the world. We are sent to the most beautiful places and are paid for the journey. We are offered a trip in a roller coaster with a parachute
40 jump at the end, and they throw down all the camping equipment we need.'

Unit 2 EXTRA PAGES

EXERCISE 1

Explain who or what these are:

1 smokejumpers
2 Montana
3 a DC-3
4 Deanne Shulman
5 Shelly Dunlap
6 Big Ernie
7 Billy Martin

EXERCISE 2

Find words from the same word families as those in brackets.

1 It's always dangerous to jump from a great … (high), even with a parachute.
2 Smokejumpers are not … (magic).
3 They have to think about their own … (safe) before they can get into their … (sleep) bags.
4 Smokejumpers are always close to … (dead) in their … (day) work.
5 A huge … (explode) is … (usual) called a 'Big Ernie'.
6 If you want to be a smokejumper, your … (weigh) cannot be more than 200 pounds.

EXERCISE 3

A reporter is writing about a forest fire. Here are some of his sentences. Put them into the passive. Use a phrase with *by* if you need to.

➡ Summer storms start most of the fires.
   Most of the fires are started by summer storms.
1 We can see thick smoke above the forest.
2 These fires kill almost a thousand people every year.
3 Someone must put them out as quickly as possible.
4 The smokejumpers brought the fire under control.
5 They have cut down some trees to save the rest of the forest.
6 The fire has destroyed a large area of the forest.

EXERCISE 4

Put in the correct forms of the words in brackets.

➡ Shelly was older (old) than most smokejumpers, but she easily (easy) passed her test.
1 Only the … (tough) of the firefighters can … (serious) expect to become smokejumpers.
2 They have to get … (very/fit), and they have to learn to work … (quick).
3 Of course the work is much … (dangerous) than an office job.
4 It is … (easy) than you might think to make a … (serious) mistake.
5 It is … (absolute/true) that most jobs are … (boring) than a smokejumper's job.
6 Be a smokejumper. Visit … (beautiful) places and have a … (simple/wonderful) time.

EXERCISE 5

Translate the third paragraph on page 72 (lines 22-31) into good German. If there are words that you don't know or don't remember, try to guess their meaning. When you do this, look at what the whole sentence might mean.

EXERCISE 6

Imagine you are a smokejumper. Last week you were a member of a team which fought a big fire in Montana. Tell your friends the story. You can use these notes.

One day – morning – hear about – fire / fly – DC-3 / see – smoke / jump – land – clearing / fight – fire – … days / hard work / have to – dig – ditch / cut down – trees / not much sleep / fire – die out / fly back / tired / ready – next fire

74 seventy-four

Gone with the Wind

→ page 160

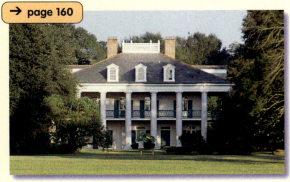

'Gone with the Wind' is a novel about white people in Georgia in the American South at the time of the Civil War. In this part of the story, 19-year-old Scarlett O'Hara has returned from Atlanta to her family's home, Tara, and
5 its cotton plantation. Union soldiers have been there and taken all the food. Scarlett's two sisters have been very ill. Most of the slaves have run away, so Scarlett, her friend Melanie and her sisters have to do some work for the first time in their lives if they are going to survive.

10 The summer lasted into November that year, and the warm days were bright days for those at Tara. The worst was over. They had a horse now, and they could ride instead of walk. They had eggs for breakfast and ham for supper, and once they even
15 had chicken.

Scarlett's visit to her neighbors had done her good. Just to know that some of the family friends and old homes had survived drove out the terrible lost and alone feeling which had weighed on her. It was the
20 tradition that neighbor helped neighbor, and they refused to take any money from Scarlett. They told her that she could give them something back next year, when Tara was on its feet again.

Every morning when Scarlett got up, she thanked
25 God for the blue sky and the warm sun, because each day of good weather put off the time when warm clothes were needed. (She knew it was dangerous to travel anywhere to buy clothes because the horse might be stolen by Yankee or
30 Confederate soldiers.) And each warm day saw more cotton in the empty slave cabins, the only place left on the plantation where they could keep it. The cabins were almost full now.

Scarlett had not intended to do any cotton picking
35 herself, but she soon saw that the others couldn't do it without her. At first it seemed unthinkable that she, an O'Hara lady, should work in the fields. She had intended that the negroes should do the field work while she and her sisters looked after the house, but
40 here she found a feeling even stronger than her own. Pork, Mammy and Prissy made clear their shock at the idea of working in the fields. They were house niggers, not field hands, they repeated. Mammy reminded Scarlett that she was born in a great
45 house, not in a slave cabin, and had slept in her mistress's bedroom, at the foot of the bed.

CHARACTERS

WHITE PEOPLE	BLACK PEOPLE
Scarlett O'Hara	Pork *(a slave)*
Suellen *(Scarlett's sister)*	Mammy *(a slave)*
Carreen *(Scarlett's sister)*	Dilcey *(a slave)*
Melanie *(Scarlett's friend)*	Prissy *(Dilcey's*
Brent *(Carreen's boyfriend)*	*daughter, a slave)*

seventy-five 75

Unit 3 — EXTRA PAGES

Scarlett refused to listen and drove them all into the cotton fields. But Mammy and Pork worked so slowly and protested so much that Scarlett sent Mammy back to the kitchen to cook and Pork to the woods and the river to catch rabbits and fish. Next she sent
5 her sisters and Melanie into the fields, but that had worked no better. Melanie picked quickly and willingly for an hour in the hot sun and then fainted and had to stay in bed for a week. Suellen pretended to faint too, but she soon woke up when Scarlett poured water in her face. Finally she refused.
10 'I won't work in the fields like a nigger! You can't make me. What if any of our friends ever heard of it?'
'I'll help you, Sissy,' said Carreen. 'I'll work for Sue and Mel too. She isn't well yet and shouldn't be out in the sun.'

Scarlett said gratefully: 'Thank you, Sugarbaby.' She felt worried
15 when she looked at her younger sister. She had been silent since her illness. She found the world very different now. She couldn't understand what had happened, but she did what she was told and worked willingly. Scarlett didn't see that Brent's death had hit Carreen hard. To Scarlett, Carreen was still 'baby sister', too
20 young to have a serious love affair.

Scarlett's back was breaking, and her hands were rough from the cotton. She needed a sister as strong as Suellen and as willing as Carreen. After an hour it was clear that Carreen was not well enough, so Scarlett sent her back to the house.

25 Now only Dilcey was left, and Dilcey's daughter Prissy. Prissy picked slowly and complained about her feet and her back and how tired she was, until her mother took a cotton stalk and beat her. After that she worked a little better. Dilcey worked silently, like a machine, and she never seemed to get tired. Scarlett's back
30 hurt, and she could feel the weight of the cotton-bag she carried. She thought that Dilcey was worth her weight in gold.

Even though Scarlett was very tired, she felt more hopeful as the cotton slowly made its way from the fields to the cabins. There was something about cotton that gave her new hope. Tara, like
35 the whole South, had become rich on cotton, and Scarlett believed that Tara and the South would rise again out of the red fields.

(adapted from Margaret Mitchell *Gone with the Wind*)

EXERCISE 1

Explain who or what they are.

➡ Georgia **Georgia** is a state in the American South.
1 the Civil War
2 Scarlett O'Hara
3 Atlanta
4 Tara
5 Yankee
6 Confederate
7 Pork and Mammy
8 Suellen and Carreen
9 Brent

EXERCISE 2

Look at the text and find the words that give you the information.

➡ There is nothing to eat at Tara. Union soldiers have taken all the food. (page 75, lines 5-6)
1 There aren't many slaves left on the plantation.
2 The white women and girls haven't done any hard work before.
3 They were afraid to go a long distance from the plantation.
4 The house slaves thought they were too good to do field work.
5 Suellen wasn't really ill, but she just wanted an excuse to stop working.
6 Carreen had not been well.
7 Carreen had been in love.
8 Dilcey didn't speak as she picked cotton.

EXERCISE 3

Find words in the text that have a similar meaning to these words.

1 finished (page 75, lines 10-15)
2 awful (page 75, lines 16-23)
3 every (page 75, lines 24-33)
4 shed (page 75, lines 24-33)
5 forest (page 76, lines 1-9)
6 important (page 76, lines 14-20)
7 protested (page 76, lines 25-31)
8 hit (page 76, lines 25-31)

EXERCISE 4

Put the words in the right group.

> back • chicken • face • faint • grateful • hands • hopeful • horse • pick • pour • rabbit • sky • sun • warm • worried

Animals	Weather	Actions	Feelings	Parts of the body
rabbit	…	…	…	…
…				

Then think of more words that belong in these groups. Write down at least two more words for each group.

EXERCISE 5

Translate these three paragraphs into good German.

Gone with the Wind is one of the most famous movies in the history of the cinema. It lasts almost four hours, and it has been called a 'Civil War soap opera'.

The movie tells the story of a beautiful young woman called Scarlett O'Hara. Scarlett comes from a family who own a cotton plantation in Georgia. She is a silly girl but at the same time a very strong character and a fighter. During the Civil War she goes to Atlanta. When the Yankees are near and the city is burning, she escapes at the last minute. She marries three times and is secretly in love with her friend's husband. Her other great love is Rhett Butler, her third husband. At the end of the movie, when Rhett leaves Scarlett, she is still hopeful. The famous last line is 'Tomorrow is another day'.

Gone with the Wind was first shown in Atlanta in December 1939, when hundreds of thousands of people were out on the streets to see the stars. The movie won nine Oscars and became probably the most popular movie ever.

EXERCISE 6

Put in the following verbs in the correct form:
get, go, hurry, pick, put, run, sit, stay, wake.

➡ After Atlanta was burned down, Scarlett **went** back to Tara.
1. The slaves all … away during the Civil War.
2. Scarlett … up early every morning.
3. Scarlett wanted to … off the time when they had to travel to buy clothes.
4. Melanie … in bed for a week.
5. Prissy was working too slowly, so Scarlett told her to … up.
6. Suellen soon … up when some cold water was poured in her face.
7. Afterwards they all … down to rest.
8. Scarlett … up the cotton-bag and took it to the cabin.

Unit 4 EXTRA PAGES   ## Headfirst into America!   → page 160

 Craig and Marlene Graham, daughter Courtney (12) and son Collier (3) were living in Wichita,
57 Kansas. Craig and Marlene were very busy with their careers and never had enough time for family
life. So they sold their home, bought a van and took their kids on a one-year tour of all 50 states of
the US. They left on Independence Day, July 4 1996, and got back home on the same day the
5 following year. It was a great adventure. Marlene wrote a book about the trip called *Headfirst into
America!* They had a website, too. Here are their answers to some frequently asked questions.

How many miles did you travel?

Craig   About 55,000 miles. We bought the van new. It's been a pretty
10   good vehicle.

Marlene   It has had a funny noise somewhere since day one, but we've had no major breakdowns.

What route did you travel?

15 Marlene   First we went north from Kansas, then across to the West, then right across the South to Florida. Then we went up the east coast to Maine and then
20   back across to Kansas.

Craig   It sounds easy, doesn't it?

Starting in Wichita, July 4th 1996

What about Alaska and Hawaii?

Marlene   We drove up through Canada to Alaska and took a ferry back down the coast.
Courtney   We flew to Hawaii from Los Angeles.

Did you have sponsors?

Marlene   We had a website sponsor but no major sponsor for the trip. We used the money from the sale of our home. We had to be pretty careful with our money, but we still spent $2,300 a month.

What about Courtney's schoolwork?

30 Marlene   We taught Courtney ourselves. Math was difficult for us, but history and geography were easier. She had classes on picnic benches, at people's homes, on ferry boats, etc. All of America was her classroom.

Didn't Courtney miss her friends?

Courtney   I stayed in contact with my Wichita friends through postcards, e-mail and phone calls.
35 Marlene   But she learned to make new friends all across America.

Did you guys ever get into arguments?

Craig   Hey, you can't travel around in a van for a year at a time and not have some major disagreements.
Marlene   I remember a big fight where we just decided to quit and go home.
40 Craig   Then Collier told us how much he was enjoying the trip, so we kept going.

Did the media find out about you?

Craig   Yes, they found out about us through the internet. We did a TV interview on CNN in Atlanta, Georgia, and suddenly we were in hundreds of newspapers across the country.
Courtney   We were interviewed on the *Today* show, too. That was in New York City.

78 seventy-eight

EXTRA PAGES Unit 4

What are some of your most interesting experiences?

Collier   We saw Keiko, the whale in *Free Willy*.
Craig   That was in Oregon. I think he's gone to Iceland now.
Courtney   We took part in a Disney World parade and waved at all the crowds. That was great.
Marlene   We visited all the state capitals, and we met 20 state governors.
Collier   One time when we woke up in the morning, there was a buffalo right outside our van. He looked in the window at us.

Were you ever in danger?

Courtney   Yes, when we got lost in some caves.
Craig   That was in Idaho. We were exploring some caves. It was getting dark, and we lost the trail.
Marlene   We had to crawl around among the rocks for about an hour until we found the way back to the van. I was scared.

A quiet road in Idaho

Where are the friendliest people?

Marlene   They're everywhere. People say Alabama and Georgia are friendly, and it's true. But we also found friendly people in the New York subways.
Craig   In Philadelphia our van was broken into and a few things stolen. That wasn't so good. But the people there were so sorry for us and so friendly and helpful. We'll never forget that.
Marlene   We were often invited to spend the night at the homes of people we met on the trip – or people who made contact with us over the internet. We stayed with about sixty families or individuals. It was fun making new friends, and we're still in contact with most of those people.

What is your favorite state?

Collier   It's Florida because that's where my grandparents live.
Craig   We all liked the national parks in the red rock country of Utah.
Marlene   Every state has something special if you take the time to really look.

(adapted from www.usatrip.org)

Bryce Canyon, Utah

EXERCISE 1

Answer the questions.

1. Where did the family's journey begin and end?
2. How many of the US states did the Grahams visit?
3. How did they travel?
4. How did they get to Hawaii?
5. Who paid for the trip?
6. What did they do about Courtney's school work?
7. How could the Grahams tell their news to friends back home?
8. How did the family become news?
9. What happened in Philadelphia?

seventy-nine 79

EXERCISE 2

Complete Marlene's sentences. Put in one of these words from the text: *careers, disagreements, experience, following, frequently, helpful, route, waved.*

1. The trip around the US was a wonderful … for all of us.
2. We had never done enough together as a family because Craig and I were too busy with our … .
3. On July 4 we … goodbye to all our friends.
4. People we met gave us a lot of … advice about places to see.
5. You can't always agree about everything. All families have their little … .
6. The kids were looking forward to our visit to Disney World the … day.
7. We were late, so we decided to take the fastest … to our destination.
8. There are some questions about our trip that people … ask us.

EXERCISE 4

Make sentences from the notes. Use *after*, the past perfect and the simple past. Be careful – most of the verbs are irregular.

▶ family – sell – home – leave – one-year tour – States
   After the family had sold their home, they left on a one-year tour of the States.

1. they – look – around – city of Wilmington – cross – into Pennsylvania
2. they – see – buffalo – kids – want – go along – some of the trails
3. Marlene – write – her notes – until – two – morning – feel – pretty tired
4. they – meet – governor – see – some of the sights
5. family – leave – Arizona – drive – Las Vegas
6. they – arrive – home – Craig and Marlene – begin – think – next trip

EXERCISE 3

Translate into German this information about a town in Washington State.

Along our route we saw beautiful mountains and dark forests. Finally we came to the popular town of Leavenworth, where we made a short stop. In the 1960s Leavenworth wanted to bring in some tourists, so the town decided to become Bavarian. Here you will find Bavarian restaurants, hotels, gift shops and even Bavarian gas stations. Several times a year Bavarian festivals take place here.

As we walked along the town's main street, the peace was suddenly broken by loud Bavarian music. We couldn't see where it was coming from because a tree was in the way, so we crossed the street quickly and looked up. There we saw a huge glockenspiel near the top of a building. I was able to get a few seconds on video before the music stopped and the doors closed behind the little people.

(adapted from Marlene Smith-Graham *Headfirst into America!*)

Main Street, Leavenworth

EXERCISE 5

Answer the following questions.

1. Which four states have a border with Mexico?
2. When the Grahams visited Cypress Gardens, which state were they in?
3. If you went as far to the north-east as you could go in the US, which state would you be in?
4. Which city in the US is not in a US state?
5. Which state lies next to four of the five Great Lakes?
6. How many states begin with the word 'New', and which are they?
7. What states are these the capitals of: Atlanta, Des Moines, Harrisburg, Montgomery, Richmond?
8. In one place you can stand in four states at once. What are the states?

PROJECTS

1 US cities

Look at this information about San Francisco.

The city of San Francisco is in California, on the west coast. It is famous for Golden Gate Bridge, and the famous cable cars that go up and down the steep hills. San Francisco was only a small place before gold was found in California in 1848. It soon became a big city as people came to look for gold. In 1906 most of San Francisco was destroyed in an earthquake. Today it is a beautiful city – and an exciting one.

Here are four interesting cities to find out about.

Work in groups. Choose a city and find some information about it. Then imagine your class is going to visit the city. Plan a sightseeing tour. Your group can be the guides for the rest of the class. Take turns to tell them about the sights they are seeing as you show them around. It will help if you have some posters or photos.

2 High schools

A Make a word map of American high schools. Put in the words you know and try to find some new words. Here are some you can add in: *auto mechanics, guidance counselor, principal, sophomore*.

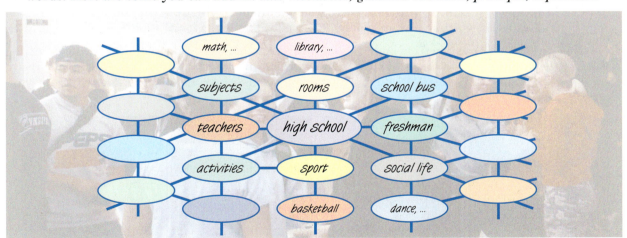

Make a wall chart with all the words you have found.

B Look on the internet and find a high school website. If you can, find a high school where German is taught. Make a wall chart with information about the school. Try to e-mail the school. Maybe you can exchange information and photos.

eighty-one 81

PROJECTS

3 Native Americans

If you've seen lots of old Hollywood movies, you might think that a Native American (an 'Indian') is like a wild animal who likes to attack people and kill them.

Navajo women

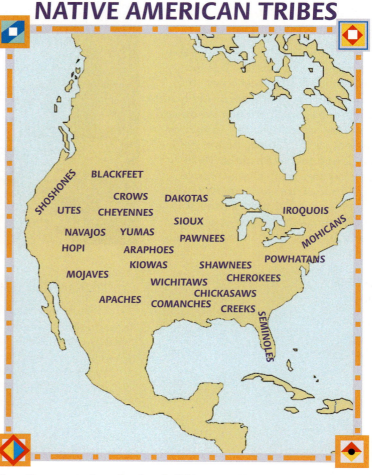
NATIVE AMERICAN TRIBES

SHOSHONES BLACKFEET
UTES CROWS DAKOTAS
CHEYENNES SIOUX IROQUOIS
NAVAJOS YUMAS PAWNEES
HOPI ARAPHOES MOHICANS
KIOWAS SHAWNEES POWHATANS
MOJAVES WICHITAWS CHEROKEES
APACHES CHICKASAWS
COMANCHES CREEKS
SEMINOLES

But real life is different.

When Europeans first came to America, there were hundreds of different tribes there, and hundreds of different languages were spoken. Each tribe had its own way of life.

Work in groups. Choose one tribe and find out all you can about it. Where did the members of the tribe live, and where do they live now? What was their traditional way of life? What were their ideas? What happened to them when the white people came? Make a wall chart and tell your classmates all about the tribe.

Shawnee

Blackfoot

Crow

Navajo

82 eighty-two

PROJECTS

4 National parks

National parks began in the US. There are over fifty of them. Here is some information about Yellowstone National Park.

Yellowstone is in the Rocky Mountains and was the first national park. It has waterfalls, mountains, forests, canyons and Yellowstone Lake. There are bears and buffalo. And Yellowstone is famous for its geysers.

There's a 140-mile road through the park, so you can drive through and look at the scenery. Or you can ride or walk along one of the trails. There are a thousand miles of them.

Most visitors walk less than a hundred meters from their car, so you can always get away from the crowds.

Choose a national park and find out about it. You could use the internet. If you search for National Park Service, you'll find links to the individual park websites. When you've got some information, your group should make a presentation and explain to the rest of the class why your park is worth a visit.

5 American football

Work in groups on these tasks.

A Make a list of all the teams in the National Football League. Draw a map of the United States and write the names on the map. The teams have names like 'Oilers' or 'Bears'. Can you translate these names into German?

B Which teams played in the last Super Bowl? What was the result? Find out as much as you can about the winners. Where do they play? Who are their best players? How many games did they win and lose last season? Make a wall chart about the team. Maybe someone has a T-shirt with the team's logo on that you can add to the display.

C What are the rules of the game? What is the aim? Find out some of the most important rules and translate them into German.

D Draw a diagram of the field of play. Make a list of all the different positions in the game like 'right guard' and 'quarterback'. Draw a diagram of a possible offensive formation and a possible defensive one. Make a list of other special football words like 'touchdown' and explain what they mean.

E Who are the big stars of American football? Choose one or two famous players and make a wall chart with photos and details about them.

eighty-three 83

REVISION

EXERCISE 1

Charles A. Lindbergh (*L*) has just made the first non-stop flight from New York to Paris. At Le Bourget airfield some reporters (*R*) are talking to him. Complete the questions.

Charles Lindbergh (on right) with his airplane 'Spirit of St. Louis' in 1927.

R How ... feel, Mr Lindbergh?
L Oh, I'm a bit tired but OK.
R ... proud you were successful?
L Well, I made it.
R ... to your family yet?
L No, I haven't spoken to them yet. But I'm going to phone them later.
R ... fly across the Atlantic?
L Well, I think I just wanted to show that it's possible.
R ... the lights of the airfield?
L Yes, I saw them from far away. They used car headlights to show me where to land.
R ... your flight take?
L It took thirty-three and a half hours.
R Is it true that you ... a prize for the first non-stop flight? ... much money ... ?
L I guess I've won $25,000, but I'm not sure.
R ... ever ... of giving up during your flight?
L Well, I wanted to give up right after the start because of the terrible weather. But when I was over Newfoundland, I just went on.
R ... any plans for your stay in Europe?
L No, I haven't really, but I want to explore Europe a bit.

EXERCISE 2

Craig and Andreas from Germany are visiting the Smithsonian Museum of American History. Andreas wants to know a lot about the first settlers. Put in the question tags.

Craig You haven't been to this museum before, ... ?
Andreas No, I haven't. It's my first time. But you've come here before, ... ?
Craig Sure. Lots of times.
Andreas The first people who settled in America came from Asia, ... ?
Craig Yes, they came about 40,000 years ago.
Andreas There were many different tribes, ... ?
Craig I think you can see the names of all the tribes in the east of the US on this map, ... ?
Andreas Oh yes. Here it says 'Powhatan'. That was the name of an Indian chief, ... ?
Craig Exactly. His daughter was Pocahontas. You've heard of her, ... ?
Andreas Well, there is this story about her and Captain Smith, ... ?
Craig You mean that she saved his life? That isn't really true, ... ?
Andreas Maybe not, but it's a nice story. You can see her picture somewhere in the museum, ... ?
Craig I don't know. But we can ask the guide ... ?
Andreas Oh, yes, she will know, ... ?

EXERCISE 3

Complete this text using the simple past or the present perfect.

Since home computers first ... (appear) in the early 1980's, technology ... (change) a lot. Before then only large companies ... (have) computers. These huge machines sometimes ... (fill) a whole room. But the first home computers ... (be) simple machines for simple things. They ... (be / not) very powerful. These early computers ... (cost / often) a lot of money and people ... (pay / sometimes) thousands of dollars for machines which actually ... (do) very little. Most people ... (use) computers as expensive typewriters or for playing games.
Times ... (change) since then. Computers ... (now / become) powerful machines which can do useful things. Software companies ... (create) a lot of different programs, which can do everything from teaching languages to drawing. Computer games are still very popular, but today's games ... (become) faster, more exciting. Many computer users ... (now / discover) the internet and the World Wide Web.

84 eighty-four

REVISION

EXERCISE 4

Sarah is on a trek in Nepal. Complete the sentences in her diary using the simple present or the present progressive.

November 12, 2001

Today ... (be) the second day of my trek up Mount Annapurna. I am exhausted and I just hope I'll be able to do the complete trek. It ... (take) much longer than I expected, but I ... (want / still) to go on. Nepal is a fascinating country, but I have a lot to learn before I can really say I know it. Everything ... (be) so different, and I ... (try) to get used to the Nepali way of life. I ... (learn) a little bit of the local language to make communication easier. Although I still ... (understand / not) very much, I think that I ... (get better / already). At the moment I ... (travel) with Geoffrey, a student from Leeds in England. He ... (be) a nice guy, but he's always in a hurry.

He ... (walk / always) ahead of me and ... (complain) that I am too slow. I usually ... (do) my best to keep up with him, but he is fitter than me.

Right now, we ... (sit) in a little inn near the bottom of the mountain. Geoffrey ... (talk) to the owner of the inn. They ... (discuss) the differences between life in England and life in Nepal. I ... (know / not) the owner's real name, but everybody ... (call / just) him Lin. Lin ... (speak) English very well and he ... (try) to teach Geoffrey some words in Nepali. Every time Lin ... (say) a new word, Geoffrey ... (try) to repeat it. Unfortunately, Geoffrey ... (seem) to have trouble learning foreign languages. I just ... (hope) we don't get lost and have to ask for directions.

eighty-five 85

REVISION

EXERCISE 5

Use the present perfect or the present perfect progressive and put in *since* or *for*.

1. Kevin is in Boston. He … in Boston … Friday.
2. I know Fiona very well. I … her … a long time.
3. Boston is in Massachusetts. It … the state capital … 1780.
4. The USS Constitution is old. She … a museum ship … 1997.
5. We're learning English. We … English … four years.
6. I like the new school I go to. I … there … six months now.
7. My brother works for Boston Adventure tours. He … for them … he was 25.
8. Our teacher is ill. He … in hospital … a week now.

◄ Old South Meeting House

USS Constitution ►

Massachusetts State House

EXERCISE 6

Complete the sentences. Use *going to* and one of these verbs: *buy, phone, rain, read, relax, sell, walk*.

1. I don't want to go home by bus. I … .
2. Don't forget your umbrella. Look at those clouds, it … .
3. Janet has just bought a magazine. She … it after tea.
4. Mum wants to talk to you. She … you this evening.
5. The Frintons don't need their car any more. They … it.
6. It's Sally's birthday tomorrow. Her boyfriend … her a present.
7. Dad feels tired. He … for half an hour.

EXERCISE 7

Della wants to see Ray, but he's very busy at work. Use *will* or *won't* and complete the telephone conversation.

Della … (you / be) at home tonight, Ray?
Ray Well, I'm not sure. I don't expect I … (be able to) finish my report before 9 o'clock so I … (not / be) home until ten.
Della Right. What about the day after tomorrow? … (you / have) time for lunch?
Ray Sorry. I … (be) in a meeting at lunchtime.
Della What time do you think …(the meeting / end)?
Ray It … (not / finish) before 2 o'clock. But what about tomorrow evening, Della? I … (be) free around 7 o'clock.
Della Great. I … (meet) you in front of your office at 7.15 then.
Ray OK. I … (see) you then. Bye.
Della Bye, Ray.

86 eighty-six

REVISION

EXERCISE 8

This interview with the American author Michael Crichton (*M.C.*) appeared in *Movie Review* (*M.R.*) in December 1999. Put the verbs in brackets in the correct tense.

M.R. This week our special guest is Michael Crichton. He … (be) the author of over a dozen best-selling novels and … (direct) several films so far. He … (win) a number of awards during the last few years. Mr Crichton, please tell us about your life.

M.C. Well, I … (be) born in Chicago on October 23, 1942, but my family … (move) to Roslyn, a suburb of New York City, when I … (be) six. I … (graduate) from Roslyn High School in 1960. Then I … (decide) to go to Harvard University and to become a writer. But I … (not/like) literature at Harvard University very much.

M.R. What … (you/do) then?

M.C. I … (begin) training as a doctor. While I … (study) at medical school, I … (start/write) thrillers under different names. During my final year at medical school I … (finish) writing *The Andromeda Strain*. It … (become) a best-seller and I … (sell) it to Hollywood.

M.R. Since that time you … (write) a number of other novels that were made into movies, haven't you?

M.C. Well, the best-known … (be) *Congo*, *Jurassic Park*, *The Lost World* and *Rising Sun*.

M.R. And what … (you/do) at the moment?

M.C. I … (just/finish) my latest novel *Timeline*.

M.R. What is it about?

M.C. It's an adventure story about some people who … (use) new technology to travel to 14th-century France to help a friend.

M.R. What … (be) your plans for the future?

M.C. We … (produce) a movie and a computer game called *Timeline*.

M.R. I'm sure it … (be) as successful as your other movies. Thank you, Mr Crichton.

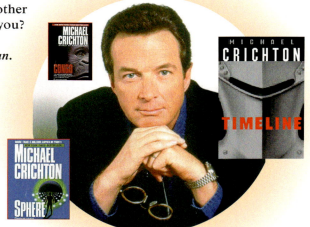

EXERCISE 9

The Trumps and their four children want to go to Florida during the summer vacation. They're going to stay at Aunt Betty's house. Complete the conversation. Put in *someone (3x), something, somewhere, anyone, anything, no one (2x), nothing, everyone, everything* and *everywhere*.

Mrs Trump	Where are all your bags and things? Put … in the back of the bus. And don't forget … .
Mr Trump	It's noon already. Can we go now? Is … here?
Cindy	No, … is missing. Guess who.
Mrs Trump	Where's Neil? Has … seen him?
Nathan	I've just been in the house. I've looked … , but he's not there.
Mrs Trump	But he must be … .
Mr Trump	Wait a minute. I'll have a look. (*Ten minutes later …*)
Mr Trump	I've asked all our neighbors, but … has seen him this morning.
Mrs Trump	We must do … . Let's ring the police.
Alicia	Wait a minute, it's OK. … is coming down the street, look. Oh yes, it's Neil.
Mrs Trump	Where have you been, Neil? What happened to you?
Neil	… really. We didn't have a present for Aunt Betty and … knew what she might like. Well, this morning at six o'clock I remembered the garage sale in Albany Street. I found this picnic basket, but I didn't have enough money. Then … told me I could have it for half the price if I helped with the sale. But I'm here now. So let's go.

REVISION

EXERCISE 10

Complete the sentences with the superlative form of these adjectives: *big, dangerous, expensive, good, old, successful.*

1   The … shark is the white shark. People often call it the man-eater.
2   At the age of 75, the actor Paul Newman was the … driver in a car race in Daytona.
3   The … guitar in the world is 11.63 m long and 4.87 m wide. You need six people to play it.
4   The bat is the animal with the … ears. It can even see with its ears.
5   *Ben-Hur* (USA 1926) was the … silent movie. It cost three million dollars.
6   The … jockey was the American Bill Shoemaker. Between 1949 and 1990 he won 8,833 horse races.

EXERCISE 11

Mrs Baxter is looking for a car. She'd like something really special, but she isn't sure exactly what. This advertisement was in the local newspaper last Saturday. Compare the three cars and complete the sentences below.

USED CARS	vintage car	limousine	sports car
How old?	1942	1999	2000
How long?	4.80 m	5.20 m	3.80 m
How heavy?	980 kg	980 kg	870 kg
How fast?	110 kph	200 kph	240 kph
Engine?	3 liters	6 liters	3,5 liters
Price?	$38,000	$25,200	$20,400

1   The sports car is … the limousine. (new)
2   The vintage car is … of the three cars. (old)
3   The vintage car is … the sports car, but not as … the limousine. (long)
4   The sports car is … of the three cars. (fast)
5   The vintage car is … the limousine. (heavy)
6   The engine of the sports car is … the one of the vintage car. (big)
7   The limousine is … the sports car (slow)
8   The vintage car isn't … as the sports car. (short)
9   The vintage car is … the limousine (expensive)
10 The … car is the sports car. (cheap)

EXERCISE 12

Rebecca has found a job. Complete the text and decide if you need an adjective or an adverb.

In May Rebecca answered an advertisement in the California Post. It was from the … (famous) MGM studios. They were looking for girls who were … (real) interested in working with the camera teams. Three weeks later a letter from MGM … (final) arrived. The … (long) and … (blue) envelope had the MGM logo on it. Rebecca opened it … (nervous). She read the … (short) letter … (quick). She was very … (excited) because it was an invitation to an interview. On the day of the interview she arrived 45 minutes … (early) but three girls were already there. Rebecca spoke to them, and they all seemed very … (nice). The two interviewers, a … (young) man and woman, spoke to her. They were very … (friendly) and Rebecca … (slow) began to feel less … (nervous) and more … (confident). The questions they asked were quite … (hard) and she had to think … (careful). When she wasn't … (sure) she answered very … (quiet) and they asked her to speak more … (loud). She soon had the feeling that the interview wasn't going … (good). At the end of the interview she could … (hard) believe her luck when they … (sudden) asked her if she was … (free) to start work the next morning.

REVISION

EXERCISE 13

Complete the sentences using subject and object pronouns.

1 …'s usually quite cold in New York in winter.
2 Jane and I are going downtown tonight. …'re going to a party. Would you like to come with … ?
3 Where are my keys? I put … on my bag a moment ago, but now …'ve disappeared.
4 I'm looking for Neil. Have … seen …? – Yes, … was over there ten minutes ago.
5 … can't drive a car in Britain until …'re 17 years old.
6 … can't do all this work on our own. – I know. The others are coming. …'ve asked … to help … .
7 Lisa likes cats, but cats don't like … .
8 What did you think of the movie, Ryan? – Well, … enjoyed … very much.

EXERCISE 14

Helen is showing her holiday photos to a friend. Join the two sentences and use *where, who, which* or *whose* where necessary.

1 That's the guide, Mrs Evans. She looked after us.
2 That's the Williams family. They stayed at the same hotel.
3 That is Mr Ferris. His wife worked in the hotel.
4 That's the Key Largo Disco. We went to it four or five times.
5 Here's the Rodrigez family. We met them in the Mexican restaurant.
6 That's Mrs White. Her husband worked in a bookshop in Orlando.
7 That's Epcot Center. I met Craig there.

EXERCISE 15

This is the story of Joseph Späh, an American comedian who survived the Hindenburg disaster in 1937.

Complete the text using the simple past or the past progressive.

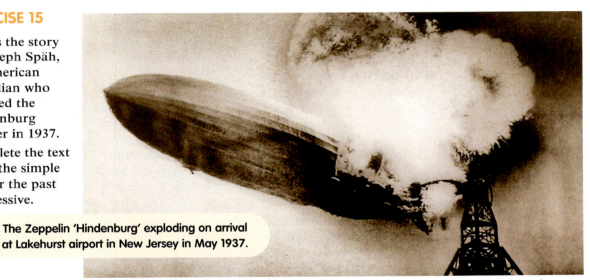

The Zeppelin 'Hindenburg' exploding on arrival at Lakehurst airport in New Jersey in May 1937.

Joseph Späh was a comedian who … (perform) under the name 'Ben Dova'. During March and April, 1937 he … (tour) a number of European cities. After his last show in Germany, Späh … (decide) to travel back to New York on the Zeppelin Hindenburg. During his journey Späh … (look forward to) his arrival in New York, where he … (live) with his wife Evelyn and three children. After 60 hours they finally … (reach) Manhattan.

A light rain … (fall) when the Hindenburg finally … (arrive) at Lakehurst airport in New Jersey on May 6, at 7 P.M. While Späh … (just / take out) his movie camera to film the arrival from one of the windows, the Zeppelin quickly … (turn) to the left. On the ground, reporter Herbert Morrisson … (get) ready for the first coast-to-coast radio program when the captain of the Hindenburg, Max Pruss, … (begin) to slow down. At that moment the disaster … (happen). At a height of 260 feet the Hindenburg suddenly … (explode). Späh … (use) his camera to break the window. He … (wait) until the ground was only forty feet below him before he … (jump). Späh's wife and children … (wait) in the car when they … (see) the ship explode. Joseph … (escape) from the burning ship just in time. His left foot … (be) broken, but he was lucky to be among the 61 people who … (survive) the disaster.

AMERICAN LITERATURE

A very short history of American literature

When the first colonists came to America and founded places like Jamestown or Plimoth Plantation, surviving was more important than reading or writing books. But after a few years the first American authors started writing diaries or reports about life in the New World.

In the 18th century people traveled west to find new land. The frontier was pushed further west and new states were created.

The first major American writer of novels was **James Fenimore Cooper (1789-1851)**. His first works were a number of sea stories, but most people remember him for his *Leatherstocking Tales*: *The Last of the Mohicans* (1826), *The Prairie* (1827) and others. These adventure stories about Indians and frontier life were the beginning of Western stories that are still popular today in films or books. In Cooper's stories Indians are not shown as cruel natives. He respected them and shared their love of nature.

Edgar Allan Poe (1809-1849) was an American author of the 19th century who also became well-known in Europe. He wrote detective stories (*The Murders in the Rue Morgue*), horror stories (*The Fall of the House of Usher*) and a number of poems (*The Raven and Other Poems*). Poe thought good stories should be short and show extreme feelings. Some people think he invented the modern 'short story'.

Nathaniel Hawthorne (1804-1864) was a descendant of one of the Puritan settlers in America. In 1850 he wrote *The Scarlet Letter*, a novel about the strict and hard life in a Puritan community.

Herman Melville (1819-1891) became popular with adventure stories and tales of the sea. His most important work is *Moby Dick* (1851). Its main character, Captain Ahab, spends years in searching for the great white whale Moby Dick, who he wants to kill. The story is based on Melville's own adventures at sea.

In 1852, the most popular book of the century appeared. *Uncle Tom's Cabin* was written as a protest against slavery. Some people think the novel was one of the reasons for the Civil War. When President Lincoln met **Harriet Beecher Stowe (1811-1896)**, he said, 'So you're the little woman who wrote the book that made this great war.'

AMERICAN LITERATURE

Illustrated scenes from 'The Adventures of Huckleberry Finn' by Mark Twain

Almost everybody knows the American writer **Mark Twain (1835-1910)**. His real name was Samuel Langhorne Clemens. His pen name Mark Twain came from the way the depth of the river was measured on the river-boats that went down the Mississippi when he was a boy. Twain wrote many different types of stories, but he is remembered most for *Tom Sawyer* (1876) and *Huckleberry Finn* (1885).

Jack London (1876-1916) is usually remembered for his books *The Call of the Wild* (1903), *The Sea-Wolf* (1904), and *White Fang* (1906). These adventure stories are still very popular with young people.

Margaret Mitchell (1900-1949) only wrote one novel, *Gone with the Wind* (1936). It is set in Georgia during the Civil War. The book and the film adaptation with Vivien Leigh and Clark Gable (1939) were enormously successful.

John Steinbeck's (1902-1968) novels tell us a lot about California at the beginning of the last century. *The Grapes of Wrath* (1939) is about the Joad family, who have to leave their farm in Oklahoma. They move to California, the land of milk and honey. Very soon they realize that life in California isn't as easy as they were told before.

Ernest Hemingway's (1899-1961) novels and short stories are often about war and fighting, but nobody ever seems to win. In *The Sun Also Rises* (1926) a group of English and American people are looking for meaning to their lives after the experience of World War I. His other important books include *A Farewell to Arms* (1929) and *For Whom the Bell Tolls* (1940), both about the Spanish Civil War. *The Old Man and the Sea* (1952) is the story of one man's struggle against nature. He also wrote many excellent short stories.

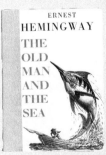

ninety-one **91**

LERNTIPPS

Presenting a paper

**1 Preparing a topic
– Everglades National Park**

Collect all the material you can find about your topic. You can use books, magazines, the internet, TV or radio programs, or talk to friends or teachers. Choose the information you need.

You can use:

- **lists**
  You can write down your ideas as they come to you.

  the EVERGLADES
  History
  Animals and plants
  Camping
  Activities
  etc

- **mind maps**
  A mind map helps you to organize your ideas from the beginning.

- **questions**
  Asking questions about your topic can help you to find new ideas. For example:
  - Who founded Everglades National Park?
  - What does the landscape look like?
  - Why are some of the animals there in danger?
  - Where can you still find Native Americans?
  - When is the best time to visit the area?

You're too tense ... You've got to learn to unwind once in a while.

* tense *angespannt*

Everglades National Park — A Tourist Guide

Mind map: the EVERGLADES
- History: Spanish explorer Ponce de León, Seminole Wars
- Geography: Florida, 1.5 million acre park
- Native Americans: Calusas, Tequestas
- Animals and plants: American alligator, Florida panther, mahogany, red mangrove, cypress
- Activities: self-guided boat tours, wildlife observation, fishing, bicycling, canoeing

92   ninety-two

LERNTIPPS

2 Structuring your paper

Normally there are three parts to a presentation.

- **Introduction**
  First you should try to get the audience interested in your topic. You can start with a picture, a cartoon, a quotation or sometimes a joke. You can also explain the structure of your presentation in a few words.

- **Main part**
  Present your main points and let each point lead naturally to the next one. Don't mention everything you know about your topic. Concentrate on the most important aspects. You can write the most important points on index cards.

- **Conclusion**
  Give a summary in a few sentences.

3 Choosing your media

Make your talk interesting by using different media. You can use transparencies, a flipchart or a presentation program on your computer.

4 Giving the presentation

It's normal to be a little nervous.
After a few sentences you'll feel better.
- Try to speak as naturally as possible.
- Keep eye contact with your audience.
- Don't talk too fast.

Always remember
- You are the expert.
- You have something important to say.

5 Discussing the topic

You can
- react to a question or point:
  You agree – *That's true. / You're right.*
  You disagree – *Sorry, I don't agree.*
  I don't think you can say (that) …
- express your opinion:
  In my opinion … / I feel … / I think … / I believe …
- give a reason:
  Let me explain …
  First … second … and then / finally …
  Let me give you an example …
  That's why …
- give a summary:
  To sum up, I'd say …

Don't forget to thank your audience at the end of your talk.

ninety-three 93

PAIR WORK

UNIT 2   EXERCISE 9

Work with a partner. One of you should look at this page, and the other should look at page 26.

Then arrange a game of tennis this weekend with your partner. Begin like this:

Partner How about a game of tennis this weekend?
You Good idea.
Partner How about Friday evening?
You Sorry, I can't on Friday. I'm going …

UNIT 4   EXERCISE 17

Work with a partner. One of you should look at this page, and the other should look at page 64.

You are Stevie Wonder. Your partner is a reporter who is going to interview you. Use the information below to answer his/her questions.

- You've been blind since you were born.
- You were born in Saginaw, Michigan.
- Your real name is Steveland Morris.
- You were ten when you got your first record contract.
- You and your wife wrote the songs on 'Where I'm coming from'.
- You first used electronic music in 1972.
- You played all the instruments yourself.
- You survived a bad automobile accident in 1973.
- Your next concert will be in September.
- You made a hit record with the English singer Paul McCartney.
- You took part in a campaign to make Martin Luther King Day a national holiday because you believe strongly in civil rights for black people.

Try to add some friendly comments to your answers. You can begin the interview like this.

Reporter May I ask you, how long have you been blind?
You Oh, since I was born. That's a long time, you know.
Reporter And where … ?

94   ninety-four

Grammatical terms Grammatikalische Fachausdrücke

active ['æktɪv]	Aktiv, Tatform	*We **bought** the new radio.*
adjective ['ædʒɪktɪv]	Eigenschaftswort, Adjektiv	*big, good, bad, dangerous, expensive, …*
adverb ['ædvɜːb]	Adverb	***very** big, **usually**, …*
adverb of frequency [ˌædvɜːb əv 'friːkwənsi]	Adverb der Häufigkeit	*always, often, never, …*
adverb of manner [ˌædvɜːb əv 'mænə]	Adverb der Art und Weise	*carefully, slowly, well, …*
article ['ɑːtɪkl]	Geschlechtswort, Artikel	*a, an, the*
auxiliary verb [ɔːgˌzɪliəri 'vɜːb]	Hilfsverb	***don't** know, **is** swimming, **has** seen*
***by*-agent** ['baɪeɪdʒənt]	Urheber einer Handlung im Passivsatz	*The phone was invented **by Bell**.*
clause [klɔːz]	Teilsatz	*He was late because he missed the last bus.*
comparative [kəm'pærətɪv]	Komparativ, erste Steigerungsform	*big**ger**, **better**, **more** interesting, …*
comparison of adjectives [kəmˌpærɪsn əv 'ædʒɪktɪvz]	Steigerung der Adjektive	*big – big**ger** – big**gest**; **as** big **as**, big**ger than***
conditional [kən'dɪʃənl]	Konditional	*I **wouldn't** do that.*
conjunction [kən'dʒʌŋkʃn]	Bindewort, Konjunktion	*and, or, but, after, when, …*
consonant ['kɒnsənənt]	Mitlaut, Konsonant	*b, c, d, f, g, k, …*
contact clause ['kɒntækt klɔːz]	Satz ohne Relativpronomen	*The girl **he met** was Lisa.*
direct object [daɪˌrekt 'ɒbdʒɪkt]	direktes Objekt, Akkusativobjekt	*He drinks **milk**. She gave him **a present**.*
emphasizing pronoun [ˌemfəsaɪzɪŋ 'prəʊnaʊn]	verstärkendes Pronomen	*I saw the accident **myself**.*
future with *going to* ['fjuːtʃə]	Futur mit *going to*	*I'm **going to leave** now.*
future with *will* ['fjuːtʃə]	Futur mit *will*	*I **will come** tomorrow.*
imperative [ɪm'perətɪv]	Befehlsform, Imperativ	*Now **listen**. **Don't talk** to your neighbour.*
indirect object [ˌɪndaɪrekt 'ɒbdʒɪkt]	indirektes Objekt, Dativobjekt	*She gave **her father** a present.*
infinitive [ɪn'fɪnətɪv]	Grundform, Infinitiv	*to go, to see, to eat, to run, to work, …*
***ing*-form** ['ɪŋfɔːm]	*-ing*-Form	*singing, dancing, sitting, …*
irregular verb [ɪˌreɡjʊlə 'vɜːb]	unregelmäßiges Verb	*do – **did** – **done**, buy – **bought** – **bought**, …*
long form ['lɒŋ fɔːm]	Langform	*He **is** reading. She **does not** work.*
main clause ['meɪn klɔːz]	Hauptsatz	***Peter isn't at school** because he's ill.*
main verb ['meɪn vɜːb]	Vollverb	*work, dance, read, write, play, …*
modal auxiliary [ˌməʊdl ɔːg'zɪliəri]	Modalverb	*can, must, could, might, ought to*
negative question [ˌneɡətɪv 'kwestʃn]	verneinter Fragesatz	***Don't** you **like** beans?*
negative statement [ˌneɡətɪv 'steɪtmənt]	verneinter Aussagesatz	*Emily **doesn't** like tennis.*
noun [naʊn]	Nomen, Substantiv	*house, book, tea, plan, idea, …*
object ['ɒbdʒɪkt]	Satzergänzung, Objekt	*She likes **pop music**.*
***of*-phrase** ['ɒvfreɪz]	Fügung mit *of*	*the name **of the game***
passive ['pæsɪv]	Passiv, Leideform	*The gangster **was caught** (by the police).*
past participle [ˌpɑːst 'pɑːtɪsɪpl]	Partizip Perfekt	*John has **called**. She hasn't **eaten** anything.*

ninety-five **95**

Grammatikalische Fachausdrücke

past perfect [ˌpɑːst ˈpɜːfɪkt]	*Past perfect* (Plusquamperfekt)	I **had seen** the film before.
past progressive [ˌpɑːst prəˈɡresɪv]	Verlaufsform der Vergangenheit	She **was reading**. We **were watching** TV.
personal passive [ˌpɜːsənl ˈpæsɪv]	persönliches Passiv	I **was offered** some sweets.
personal pronoun [ˌpɜːsənl ˈprəʊnaʊn]	persönliches Fürwort, Personalpronomen	I, you, she, … , me, us, them, …
phrasal verb [ˌfreɪzl ˈvɜːb]	Verbindung Verb–Adverb, Verb–Präposition	to put **on**, to take **away**, to listen **to**, …
plural [ˈplʊərəl]	Mehrzahl, Plural	book**s**, letter**s**, dog**s**, wom**en**, child**ren**, **feet**
positive [ˈpɒzətɪv]	Positiv, Grundform des Adjektivs	good – better – best, **interesting** – more interesting – most interesting
positive statement [ˌpɒzətɪv ˈsteɪtmənt]	bejahter Aussagesatz, Erzählsatz	I **speak** English and French.
possessive adjective [pəˌzesɪv ˈædʒɪktɪv]	adjektivisch gebrauchtes, besitzanzeigendes Fürwort, Possessivpronomen	my, your, his, her, its, our, your, their
possessive form [pəˌzesɪv ˈfɔːm]	besitzanzeigende Form, *s*-Genitiv	Adam**'s** computer, his friends**'** books
possessive pronoun [pəˌzesɪv ˈprəʊnaʊn]	nominal gebrauchtes Possessivpronomen	mine, yours, his, hers, ours, yours, theirs
preposition [prepəˈzɪʃn]	Verhältniswort, Präposition	in, at, on, with, because of, …
preposition of direction [prepəˌzɪʃn əv dəˈrekʃn]	Präposition der Richtung	**to** school, **onto** the table, **into** the water, …
preposition of place [prepəˌzɪʃn əv ˈpleɪs]	Präposition des Ortes	**at** the bus stop, **on** the wall, **in** the house, …
preposition of time [prepəˌzɪʃn əv ˈtaɪm]	Präposition der Zeit	**at** seven o'clock, **on** Sunday, **in** winter, …
present participle [ˌpreznt ˈpɑːtɪsɪpl]	Partizip Präsens	He is **going** home. It's **freezing** cold.
present perfect [ˌpreznt ˈpɜːfɪkt]	*Present perfect* (Perfekt)	We **have finished** the lesson.
present perfect progressive [ˌpreznt pɜːfɪkt prəˈɡresɪv]	Verlaufsform des *present perfect*	We **have been reading** for two hours.
present progressive [ˌpreznt prəˈɡresɪv]	Verlaufsform des Präsens	I **am watching** TV.
pronoun [ˈprəʊnaʊn]	Fürwort, Pronomen	I, me, my, this, …
proper noun [ˌprɒpe ˈnaʊn]	Eigenname	Mr Smith, Munich, the Thames
propword [ˈprɒpwɜːd]	Stützwort	Do you want the red **one** or the green **ones**?
question [ˈkwestʃn]	Frage, Fragesatz	**Is Adam at school?** – No, he isn't. – **Where is Adam?**
question tag [ˈkwestʃn tæɡ]	Frageanhängsel	It's cold today, **isn't it?**
question word [ˈkwestʃn wɜːd]	Fragewort	what, when, where, who, whose, why, which, how
reflexive pronoun [rɪˌfleksɪv ˈprəʊnaʊn]	Reflexivpronomen, rückbezügliches Fürwort	He hurt **himself**.
regular verb [ˌreɡjʊlə ˈvɜːb]	regelmäßiges Verb	call – called – called, …
relative clause [ˌrelətɪv ˈklɔːz]	Relativsatz	The girl **who phoned** was Mary.
relative pronoun [ˌrelətɪv ˈprəʊnaʊn]	Relativpronomen	who, that, which, whose
sentence [ˈsentəns]	Satz, Satzgefüge	I love Star Trek. Do you speak French?

Grammatikalische Fachausdrücke

short answer [ˈʃɔːt ˌɑːnsə]	Kurzantwort	*Do you understand? – **Yes, I do**.*
short form [ˈʃɔːt ˌfɔːm]	Kurzform	*I'**ve** got a rabbit. **She's** over there.* *– **I can't** see her.*
simple past [ˌsɪmpl ˈpɑːst]	einfache Form der Vergangenheit	*I **called** Katie. She **bought** a new skirt.*
simple present [ˌsɪmpl ˈpreznt]	einfache Form des Präsens	*She **reads** love stories every day.*
singular [ˈsɪŋɡjʊlə]	Einzahl, Singular	*book, letter, dog, woman, child, foot*
statement [ˈsteɪtmənt]	Aussage, Aussagesatz	*She likes cats. I don't like dinosaurs.*
subject [ˈsʌbdʒɪkt]	Satzgegenstand, Subjekt	***Jessica** likes maths. **The girl over there** is Sophie.*
subject question [ˈsʌbdʒɪkt ˌkwestʃn]	Frage nach dem Subjekt	***Who** phoned you?*
superlative [suːˈpɜːlətɪv]	Superlativ, höchste Steigerungsform	*big**gest**, **best**, **most** interesting, …*
tense [tens]	grammatische Zeit, Tempus	*present tense, past tense, …*
time [taɪm]	(wirkliche) Zeit	*past, present, future*
verb [vɜːb]	a) Zeitwort, Verb b) Satzaussage, Prädikat	*be, love, play, get up, … ; can, will, do, …* *She **likes** yoghurt. We **can play** cards.*
vowel [ˈvaʊəl]	Vokal, Selbstlaut	*a, e, i, o, u*
word order [ˈwɜːd ˌɔːdə]	Wortstellung	*subject – verb – object (S – V – O)*
yes/no question [ˌjesnəʊ ˈkwestʃən]	Entscheidungsfrage	***Is Adam at home?** – Yes, he is. / No, he isn't.*

LERNTIPP: Vokabelkartei

Eine hervorragende Möglichkeit zum planmäßigen Testen und Wiederholen bietet eine Lernkartei:

So arbeitest du mit der Lernkartei:

- ➡ Auf die Vorderseite eines Kärtchens schreibst du das deutsche Stichwort und eventuelle Symbole für *synonyms* oder *opposites*; auf die Rückseite die englische Entsprechung und *synonyms, opposites* etc. aus der dritten Spalte im Vokabelverzeichnis von ***GO AHEAD***.
- ➡ Die fertigen Karteikarten wandern ins erste Fach. Sobald dieses gefüllt ist, wird es Zeit, mit dem Wiederholen zu beginnen. Karten mit gemerkten Vokabeln werden hinten ins zweite Fach gesteckt, vergessene Vokabeln kommen auf die Rückseite des Stoßes im ersten Fach.
- ➡ Nach einiger Zeit füllt sich auch das zweite Fach. Nun wird hier nach dem gleichen System verfahren: Gemerkte Vokabeln steckt man hinten in das dritte Fach, vergessene Wörter kommen zurück in das erste Fach.
- ➡ Entsprechend geht es mit den anderen Fächern weiter. Grundregel: Alle Vokabeln, die beherrscht werden, wandern ein Fach weiter. Alle vergessenen Vokabeln müssen zurück ins erste Fach.
- ➡ Wichtig: Werden die Fächer zwei bis vier zu voll, solltest du immer nur einen Finger breit von vorn nach hinten leerräumen. Es wäre falsch, aus Ehrgeiz das gesamte Fach zu bearbeiten.

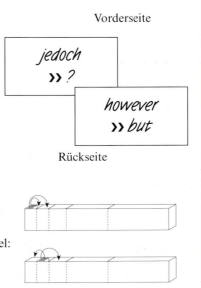

UNIT 1
GRAMMATIKANHANG

1 modal auxiliaries and their substitutes

Modale Hilfsverben und ihre Ersatzformen

Kazuko lives in Bavaria.
She **can** speak German and Japanese.

... verwenden wir, um auszudrücken, dass

◆ etwas geschehen oder sein **kann**, **darf**, **soll**, **muss** etc. Auf das modale Hilfsverb folgt ein Vollverb.

Beachte: Sie **kann** Französisch.
She **can** **speak** *French.*

May I **see** your passport? (*Darf ich … sehen?*)
They **might invite** us. (*Sie könnten uns vielleicht einladen.*)
We really **must leave** now. (*Wir müssen … gehen.*)
You **mustn't forget** the tickets. (*Ihr dürft … nicht vergessen.*)
He **needn't help** me. (*Er braucht mir nicht zu helfen.*)
You **ought to go** there. (*… solltest … gehen*)
And she **should go**, too. (*… sollte … gehen*)
It **will rain** tomorrow. (*… wird … regnen*)
Would you **close** the door, please? (*Würdest du … schließen?*)

Einige modale Hilfsverben kennst du bereits:
can – may – might – must – mustn't – needn't – ought to – should – will – would

Diese werden **immer** mit dem *infinitive without to* verbunden.

Beachte aber: *ought* **to** – You **ought to** think of other people.

| I
You
He/She/It
We
You
They | can | swim very well. |

Sie sind unveränderlich, d.h., man kann kein *-s*, *-ed*, *-ing* anhängen.

Und was ist mit „*he*, *she*, *it*, ein *-s* muss mit"?

Ach so!

Das gibt es nur im *simple present* bei Vollverben, nicht bei modalen Hilfsverben.

He **can't** come tonight.
May I **go** to the cinema?

I **must** write some postcards.
We **had to** do a history test last week.
Jane **will have to** do one when she's back at school.

Sie bilden **Frage und Verneinung ohne do**. In verneinten Sätzen folgt *not* oder *n't*; in Fragen steht das Modalverb vor dem Subjekt.

Sie können **nicht alle Zeitformen** bilden. Es gibt jedoch zu bestimmten Modalverben **Ersatzformen** mit ähnlicher Bedeutung. Von diesen lassen sich alle Zeitformen bilden.

ninety-eight

können

can, could, be able to

can hat, je nach Sprechabsicht, sehr unterschiedliche Bedeutungen.
In der Gegenwart drücken wir z.B. mit *can* und *is/are/am able to* aus, dass wir etwas tun können (**Fähigkeit**).

Beachte: *can* wird hier häufiger verwendet.

Die **verneinten Formen** lauten *cannot* ['kænɒt] oder *can't* [kaːnt] und *am/are/is not able to*.

Beachte: *cannot* wird zusammengeschrieben.

In **Fragen** benutzt man meistens *can*.

Wir können *could* oder *was/were able to* verwenden, um eine Fähigkeit in der **Vergangenheit** auszudrücken.

Allerdings wird *was/were able to* bevorzugt, wenn wir sagen wollen, dass jemandem etwas zu einem bestimmten Zeitpunkt in der Vergangenheit gelungen ist.

Bei **Verben der Sinneswahrnehmung** (*see*, *hear*, *feel* etc.) verwenden wir *could*.

In **Fragesätzen** und **verneinten Sätzen** können wir beide Formen verwenden, doch *could* und *couldn't* sind die häufigeren Formen.

will (not) be able to wird verwendet, um eine Fähigkeit in der **Zukunft** auszudrücken.

Ist eine Zeitangabe der Zukunft vorhanden, so kann man auch *can* verwenden.

PRESENT

Some people | **can** / **are able to** | walk on their hands.

Sorry, I | **cannot** / **can't** / **am not able to** | help you.

Can he drive a car?
(**Is** he **able to** drive a car?)

PAST

He **could**/**was able to** read when he was five years old.

We **were able to** get to the station in time.
(managed to = *schafften es*)

I **could hear** a strange noise outside.
We **could see** a light in the apartment.

Could you get in/**Were you able to** get in with that key?
No, I **couldn't**/**wasn't able to** get in.

FUTURE

I **will be able to** finish this job by Monday.
She **won't be able to** come next Friday.

She **can't** come next Friday.

UNIT 1   Grammatikanhang

b **can, may, be allowed to**   **dürfen**

PRESENT

We	**can**	swim here.
You	**are allowed to**	take photos.

We	**cannot/can't**	leave the hotel.
You	**are not allowed to**	take photos.

can und *is/are/am allowed to* beziehen sich auf eine **Erlaubnis** in der **Gegenwart**.

Wird die Erlaubnis nicht gewährt, so verwendet man *cannot/can't* oder *am/are/is not allowed to*.

Beachte: Bei einem echten **Verbot** (Zwang) steht *must not*: *You **mustn't** copy your neighbour's homework.*

Can	I	use your camera?
May	we	take photos in the museum?

Wenn man **um Erlaubnis bittet**, verwendet man *Can I/we … ?* oder *May I/ we … ?*

Beachte: *May I/we … ?* ist förmlicher.

PAST

He **was allowed to** go to the party.
We **weren't allowed to** swim in the pool.

In der **Vergangenheit** muss man *was/were (not) allowed to* verwenden.

FUTURE

I hope we **will be allowed to** stay up late.
She **won't be allowed to** go to the disco.

will (not) be allowed to wird verwendet, um über eine Erlaubnis in der **Zukunft** zu sprechen.

100 one hundred

Fragesätze

Fragesatzarten

Es lassen sich zwei Arten von Fragesätzen unterscheiden:

- **Entscheidungsfragen** (*yes/no questions*)
  Sie können mit ja oder nein beantwortet werden und beginnen mit einem Hilfsverb (*have*, *do*) oder Modalverb (*can*).

- **Fragesätze mit Fragewörtern** (*wh-questions*)
  Es werden dabei bestimmte Informationen erfragt. Die Fragewörter sind *who, what, when, where, how, why, which, whose*.

Bejahte Fragen

Man bildet einen Fragesatz, indem man das **Hilfsverb** des Aussagesatzes **vor das Subjekt** stellt.

Ausnahme: Fragen nach dem Subjekt
(*Daniel likes heavy metal music.*)
Who *likes heavy metal music?*

Fragewörter stehen am Satzanfang.

Ist im Aussagesatz kein Hilfsverb vorhanden, so wird im Fragesatz *do*, *does* oder *did* **vor das Subjekt** gestellt. Das **Verb** steht dann immer in der **Grundform**.

Beachte: Auch Fragen mit dem Vollverb *do* werden mit *do*, *does* oder *did* verbunden:
(*Jane does her homework in the evenings.*)
*When **does** Jane **do** her homework?*

questions

types of questions

Have you ever been to Chinatown?
– **Yes**, lots of times.
Do you speak Chinese? – **No**, I don't.
Can you read this sign? – **No**, I can't.

When did you go to New York? – I went **last summer**.
Where did you stay? – **At a hotel**.

positive questions

		(Daniel	was	looking at the guitars.)
	Was	Daniel		looking at the guitars?

		(You	have	bought something.)
What	**have**	you		bought?

		(You	know	her name.)
	Do	you	**know**	her name?

		(She	met	somebody.)
Who	**did**	she	**meet**?	

Bei Fragen stellt man also immer das Hilfsverb vor das Subjekt?

Ja.

Und was macht man, wenn kein Hilfsverb im Aussagesatz steht?

Dann nimmt man *do*, *does* oder *did*.

UNIT 1   Grammatikanhang

c **negative questions**

Why	**didn't**	she	ring me?
	Haven't	you	seen the film?

Who	**wasn't**	here last night?
Why	**don't**	we walk?
	Can't	you swim?

Verneinte Fragen

Verneinte Fragesätze werden mit einem **Hilfsverb** und *n't* gebildet.

Sie werden verwendet, um
◆ Informationen zu erfragen
◆ einen Vorschlag zu machen
◆ Überraschung auszudrücken.

3 the future

a the future with 'will'

Möglichkeiten, zukünftiges Geschehen auszudrücken

Das future mit „will"

It **will be** hot in South Wales tomorrow.
But the sunshine **won't last** very long.

I**'ll help** you with your math problem.
I think I**'ll have** another hamburger.

verwendet man, um

◆ eine **Vorhersage** über Zukünftiges zu machen, auf das der Sprecher keinen Einfluss hat

◆ ein **Angebot** oder eine **spontane Entscheidung** auszudrücken.

b the future with 'be going to'

I**'m going to buy** some shoes today.

Look at the clouds. It**'s going to rain**.

The repairs **will cost** a lot.
The repairs **are going to cost** a lot.

She **is going to join** the drama class.

Das future mit „be going to"

verwendet man, um auszudrücken,

◆ dass jemand etwas vorhat oder plant

◆ dass etwas bald geschehen wird, da es schon Anzeichen dafür gibt.

Beachte: Es gibt viele Fälle, in denen man sowohl *will* als auch *be going to* verwenden kann.

Will man aber eine **Absicht** ausdrücken, so kann *will* nicht verwendet werden.

Grammatikanhang UNIT 1

Das present progressive

verwendet man, um auszudrücken,

◆ dass jemand etwas bereits **fest geplant** oder **arrangiert** hat. Ort und Zeit sind dabei meistens schon festgelegt.

Das simple present

verwendet man, um über ein

◆ durch **Fahrplan** oder **Terminplan** festgelegtes Geschehen zu sprechen.

Beachte: Meist steht diese Zeitform zusammen mit einer **Zeitbestimmung**, z.B. *tomorrow, at ten-thirty* etc.

the present progressive   c

We**'re flying** to the USA **next Monday**.
My sister **is having** a party **tomorrow**.
What **are** we **having** for tea?

the simple present   d

England **plays** Germany **on Saturday**.
It**'s** school **tomorrow**.
The next train **arrives** at ten-thirty.

UNIT 2

Das Passiv   the passive   1

Aktiv und Passiv   active and passive   a

Viele Vorgänge lassen sich mit einem Aktivsatz oder mit einem Passivsatz darstellen:

Im **Aktivsatz** wird betont, **wer** (oder **was**) **etwas tut**. Das Subjekt des Aktivsatzes führt die Handlung aus.
Für den Sprecher ist es also wichtig zu sagen, was Kolumbus tat.

Columbus **discovered** America in 1492.
Kolumbus entdeckte 1492 Amerika.

Im **Passivsatz** wird hervorgehoben, **mit wem** (oder **womit**) **etwas geschieht**. Im Passivsatz wird etwas mit dem Subjekt getan. Der Sprecher sagt also, was mit Amerika geschehen ist.

America **was discovered** in 1492.
Amerika wurde 1492 entdeckt.

one hundred and three   **103**

UNIT 2   Grammatikanhang

b form

SIMPLE PRESENT

Cheese **is produced** in Tillamook.
    (… *wird hergestellt*)

SIMPLE PAST

A lot of cheese **was produced** last year.
    (… *wurde hergestellt*)

PRESENT PERFECT

Cheese **has been produced** here since 1909.
    (… *ist hergestellt worden*)

PAST PERFECT → page 106

Cheese **had been produced** in Tillamook before.
    (… *war hergestellt worden*)

FUTURE WITH WILL

More cheese **will be produced** next year.
    (… *wird hergestellt werden*)

MODAL VERBS

Different cheese **can be produced**.
    (… *kann hergestellt werden*)
Cheese **must be produced** every day.
    (… *muss hergestellt werden*)

c use

SUBJECT	VERB	OBJECT
The English	established	a colony in Jamestown.

A colony   was established   in Jamestown.

300 passengers **were killed** in a plane crash in Italy.
Yesterday a boy **was injured** in a road accident. He **was taken** to hospital.

English **spoken** = English **is spoken** here.
Popstar **killed** in plane crash = A popstar **has been killed** in a plane crash

Formen

Passivformen werden mit *be + past participle* gebildet.

Die Zeitformen werden wie im Aktiv verwendet.

I've told you hundreds of times … you can't watch TV.

Why not?

It hasn't been invented yet.

Beachte: Im Deutschen verwenden wir **werden** für das Passiv und das Futur:
'The Simpsons' **is shown** twice a week. (Passiv)
    (wird … gezeigt)
CNN **will show** the news at 9 o'clock. (Futur)
    (wird … zeigen)

Verwendung

Wenn ein Aktivsatz ein Objekt enthält, so kann man in der Regel daraus einen Passivsatz bilden. Das **Objekt** des **Aktivsatzes** wird zum **Subjekt** des **Passivsatzes**.
Man verwendet das Passiv, um zu sagen, was mit einer Person oder einer Sache **getan wird**. **Wer** die Tätigkeit ausführt, ist oft **unwichtig**.

Deshalb findet man das Passiv häufig in
◆ Berichten über (Natur-)Katastrophen
◆ Berichten über Unfälle und Verbrechen
◆ Anleitungen und wissenschaftlichen oder technischen Beschreibungen.

Auf Schildern und in Zeitungsschlagzeilen kommt das Passiv oft verkürzt (ohne die Form von *be*) vor.

Grammatikanhang UNIT 2

Passivsätze mit „by"

Muss oder will man trotzdem in einem Passivsatz erwähnen, **von wem** etwas getan wird, so fügt man die Information mit der Präposition *by* an (***by-agent***).

Einige Sätze ergeben ohne einen *by-agent* keinen Sinn.

passive sentences with 'by'   d

A lot of voyages were made **by Europeans**.
(… *wurden von Europäern unternommen.*)

Robinson Crusoe was written **by Daniel Defoe**.

Wann nimmt man dann *from*?

Ah ja!

From bedeutet, von wo etwas kommt: *A letter from America* ist ein Brief aus Amerika.

Verben mit einem Objekt

Einige englische Verben mit direktem Objekt können, im Gegensatz zum Deutschen, ein Passiv bilden.

Da meist eine Person zum Subjekt des Passivsatzes wird, nennt man es **persönliches Passiv**. Dazu gehören: *to help sb, to answer sb, to follow sb, to join sb, to remember sb/sth.*

verbs with one object   e

SUBJECT	VERB	OBJECT	
They	helped	**me**	at once.
I	**was helped**		at once.

Verben mit zwei Objekten

Verben, die im Aktiv gewöhnlich mit einem indirekten Objekt (Person) und einem direkten Objekt (Sache) verbunden werden (*give, offer, tell, pay, promise, send, show, teach, lend*), bilden ebenfalls meist ein **persönliches Passiv**; d.h. **das indirekte Objekt** (Person) des **Aktivsatzes** wird zum **Subjekt des Passivsatzes**.

Es ist auch möglich, das direkte Objekt (Sache) des Aktivsatzes zum Subjekt des Passivsatzes zu machen. Das persönliche Passiv wird jedoch bevorzugt.

Beachte: *I was given a letter.*
Mir wurde ein Brief gegeben.
Besser: **Man** gab **mir** einen Brief.

verbs with two objects   f

SUBJECT	VERB	INDIRECT OBJECT	DIRECT OBJECT
They	gave	**us**	a book.
We	were given		a book.

(*Uns wurde ein Buch gegeben./Man gab uns ein Buch.*)

SUBJECT	VERB	INDIRECT OBJECT	DIRECT OBJECT
They	gave	us	**a ticket**.
A ticket	was given	**to** us.	

one hundred and five   **105**

UNIT 2 Grammatikanhang

g **verbs + preposition or adverb**

Tourists **threw away** empty bottles.
Empty bottles **were thrown away** by tourists.

(*Leere Flaschen wurden … weggeworfen.*)

Verben mit Präposition oder Adverb

Das Passiv lässt sich auch von Verben bilden, die fest mit einer **Präposition** oder einem **Adverb** verbunden sind, z.B. *look after, think of, shoot at, throw away* etc.

Die Präposition oder das Adverb **folgt** dabei immer **auf das Verb**.

UNIT 3

1 **the past perfect**

Das past perfect

verwenden wir, um auszudrücken, dass eine **Handlung vor** einer anderen Handlung oder **vor** einem bestimmten **Zeitpunkt in der Vergangenheit** stattfand.

The Pilgrims **landed** near Plymouth Rock.
They **had been** at sea for six weeks.

a **positive statements**

| I/You
He/She/It
We/You
They | had | worked
seen | there before.
the film. |

Bejahte Aussagesätze

Das *past perfect* bildet man mit *had* und dem *past participle* (Partizip Perfekt).

Regelmäßige Verben bilden das *past participle* auf *-ed* (*work**ed***), die dritte Form der unregelmäßigen Verben (*seen*) findest du auf den Seiten 138–139.

Beachte: Im Deutschen verwendet man **hatte** oder **war**.
*I **had been** there and **had seen** the castle.*
  (war … gewesen)   (hatte … gesehen)

106 one hundred and six

Grammatikanhang UNIT 3

Verneinte Aussagesätze

werden mit *had not* oder *hadn't* und dem *past participle* gebildet.

negative statements   b

| I/You
He/She/It
We/You/They | **had not worked**.
hadn't seen the sign. |

Fragen

im *past perfect* werden mit *had* und dem *past participle* gebildet; *had* steht vor dem Subjekt.

Die Kurzantwort auf Entscheidungsfragen (*yes/no questions*) lautet normalerweise:
Yes, she had.
No, we hadn't.

Fragewörter (*where, when, why* …) stehen am Anfang des Satzes.

questions   c

| **Had** | I
you
he
she
it
we
you
they | **closed** the gate?
been there? |

What time **had** you **finished**?
When **had** she **seen** the film?

Simple past und past perfect

Mit dem *simple past* drücken wir aus, dass etwas zu einem bestimmten Zeitpunkt in der Vergangenheit stattfand:

Die Boston Tea Party ereignete sich im Jahre 1773.

Vorher war bereits etwas anderes geschehen: Die britische Regierung hatte eine neue Steuer auf Tee erhoben. Was vorher geschehen war, steht im *past perfect*.

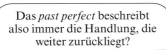

Das *past perfect* beschreibt also immer die Handlung, die weiter zurückliegt?

Stimmt!

Hier hatte der Film bereits begonnen, bevor Katie ankam. Sie versäumte den Anfang.

In diesem Fall begann der Film erst, als sie ankam. Sie kam rechtzeitig.

simple past and past perfect   2

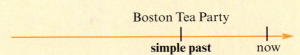

The Boston Tea Party **happened** in 1773.

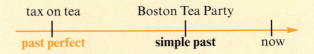

It **happened** because the British government **had put** a new tax on tea.

The movie **had started** when Katie **arrived**.
(*Der Film hatte angefangen, als Katie kam.*)

The movie **started** when Katie **arrived**.
(*Der Film fing an, als Katie kam.*)

one hundred and seven **107**

UNIT 3   Grammatikanhang

3 reflexive pronouns — Reflexivpronomen

He's so much in love with **himself**.

I looked at **myself** in the mirror.
Be careful, you'll make **yourself** ill.
He fell down and hurt **himself**.
She got **herself** a new dress.
The machine switches **itself** off.

We enjoyed **ourselves** at the party.
Help **yourselves** to sandwiches.
They had the whole hotel to **themselves**.

The tourists **complained** about the food.

I can't **remember** her name.

beziehen sich auf das **Subjekt** des Satzes. Sie bezeichnen **dieselbe Person** oder Sache wie das Subjekt. Man nennt es deshalb **rückbezüglich** (= reflexiv).

Vergleiche:
*I've hurt **myself**.* Ich habe mich verletzt.
*He hurt **me**.* Er hat mich verletzt.

Die Pronomen im
◆ Singular enden auf *-self*

◆ Plural auf *-selves*.

Beachte: Die Betonung liegt auf der zweiten Silbe: *my**self*** [maɪˈself].

Beachte: Bei einigen Verben benötigen wir in der deutschen Übersetzung kein Pronomen:
Enjoy yourself. Viel Spaß! *Help yourself.* Greif zu!

Umgekehrt stehen die folgenden Verben (im Deutschen reflexiv) ohne Reflexivpronomen:

to **argue**	sich streiten
to **borrow**	sich ausleihen
to **change**	sich (ver)ändern
to **complain**	sich beschweren
to **develop**	sich entwickeln
to **divorce**	sich scheiden lassen
to **feel**	sich fühlen
to **hide**	sich verstecken
to **hurry**	sich beeilen
to **imagine**	sich vorstellen
to **join**	sich anschließen
to **lie down**	sich hinlegen
to **look forward to**	sich freuen auf
to **meet**	sich treffen
to **move**	sich bewegen
to **open**	sich öffnen
to **refuse**	sich weigern
to **relax**	sich erholen
to **remember**	sich erinnern
to **sit down**	sich hinsetzen
to **wonder**	sich fragen
to **worry**	sich Sorgen machen

Grammatikanhang UNIT 3

Verstärkende Pronomen

emphatic pronouns 4

heben ein Nomen oder Pronomen im Satz besonders **hervor**.
Sie haben dieselben Formen wie Reflexivpronomen (*myself*, *yourself*, …).

Beziehen sie sich auf das Subjekt, so stehen sie gewöhnlich am Satzende. Sonst stehen sie hinter dem Wort, das sie hervorheben.

Beachte: Verstärkende Pronomen kann man weglassen, Reflexivpronomen nicht:

He decorated the flat **himself**.

The Queen herself spoke to me.

He told me about it **himself**. (*verstärkend*)
He told me about it.

He cut **himself**. (*reflexiv*)

each other

each other 5

drückt eine **wechselseitige Beziehung** zwischen mindestens zwei Personen aus.

The tourists were taking photos of **each other**.
Lisa and Mia are very good friends.
They see **each other** a lot.

Vergleiche:
Lisa and Mia are looking at **each other**.

They are looking at **themselves**.

Anstelle von *each other* kann auch *one another* stehen, denn *each other* und *one another* (einander, sich gegenseitig) sind bedeutungsgleich.

one hundred and nine **109**

UNIT 4   Grammatikanhang

1 conditional sentences — Bedingungssätze

If you **don't hurry**, we **will miss** the bus.

Ein Bedingungssatz besteht aus zwei Teilen: einem Nebensatz mit *if* und einem Hauptsatz. Ein Bedingungssatz gibt die **Bedingung** an (Wenn du dich nicht beeilst,), unter der ein bestimmtes Ereignis (verpassen wir den Bus.) stattfindet.

a open condition – type 1 (revision) — Offene, erfüllbare Bedingung – Typ 1 (Revision)

IF-CLAUSE	MAIN CLAUSE
If we **leave** now,	we'**ll** catch the bus.
If we **go** to Florida,	I **can** practice my English.
If you **climb** a mountain,	you **must** be careful.
If you **feel** tired,	you **should** go to bed.
If you **want** to come,	please **tell** us.

Wir verwenden im

IF-SATZ	HAUPTSATZ
simple present	*will*-future
	Modalverb can + Infinitiv
	must + Infinitiv
	should + Infinitiv
	Befehlsform

◆ **Was ist, wenn …**
Diese *if*-Sätze drücken aus, was unter bestimmten Bedingungen geschehen **wird**, **kann** oder **soll**.

Willst du nicht die Briten schrecken, so darf kein *will* im *if-clause* stecken!

b unreal condition – type 2 — Unwahrscheinliche, nicht erfüllbare Bedingung – Typ 2

IF-CLAUSE	MAIN CLAUSE
If I **had** more money,	I'**d** buy a new computer.
If we **had** £10,000,	I **could** buy a car.
If he **tried** harder,	he **might** do better at school.

Wir verwenden im

IF-SATZ	HAUPTSATZ
simple past	Modalverb *would* + Infinitiv
	Modalverb *could* + Infinitiv
	Modalverb *might* + Infinitiv

◆ **Was wäre, wenn …**
Diese *if*-Sätze drücken aus, dass es sich nur um eine Annahme handelt. Die Bedingung ist **nicht erfüllbar** oder wird **wahrscheinlich nicht erfüllt**.

Grammatikanhang UNIT 4

Was muss man sich merken?

Im *if-clause* von Typ 2 kein *would*, sonst ist der ganze Satz kaputt.

Ah ja!

Beachte: die Redewendung *If I were you …*

If I were you, I would buy the mountain bike.
Ich an deiner Stelle würde …

Vergleiche die Bedingungssätze:

TYP 1

Der Sprecher hält es für **wahrscheinlich**, dass sie ihn um Hilfe bittet.

TYP 2

Der Sprecher hält es für **unwahrscheinlich** oder **unmöglich**, dass sie ihn um Hilfe bittet.

TYPE 1

If she **asks** me,   **I'll help** her.
(Perhaps she'll ask me.)

TYPE 2

If she **asked** me,   **I'd help** her.
(But she won't ask me.)

Wortstellung in Fragesätzen

Du weißt bereits, dass in Fragesätzen das Hilfsverb vor dem Subjekt steht (Vgl. S. 101).

word order in questions   2

	AUX	SUBJECT	
	Do	**you**	know where she is?
	Is	**she**	visiting Washington?
What	**is**	**she**	doing there?
When	**will**	**they**	come back?

Wortstellung in Fragen nach dem Subjekt

In Fragen nach dem Subjekt (**wer** oder **was**?), bleibt allerdings die Wortstellung wie im Aussagesatz (*subject – verb*).

Das Fragewort nimmt einfach die Stelle des Subjekts ein.

word order in subject questions   a

SUBJECT	VERB	
Andrew	phoned	you.
↓		
Who	phoned	you?
The problem	made	him nervous.
↓		
What	made	him nervous?

one hundred and eleven **111**

UNIT 4   Grammatikanhang

SUBJECT QUESTION

Jeff loves Fiona.
Who loves Fiona?
(*Wer mag Fiona?*)

The cat ate the mouse.
What ate the mouse?
(*Wer fraß die Maus?*)

OBJECT QUESTION

Jeff loves **Fiona**.
Who does Jeff **love**?
(*Wen mag Jeff?*)

The cat ate **the mouse**.
What did the cat **eat**?
(*Was/wen fraß die Katze?*)

Mit *who*, *what*, *which* etc. kann man sowohl nach dem Subjekt als auch nach dem Objekt fragen. Fragen nach dem Subjekt werden ohne *do*, *does*, *did* gebildet.

Das ist aber kompliziert!

Ich merke mir einfach: Bedeutet *who* oder *what* „wer oder was", so wird die Frage ohne *do*, *does*, *did* gebildet.

Hmm!

b   prepositions in questions

Brian **comes from** Detroit.

Where does Brian **come from**?
(*Woher kommt Brian?*)

She's **thinking of** her vacation in Wales.

What is she **thinking of**?
(*Woran denkt sie?*)

Präpositionen in Fragesätzen

Eine im Deutschen zum Fragewort gehörende Präposition steht im Englischen in der Regel am Ende des Fragesatzes.

Das ist doch ganz einfach!

Wieso?

Die Präposition bleibt immer am Verb kleben!

Na klar.

English sounds Erklärung der Lautschriftzeichen

Vowels
Selbstlaute, Vokale

[iː]	eat, week, he
[i]	party, very, ready
[ɪ]	in, give, film
[e]	end, get, many
[æ]	add, man, black
[ʌ]	under, come
[ɑː]	ask, half, car
[ɒ]	often, what, coffee
[ɔː]	all, four, door
[ʊ]	put, good, woman
[u]	situation, unite, actual
[uː]	who, June, blue
[ɜː]	learn, girl, work
[ə]	again, policeman, sister
[eɪ]	eight, table, play
[aɪ]	I, nice, by
[ɔɪ]	boy, toilet
[əʊ]	old, road, know
[aʊ]	out, house, now
[ɪə]	we're, here, near
[eə]	wear, chair, there
[ʊə]	your, pure, sure

Consonants
Mitlaute, Konsonanten

[p]	pen, speak, map
[b]	book, rabbit, job
[t]	table, letter, sit
[d]	desk, radio, old
[k]	car, basketball, back
[g]	get, bigger, bag
[f]	father, left, cliff
[v]	very, every, have
[θ]	thank, birthday, bath
[ð]	this, father, with
[s]	see, classes, dance
[z]	zoo, thousand, please
[ʃ]	shop, sugar, English
[ʒ]	television, usually
[tʃ]	child, kitchen, watch
[dʒ]	jam, June, arrange
[h]	help, who, home
[m]	mouse, number, film
[n]	name, window, pen
[ŋ]	sing, morning, long
[l]	like, blue, all
[r]	read, borrow, very
[j]	yes, you, year
[w]	walk, where, quiz

The English alphabet
Das englische Alphabet

a	[eɪ]
b	[biː]
c	[siː]
d	[diː]
e	[iː]
f	[ef]
g	[dʒiː]
h	[eɪtʃ]
i	[aɪ]
j	[dʒeɪ]
k	[keɪ]
l	[el]
m	[em]
n	[en]
o	[əʊ]
p	[piː]
q	[kjuː]
r	[ɑː]
s	[es]
t	[tiː]
u	[juː]
v	[viː]
w	['dʌbl juː]
x	[eks]
y	[waɪ]
z	[zed]

Erklärung der Symbole im Wörterverzeichnis

Act	=	Activities	Proj	=	Project	WP	=	Words and Pictures
Com	=	Communication	Read	=	Reading	❭	=	definition
Ex	=	Exercise	Rev	=	Revision	❭❭	=	synonym
Intro	=	Introduction	Sit	=	Situation	❭❬	=	opposite
List	=	Listening	T	=	Text			
Lit	=	Literature	TYE	=	Test your English			

one hundred and thirteen **113**

British and American English   Britisches und amerikanisches Englisch

Die Hauptunterschiede zwischen britischem Englisch (BE) und amerikanischem Englisch (AE) zeigen sich in der Aussprache und im Wortschatz. Abweichungen finden sich aber auch in den Bereichen Schreibung und Grammatik. Im Rahmen der Globalisierung (z.B. durch das Internet) verwischen die Grenzen besonders beim Wortschatz mehr und mehr.

Unterschiede in der Aussprache

BE		AE
[ɑː]	ask, dance, glass, pass	[æ]
[ɒ]	body, dollar, hot	[ɑː]
[juː]	duty, new, stupid, Tuesday	[uː]
[t]	better, capital, water	[d] (innerhalb eines Wortes)
[fɑː], [fɔː], [hɪə], [ʃɜːt]	far, for, hear, shirt	[fɑːr], [fɔːr], [hɪr], [ʃɜːrt]

Unterschiede in der Betonung

[ə'dres]	address	['ædres]
[əd'vɜːtɪsmənt]	advertisement	[ˌædvɜːr'taɪzmənt]
['gærɑːʒ]	garage	[gə'rɑːʒ]

Unterschiede im Wortschatz

Unterschiedliche Bezeichnungen gibt es in fast allen Lebensbereichen, z.B.:

BE	AE	
petrol station	gas station	◆ **Verkehr**
lorry, truck	truck	
car	car, automobile	
windscreen	windshield	
railway	railroad	
trousers	pants	◆ **Kleidung**
handbag	purse	
chips	french fries	◆ **Nahrungsmittel**
sweets	candy	
lift	elevator	◆ **Technik**, **Bauwesen**
ground floor	first floor	
postman	mailman	◆ **öffentliches Leben**

114   one hundred and fourteen

Unterschiede in der Schreibung

	BE	AE
◆ Wörter, die im BE auf *-re* enden, werden im AE meistens *-er* geschrieben.	cent**re** theat**re**	cent**er** theat**er**
◆ Substantive, die im BE *-our* aufweisen, haben im AE fast immer die Endung *-or*.	col**our** neighb**our** harb**our**	col**or** neighb**or** harb**or**
◆ Bei einigen Wörtern wird die BE Endung *-ence* zu AE *-ense*.	def**ence** lic**ence**	def**ense** lic**ense**
◆ Im BE wird ein End-*l* in unbetonten Silben vor *-ing*, *-ed*, *-er* verdoppelt. Im AE nicht.	trave**ll**ing quarre**ll**ing dia**ll**ed	trave**l**ing quarre**l**ing dia**l**ed
◆ Manche Wörter werden in ihrer Schreibung im AE vereinfacht.	progra**mme** dialo**gue** che**que**	progra**m** dialo**g** che**ck**
(noun: pract**i**ce *BE/AE*)	to practi**se**	to practi**ce**
◆ Extreme Vereinfachungen kommen in der Werbung vor (eigentlich inkorrekt).	li**ght** ni**ght**	li**te** ni**te**

Unterschiede in der Grammatik

	BE	AE
◆ Im AE ist in der Bedeutung „haben, besitzen" die Form *Do you have …?* üblich.	**Has she got** blue eyes? **Have you got** any children?	**Does she have** blue eyes? **Do you have** any children?
◆ Im AE wird anstelle des *present perfect* manchmal das *simple past* verwendet.	We **have** just **come** home. **Have** you ever **played** baseball?	We just **came** home. **Did** you ever **play** baseball?
◆ Im BE lautet die *past participle*-Form *got*. Das AE verwendet für Vorgänge *gotten*.	His singing has **got** better.	His singing has **gotten** better.
◆ In der Umgangssprache verwendet das AE manchmal ein **Adjektiv** anstelle eines Adverbs.	We had some **really** nice weather.	We had some **real** nice weather.
◆ **Präpositionen** werden im AE oft anders verwendet als im BE.	Jim will be here **from** Monday **to/till** Saturday. This cap is **different from** the others. We stayed **at** home.	Jim will be here **from** Monday **through** Saturday. This cap is **different from/than** the others. We stayed home.
◆ Nach *hundred* kann im AE *and* weggelassen werden.	It's about a hundred **and** sixty miles.	It's about **a hundred sixty** miles.
◆ Auch bei **Zeitangaben** unterscheidet sich das AE.	It's twenty **to** eight. Let's meet at ten **past** one.	It's twenty **to/of** eight. Let's meet at ten **past/after** one.

one hundred and fifteen **115**

Wörterverzeichnis

Unit 1

WP	**skyline** ['skaɪlaɪn]	Silhouette, Skyline	*the Manhattan **skyline***
	statue ['stætʃuː]	Statue	*the **Statue** of Liberty*
	liberty ['lɪbəti]	Freiheit	
	empire ['empaɪə]	Reich, Imperium	*the **Roman Empire**,*
			*the **British Empire***
	borough ['bʌrə]	(Stadt)Bezirk	*the **borough** of Queens in New York City*

Chinese [tʃaɪˈniːz]	chinesisch; Chinese, Chinesin	
southern ['sʌðən]	südlich; Süd-	
Jew [dʒuː]	Jude, Jüdin	
Hispanic [hɪˈspænɪk]	hispanisch; Hispanoamerikaner/in	

	apartment [əˈpɑːtmənt] *esp AE*	Wohnung	≫ *flat BE*
	condition [kənˈdɪʃn]	Bedingung, Zustand, Verhältnisse	❯ *the situation in which people live or work*
Sit1	**capital** ['kæpɪtl]	Hauptstadt	*Paris is the **capital** of France.*
	to be able to [bi ˈeɪbl tə]	können, in der Lage sein	*Stacy **won't be able to** come to the party on Friday. She's ill.*
	could [kʊd]	konnte	*It was so noisy that they **couldn't** hear anything.*
	opportunity [ˌɒpəˈtjuːnəti]	Gelegenheit, Chance	≫ *chance* ❯ *a time when it is possible to do sth*
	opportunity to do sth [ˌɒpəˈtjuːnəti tə]	Gelegenheit, Chance, etwas zu tun	*I had no **opportunity to** phone him this morning.*
	dollar ['dɒlə]	Dollar	

	clothing ['kləʊðɪŋ]	Bekleidung, Kleidung	≫ *clothes*
	store [stɔː] *AE*	Laden, Geschäft	≫ *shop BE*
	so that ['səʊ ðət]	sodass, damit	
	metal ['metl]	Metall	Betonung: 1. Silbe *metal* ●●
	heavy metal [ˌhevi 'metl]	Heavy Metal	
	loud [laʊd]	laut	❳❲ *quiet*
	to fall over [ˌfɔːl ˈəʊvə] **fell, fallen** [fel, ˈfɔːlən]	hinfallen, umkippen	❯ *to fall to the ground*
Ex1	**instead of** [ɪnˈsted əv]	anstatt	*Let's buy a CD **instead of** some flowers for Jane's birthday.*
Sit2	**to plan** [plæn]	planen	*We're **planning** a holiday in the USA.*
	to plan to do sth [plæn]	planen, etwas zu tun	*She **plans to** get a job as a teacher.*
	to book [bʊk]	buchen	
	trouble ['trʌbl]	Mühe, Umstände	*It's **no trouble**.*
	certain ['sɜːtn]	sicher	≫ *sure*
	certainly ['sɜːtnli]	sicherlich	≫ *surely*
	to like to do sth [laɪk]	etwas gerne tun	*I really **like to** travel.*

116 one hundred and sixteen

Wörterverzeichnis UNIT 1

> **MERKE:** **Verb + Infinitive with to**   oder   **Verb + Verb-*ing***
> I **like to read** in bed.   I **like read**ing in bed.
> Ann **hates to clean** the car.   Ann **hates clean**ing the car.
>
> Nach **like**, **love** und **hate** kann sowohl der **infinitive with to** als auch die **-ing**-Form folgen.
>
> **Nur Verb + Infinitive with to**
> I'd **like to read** Michael Crichton's new novel.
> I **would love to come** to your birthday party.
>
> Nach **would like**, **would love**, **would hate** und **would prefer** steht nur der **infinitive with to**.   → page 120, 130

to **shop** [ʃɒp]	einkaufen (gehen), Einkäufe machen	We **shop** twice a week. Where do you **shop for** food?
till [tɪl]	bis	❯❯ *until*
T1 **skyscraper** ['skaɪskreɪpə]	Wolkenkratzer	❯ *a very tall building*
to **hold** [həʊld] **held, held** [held, held]	enthalten, fassen	
to **reach** [riːtʃ]	erreichen	❯ *to get to a place*
midtown Manhattan [ˌmɪdtaʊn mæn'hætn]	Stadtteil von Manhattan	(zwischen der 42. und 59. Straße)
subway ['sʌbweɪ] *AE*	U-Bahn	❯❯ *underground/tube BE*
to **park** [pɑːk]	parken	❯ *to leave a car, lorry, etc somewhere for some time*
line [laɪn] *AE*	Reihe, Schlange	❯❯ *queue BE*
elevator ['elɪveɪtə] *AE*	Aufzug, Lift	
to **change** [tʃeɪndʒ]	umsteigen	❯ *to go from one train, bus, etc to another*
floor [flɔː]	Stockwerk, Etage	**on** the 22nd **floor** = **im** 22. Stock

floor	=	Stockwerk, Fußboden
Flur	=	**hall, corridor**

spectacular [spek'tækjələ]	sensationell, atemberaubend	❯ *wonderful to watch* **spectacular** views
crowded ['kraʊdɪd]	voll, überfüllt	❯❮ *empty* ❯ *full of people* There are a lot of people on the bus. It's **crowded**.
wait [weɪt]	Warten, Wartezeit	We had a long **wait** for the next subway.
stop [stɒp]	Halt(en), Haltestelle; Aufenthalt	

litter ['lɪtə]	Abfall	
graffiti [grə'fiːti]	Graffiti, Wandschmierereien	
copper ['kɒpə]	Kupfer; kupfern	
step [step]	Stufe; Schritt	Do the project **step by step**. (Schritt für Schritt)
crown [kraʊn]	Krone	
P.M./p.m./pm [ˌpiː 'em]	nach 12 Uhr mittags	❯ *after 12 o'clock*
to **have a look (at)** [ˌhæv ə 'lʊk]	etwas ansehen	**Have a look at** my new car.
sidewalk *AE* ['saɪdwɔːk]	Gehsteig, Bürgersteig	
to **be afraid of** do**ing** sth [bi ə'freɪd əv]	Angst davor haben, etwas zu tun	Amy **is afraid of** going out alone at night.

one hundred and seventeen **117**

UNIT 1   Wörterverzeichnis

MERKE: Adjective + Preposition + Verb-*ing*

She's **afraid of meeting** her new boss.   I'm **tired of telling** you again and again.

Du kennst außerdem: to be **interested in doing** sth   *Interesse haben, etwas zu tun*
                       to be **good at doing** sth   *etwas gut können*
                       to be **proud of doing** sth   *auf etwas stolz sein*
                       to be **worried about doing** sth   *sich um etwas Sorgen machen*
                       to be **bored with doing** sth   *etwas satt haben*

---

direction [də'rekʃn]	Richtung	to **ask for directions** = nach der Richtung fragen; nach Anweisungen fragen
corner ['kɔːnə]	Ecke	*in the corner*
courage ['kʌrɪdʒ]	Mut	*on the corner*
Ex5 **summary** ['sʌməri]	Zusammenfassung	
Ex6 **purpose** ['pɜːpəs]	Zweck, Ziel, Absicht	*What's the **purpose** of your visit? = Why are you here?*

MERKE: Purpose

Most people work **to earn** money.   I'll post the card today **so that it gets** there in time.
          (*um … zu verdienen*)   (*damit sie … ankommt*)
We went to the bookshop **to buy** some books.   I gave him the map **so that he could find** the way.
          (*um … zu kaufen*)   (*damit er … finden konnte*)

Wir verwenden einen **infinitive with to**, um   Nach **so that** verwenden wir ein Subjekt und
den Zweck einer Handlung auszudrücken.   ein Verb (**it gets**, **he could find**).

Ex7 **natural history** [ˌnætʃrəl 'hɪstri]	Naturkunde, Naturgeschichte	
trade [treɪd]	Handel	❯ *buying and selling things between countries*
pattern ['pætn]	Muster	
avenue ['ævənjuː]	Boulevard, breite Straße, Allee	❯ *a road in a town* *The hotel is **on** 11th **avenue**.*
to **divide** [dɪ'vaɪd]	teilen, aufteilen; trennen	***Divide** the cake into four pieces.*
block [blɒk] *AE*	Häuser-, Wohnblock	
downtown *esp AE* ['daʊntaʊn]	(im/ins) Stadtzentrum	❯ *(in or to) the center (AE) of a city*
business ['bɪznəs]	Geschäft; Betrieb	
district ['dɪstrɪkt]	Gebiet, Bezirk, Stadtviertel	❯ *an area in or around a town*
area ['eəriə]	Gebiet; Bereich	
Ex8 **desk clerk** ['desk klɜːrk]	Empfangschef/in	
Sit3 to **be allowed to** do sth [bi ə'laʊd]	etwas tun dürfen	*Are you **allowed to** watch horror movies?*
license ['laɪsns] *AE*	Erlaubnis; Führerschein	*You must have a **driver's license**/**driving licence** (BE) before you are allowed to drive a car.*

Wörterverzeichnis UNIT 1

	to **pass** [pɑːs]	bestehen (Prüfung)	✘ *to fail*
	freedom ['friːdəm]	Freiheit	≫ *liberty* ⚠ *liberty* klingt förmlich!
Ex9	**visa** ['viːzə]	Visum, Sichtvermerk	
	to **enter** ['entə]	eintreten (in)	≫ *to go in(to), to come in(to)*
Ex10	**service** ['sɜːvɪs]	Dienst	
	bus service ['bʌs sɜːvɪs]	Busverbindung	*plane service, train service*
	A.M./a.m./am [ˌeɪ 'em]	vor 12 Uhr mittags	

	arrival [ə'raɪvl]	Ankunft	✘ *arrival*
	departure [dɪ'pɑːtʃə]	Abfahrt, Abreise	
Ex11	to **note down** [ˌnəʊt 'daʊn]	notieren, aufschreiben	› *to write sth down to remember it*
	math [mæθ] *AE*	Mathematik	≫ *maths BE*
T2	**bright** [braɪt]	hell; strahlend, klar	*It was a **bright**, sunny day.*
	classmate ['klɑːsmeɪt]	Klassenkamerad/in	› *someone in the same class as you at school*
	to **correct** [kə'rekt]	verbessern, korrigieren	*This sentence is wrong. Can you **correct** it?*
	to **discuss** [dɪ'skʌs]	besprechen, diskutieren	*Tomorrow we'll **discuss** the problem in class.*
	stay [steɪ]	Aufenthalt	*He's back from a short **stay** with his aunt.*
	studio ['stjuːdiəʊ] *pl* **studios**	Studio	
	flashing ['flæʃɪŋ]	blinkend, blitzend	
	soda ['səʊdə]	Soda(wasser)	
	alcohol ['ælkəhɒl]	Alkohol	

	nachos ['nætʃəʊz]	Nachos	*(gebackene Tortilla-Chips aus Maismehl und Pflanzenöl)*
	somehow ['sʌmhaʊ]	irgendwie	
	hip hop ['hɪp hɒp]	Hip-Hop	
	even though ['iːvn ðəʊ]	obwohl	≫ *although* *We went swimming **even though** it was cold.*
	in fact [ˌɪn 'fækt]	eigentlich, tatsächlich	≫ *really*
	rap [ræp]	Rap	
	way of life [ˌweɪ əv 'laɪf]	Lebensart, Lebensweise	

	break-dancing ['breɪk dɑːnsɪŋ]	Breakdancing	
	hip-hop magazine ['hɪphɒp ˌmægə'ziːn]	Hip-Hop Zeitschrift	
	violence ['vaɪələns]	Gewalt	*There is too much **violence** on TV.*
	violent ['vaɪələnt]	gewalttätig	***violent** crime*
	gangster ['gæŋstə]	Gangster, Verbrecher	
	midnight ['mɪdnaɪt]	Mitternacht	*at **midnight** = at 12 o'clock at night*
	to **return** [rɪ'tɜːn]	zurückkehren	≫ *to go back, to come back*
Ex12	**false** [fɔːls]	falsch, unrichtig	✘ *true, right*
Ex13	to **clean** [kliːn]	sauber machen	*We **clean** the apartment every Saturday.*
Ex14	**ending** ['endɪŋ]	Endung, Ende	
Ex15	**pavement** ['peɪvmənt] *BE*	Gehsteig	≫ *sidewalk AE*
	detail ['diːteɪl]	Einzelheit, Detail	*He told us his plan **in detail**.*

one hundred and nineteen 119

UNIT 1   **Wörterverzeichnis**

Ex16 to **practice** do**ing** sth   üben, etwas zu tun   **»** *to practise BE*
['præktɪs] *AE*

MERKE: Verb + Verb-*ing*

Bestimmte Verben haben als Ergänzung eine *-ing*-Form:

| Vergleiche: | He **practiced** | the dance. | He **started** | a new job | yesterday. |
| | He **practiced** | danc**ing**. | He **started** | work**ing** | yesterday. |

Du kennst außerdem: to **like** do**ing** sth   to **start** do**ing** sth
to **enjoy** do**ing** sth   to **keep** do**ing** sth   → **page 117, 130**

---

to **arrange** [ə'reɪndʒ]   vereinbaren;
anordnen

to **arrange to** do sth   vereinbaren, etwas   *We **arranged to** meet at 6 P.M.*
[ə'reɪndʒ]   zu tun

MERKE: Verb + Infinitive with to

Bestimmte Verben können als Ergänzung ein weiteres Verb im Infinitiv haben:

| Vergleiche: | I **arranged** | a trip to Canada. | He **tried** | a new computer game | yesterday. |
| | I **arranged** | **to** work in a bank. | He **tried** | **to** play it | yesterday. |

Du kennst außerdem: to **need to** do sth   to **begin to** do sth   **would like to** do sth
to **decide to** do sth   to **learn to** do sth   **would love to** do sth
to **hope to** do sth   to **like to** do sth   **would hate to** do sth
to **agree to** do sth   to **plan to** do sth   to **want to** do sth   → **page 128**

---

to **create** [kri'eɪt]   (er)schaffen,   **›** *to make sth happen or exist*
hervorbringen;
verursachen

Com **single** ['sɪŋgl]   einzeln; Einzel-   *Do you want a **single** or a double room?*
TYE **immigration** [ˌɪmɪ'greɪʃn] Einwanderung
movement ['muːvmənt]   Bewegung   *eye **movement**, women's **movement***
immigrant ['ɪmɪgrənt]   Einwanderer,   Betonung : 1. Silbe ***immigrant*** ●●●
Einwanderin

eastern ['iːstən]   östlich; Ost-

religion [rɪ'lɪdʒən]   Religion
passenger ['pæsɪndʒə]   Fahrgast,
Passagier/in   **›** *someone traveling (AE) on a bus, train, plane or ship*
to **examine** [ɪg'zæmɪn]   untersuchen   **›** *to look at someone or something carefully*
TYE2 **interpreter** [ɪn'tɜːprɪtə]   Dolmetscher/in   *I couldn't speak Italian, so my wife was my **interpreter**.*
TYE3 **great-grandfather**   Urgroßvater   *My mother's grandfather is my **great-grandfather**.*
[ˌgreɪt'grænfɑːðə]
great-great-grandfather Ururgroßvater
[ˌgreɪt ˌgreɪt 'grænfɑːðə]
TYE4 **voyage** ['vɔɪɪdʒ]   Seereise   **›** *a long journey in a ship*
Italian [ɪ'tæliən]   italienisch; Italiener/in

120 **one hundred and twenty**

Wörterverzeichnis UNIT 1

Read **robber** ['rɒbə] — Räuber/in — ❯ *someone who steals things from a bank or shop*

Federal Bureau of Investigation/FBI [ˌfedərəl ˌbjuːrəʊ əv ɪnvestɪ'geɪʃn, ˌef biː 'aɪ] — FBI (Bundeskriminalamt)

to **mug** [mʌg] — überfallen und ausrauben — ❯ *to attack someone and take their money*

grocery (store) ['grəʊsəri stɔː] — Lebensmittelgeschäft — ❯ *a small food shop*

jail [dʒeɪl] *esp AE* — Gefängnis — ❯❯ *prison esp BE*

to **form** [fɔːm] — formen, bilden — ❯ *to start a group, to make something*

gang [gæŋ] — Bande, Gang — ❯ *a group of people who do illegal things*

to **rob** [rɒb] — berauben, ausrauben — *He robbed a bank and went to jail.*

to **smuggle (into)** ['smʌgl] — (ein)schmuggeln (in)

alarm [ə'lɑːm] — Alarm — ❯ *a loud noise or signal that warns people of danger*

handsome ['hænsəm] — gut aussehend

MERKE:

Man	Woman	Child	Thing
a **handsome** boy			a **handsome** house
	his **beautiful** girlfriend	a **beautiful** child	a **beautiful** house
	a **pretty** girl	a **pretty** child	a **pretty** picture
a **good-looking** man	a **good-looking** woman		
an **attractive** young man	an **attractive** model		an **attractive** town

---

charming ['tʃɑːmɪŋ] — charmant, bezaubernd — ❯❯ *very attractive (looks and character)*

killer ['kɪlə] — Mörder/in

fake [feɪk] — unecht; Fälschung — *He paid with fake money.   The painting was a fake.*

to **fool** [fuːl] — zum Narren halten

agent ['eɪdʒənt] — Agent/in, Detektiv/in

to **surround** [sə'raʊnd] — umzingeln, umgeben — ❯ *to go or be all around sb or sth*

nephew ['nevjuː] — Neffe — *The son of your brother or sister is your nephew.*

to **recognize** ['rekəgnaɪz] — erkennen, anerkennen — *I recognized her but I couldn't remember her name.*

electric [ɪ'lektrɪk] — elektrisch

shot [ʃɒt] — Schuss

MERKE: Wortbildung mit Vorsilben

Durch **Vorsilben** ändert sich zwar die Wortbedeutung, die Wortart bleibt jedoch meist erhalten.

sub-	*unter*	subway (*U-Bahn*), submarine (*U-Boot*)	• Diese Vorsilben drücken einen **räumlichen Bezug** oder einen höheren bzw. geringeren **Grad** aus.
inter-	*zwischen*	inter-school, intercontinental	
trans-	*hinüber*	transport, translate (*übersetzen*)	
super-	*über*	superman, supermarket	
mini-	*klein*	minibus, miniskirt (*Minirock*)	
pre-	*vor*	pretend (*vorgeben*), prepare	• Durch diese Vorsilben werden **zeitliche Beziehungen** ausgedrückt.
post-	*nach*	post-war (*nach dem Krieg*)	
re-	*wieder*	rebuild, reuse	

one hundred and twenty-one   121

UNIT 2   Wörterverzeichnis

Unit 2

WP to **celebrate** ['selɪbreɪt]   feiern
    independence   Unabhängigkeit
    [ˌɪndɪ'pendəns]

    calendar ['kælɪndə]   Kalender

a diary (Taschenkalender)   *a calendar* (Wandkalender)

    flag [flæg]   Flagge
    to **discover** [dɪ'skʌvə]   entdecken
    parade [pə'reɪd]   Umzug, Festzug, Parade

*Did Columbus **discover** America?*

    Thanksgiving   Erntedankfest
    ['θæŋksɡɪvɪŋ]
    turkey ['tɜːki]   Truthahn
    European [ˌjʊərə'piːən]   europäisch; Europäer/in
    settler ['setlə]   Siedler/in
    to **survive** [sə'vaɪv]   überleben
    population [ˌpɒpju'leɪʃn] Bevölkerung

Einer der höchsten Feiertage in den USA; wird am vierten Donnerstag im November gefeiert.

*Four people died in the accident. Only one person **survived**.*
› *all the people of a town or country*

    Mardi Gras   Mardi Gras (Karneval)
    [ˌmɑːdi 'ɡrɑː]
    carnival ['kɑːnɪvl]   Volksfest; Karneval, Fasching

In einigen Gegenden im Süden der USA (New Orleans, Biloxi, Mobile) feiert man Mardi Gras. New Orleans war früher Hauptstadt der französischen Kolonie Louisiana.

Sit1 **breeze** [briːz]   Brise
    sample ['sɑːmpl]   Kostprobe, Muster
    product ['prɒdʌkt]   Produkt

› *a small piece that shows what the rest is like*
Betonung: **product** ● ●

MERKE: Unregelmäßige Verben

to **sell, sold, sold**	verkaufen	to **pay, paid, paid**	bezahlen
to **teach, taught, taught**	unterrichten	to **throw, threw, thrown**	werfen
to **mean, meant, meant**	bedeuten, meinen	to **wear, wore, worn**	tragen (Kleidung)
to **give, gave, given**	geben	to **show, showed, shown/showed**	zeigen

Alle unregelmäßigen Verben findest du auf den Seiten 138–139.

---

    counter ['kaʊntə]   Ladentisch, Tresen
    yummy ['jʌmi]   lecker, schmackhaft
    typical (of) ['tɪpɪkl]   typisch (für)
    to **serve** [sɜːv]   servieren, bedienen
    altogether [ˌɔːltə'ɡeðə] insgesamt, im Ganzen
Ex1 to **milk** [mɪlk]   melken
Sit2 to **injure** ['ɪndʒə]   verletzen
    biology [baɪ'ɒlədʒi]   Biologie
    period ['pɪəriəd] *esp AE* (Unterrichts-)Stunde
    physics ['fɪzɪks]   Physik
Ex2 **chat room** ['tʃæt ruːm]   Chatroom (Internet)
    article ['ɑːtɪkl]   Artikel, Beitrag

› *very good to eat*
*Spaghetti is **typical of** Italian cooking.*
› *to give a meal to someone*

*When does the farmer **milk** the cows?*
›› *to hurt someone/something*

›› *lesson BE*
⚠ *physics* ist immer im Singular!

*Did you read the **article** in 'The European'?*

122   one hundred and twenty-two

Wörterverzeichnis UNIT 2

T1	**pen pal** ['pen pæl] *AE*	Brieffreund/in	›› *penfriend BE*
	junior ['dʒu:niə] *AE*	Student/in im vorletzten Studienjahr	
	senior ['si:niə] *AE*	Student/in im letzten Studienjahr	
	to **graduate** ['grædʒuət]	die Abschlussprüfung bestehen	› *to pass the final exam* (Prüfung) *at college / high school*
	schedule ['skedʒu:l] *AE*	Stundenplan, Zeitplan	›› *timetable BE* ['ʃedju:l]
	annual ['ænjuəl]	jährlich; Jahres-	› *happening or done once every year*
	production [prə'dʌkʃn]	Herstellung, Produktion	
	yearbook ['jɪəbʊk]	Jahrbuch	
	cafeteria [,kæfə'tɪəriə]	Cafeteria	
	to **take part (in)** [teɪk 'pɑ:t] **took, taken** [tʊk, 'teɪkən]	teilnehmen an	to **take part in** *a discussion*
	volleyball ['vɒlibɔ:l]	Volleyball	
	season ['si:zn]	Jahreszeit; Saison	*the four seasons, the football season, the holiday season*
	cheerleader ['tʃɪəli:də]	Cheerleader	
	to **lead** [li:d] **led, led** [led, led]	führen, leiten	*The teacher led the pupils into the classroom.* *They lead a very busy life.*
	drive [draɪv]	Aktion, Kampagne	
	boxing ['bɒksɪŋ]	Boxen, Box-	
	cent [sent]	Cent	
	total ['təʊtl]	(End)Summe, Gesamtmenge	
	dance [dæ:ns]	Tanz, Tanzen; Tanzveranstaltung	
	formal ['fɔ:ml] *AE*	Tanzveranstaltung	(Gesellschaftskleidung ist vorgeschrieben)
	seafood ['si:fu:d]	Meeresfrüchte	
	theme [θi:m]	Thema, Motto	›› *subject*
	decorate ['dekəreɪt]	schmücken; tapezieren	*We decorated the apartment for Christmas.* (schmückten) *He decorated the kitchen.* (tapezierte)
	snow [snəʊ]	Schnee	
	DJ [,di: 'dʒeɪ]	Discjockey	
Ex7	**Indian** ['ɪndiən]	indianisch; Indianer/in; Inder/in	
Ex8	to **cut out** [,kʌt 'aʊt] **cut, cut** [kʌt, kʌt]	ausschneiden	
Ex9	**how about …?** [,haʊ ə'baʊt]	wie wär's mit …?	*How about going by train? – Yes, good idea.*
Sit3	**amount** [ə'maʊnt]	Betrag; Menge	
	to **treat** [tri:t]	behandeln	*He treated his wife and children very badly.*
	inter-school [,ɪntə'sku:l]	zwischen Schulen	› *between schools*
	event [ɪ'vent]	Ereignis, Veranstaltung	› *sth important that happens*
	local ['ləʊkl]	örtlich, am Ort, Lokal-	› *near or belonging to the place where you live*
Ex10	**bomb** [bɒm]	Bombe	⚠ Aussprache: stummes b [bɒm]

UNIT 2   Wörterverzeichnis

Sit4	to **beat** [biːt] beat, beaten [biːt, ˈbiːtn]	schlagen; klopfen	❯ to hit sb or sth ❯ to defeat sb in a game or competition
Ex11	**headline** [ˈhedlaɪn]	Schlagzeile	
Sit5	**cost** [kɒst]	Kosten	❯ the money that you must pay for something
	daily [ˈdeɪli]	täglich; Tages-	You can buy a **daily** newspaper every day.
	to **increase** [ɪnˈkriːs]	zunehmen, anwachsen	❯ to become greater in amount or number
	season ticket [ˈsiːzn tɪkɪt]	Dauerkarte	
	individual [ˌɪndɪˈvɪdʒuəl]	einzeln, individuell	❯ for one person only
Ex12	to **touch** [tʌtʃ]	berühren	
	to **bounce** [baʊns]	aufprallen lassen	
	backwards [ˈbækwədz]	rückwärts	❯❮ forwards
	aim [eɪm]	Ziel	Her **aim** is to find a good job.
	touchdown [ˈtʌtʃdaʊn]	Versuch	(Niederlegen des Balls hinter der goal line des Gegners.)
	to **tackle** [ˈtækl]	angreifen	
	goalkeeper [ˈɡəʊlkiːpə]	Torwart	

T2	**Super Bowl** [ˈsuːpə bəʊl]	Super Bowl	
	professional [prəˈfeʃənl]	Berufs-, Fach-, Profi-	
	championship [ˈtʃæmpiənʃɪp]	Meisterschaft (Sport)	the World/European **Championships**
	play-off [ˈpleɪɒf]	Entscheidungsspiel	
	winner [ˈwɪnə]	Gewinner/in	❯ someone who wins in a game
	to **take place** [teɪk ˈpleɪs] took, taken [tʊk, ˈteɪkən]	stattfinden	

to **take place**	=	stattfinden
Platz nehmen	=	to **take a seat**, to **sit down**

	host [həʊst]	Gastgeber/in; Moderator/in	
	however [haʊˈevə]	jedoch	❯❯ but
	entertainment [ˌentəˈteɪnmənt]	Unterhaltung	
	superstar [ˈsuːpəstɑː]	Superstar	❯ a really famous actor, sportsperson, etc.
	tension [ˈtenʃn]	Anspannung, Spannung	
	close [kləʊs]	knapp	a **close** match, a **close** finish
	confident [ˈkɒnfɪdənt]	zuversichtlich, selbstsicher	Helen is **confident** that she'll pass the test.
	defense [dɪˈfens] *AE*	Verteidigung	❯❯ defence BE
	to **give away** [ˌɡɪv əˈweɪ] gave, given [ɡeɪv, ˈɡɪvn]	abgeben, verschenken	If you don't want the ticket, **give** it **away**.
	point [pɔɪnt]	Punkt	
	worldwide [ˈwɜːldwaɪd]	weltweit	❯ all over the world
	network [ˈnetwɜːk]	Sendenetz (TV, Radio)	
	commercial [kəˈmɜːʃl]	Werbespot	❯ a short film that helps to sell a product
	because of [bɪˈkɒz əv]	wegen	There were lots of accidents **because of** the storm.
	to **develop** [dɪˈveləp]	(sich) entwickeln	
	ultimate [ˈʌltɪmət]	perfekt, vollendet	❯❯ greatest

124   one hundred and twenty-four

Wörterverzeichnis UNIT 2

between the players

among the players

	among [əˈmʌŋ]	zwischen, unter	
	to **advertise** [ˈædvətaɪz]	Werbung machen (für)	
	to **deny** [dɪˈnaɪ]	bestreiten, leugnen	❯ to say that something isn't true
Ex14	**heading** [ˈhedɪŋ]	Überschrift	
Ex17	**example (of)** [ɪgˈzɑːmpl]	Beispiel (für)	Football is a typical **example of** a popular sport. **for example** = zum Beispiel
Ex18	**beginner** [bɪˈgɪnə]	Anfänger/in	
Com	**way of** do**ing** sth [ˈweɪ əv]	Art und Weise, etwas zu tun	Do you know a good **way of** earn**ing** money?
	could [kʊd]	könnte	**Could** I use your phone, please?

> **MERKE: Could**
>
> Ron **could** read when he was 5 years old.   It **could** snow tomorrow.
> My grandma **couldn't** swim.   **Couldn't** we leave earlier?
> **Could** grandpa play the guitar?   **Could** I have another piece of cake, please?
>
> **k**onnte   k**ö**nnte

TYE	to be **good at** do**ing** sth [ˈgʊd ət]	gut sein in, etwas gut können	Zoe is **good at** learn**ing** languages.
	to **invent** [ɪnˈvent]	erfinden	❯ to create sth that hasn't existed before
	automobile [ˈɔːtəməbiːl] *AE*	Auto, Automobil	❯❯ car
	invention [ɪnˈvenʃn]	Erfindung	
	to **refuse** [rɪˈfjuːz]	sich weigern	I asked Jack to help me but he **refused**.
	to **settle** [ˈsetl]	sich ansiedeln, sich niederlassen	❯ to make your home in a new place
	Dutch [dʌtʃ]	holländisch, niederländisch	❯ Pennsylvania Dutch (englisch-deutscher Dialekt, der von den Amisch gesprochen wird)
	jewelry [ˈdʒuːəlri] *AE*	Schmuck, Juwelen	❯❯ jewellery *BE*
	souvenir [ˌsuːvəˈnɪə]	Andenken, Souvenir	He brought back a cowboy hat as a **souvenir** of the USA.
TYE1	to **mention** [ˈmenʃn]	erwähnen	❯ to say or write about something in a few words
TYE4	**witness** [ˈwɪtnəs]	Zeuge, Zeugin	The **witness** has said she heard shots.
	to **witness** [ˈwɪtnəs]	Zeuge sein von	❯ to see something happening
	murder [ˈmɜːdə]	Mord	
	corrupt [kəˈrʌpt]	bestechlich, korrupt	
Read	**flat** [flæt]	flach	
	to **realize** [ˈrɪəlaɪz]	erkennen, begreifen, klar werden	❯❯ to understand
	geography [dʒiˈɒgrəfi]	Geografie	
	turn [tɜːn]	Kurve, Abzweigung	❯ a change in direction

murder	=	Mord
Mörder	=	**murderer**

one hundred and twenty-five 125

UNIT 2   Wörterverzeichnis

signpost ['saɪnpəʊst]	Wegweiser	
bend [bend]	Kurve, Biegung	
intersection [ˌɪntə'sekʃn]	Kreuzung, Autobahnkreuz	❯ *a place where two or more roads meet*
expressway [ɪk'spreswer] *AE*	Autobahn	
junction ['dʒʌŋkʃn] *esp BE*	Straßenkreuzung, Verkehrsknotenpunkt	❯ *a place where two or more roads or railroad lines meet*
No U-turn [nəʊ 'juː tɜːn]	Wenden verboten	
to **brush** [brʌʃ]	bürsten, putzen	*She **brushed** her hair, her teeth and her shoes.*
tooth [tuːθ] *pl* **teeth** [tiːθ]	Zahn	
cork [kɔːk]	Kork(en)	
amusement park [ə'mjuːzmənt pɑːk]	Vergnügungspark	
freeway ['friːweɪ] *AE*	(gebührenfreie) Autobahn	
chain-link fence [ˌtʃeɪnlɪŋk 'fens]	Maschendrahtzaun	
for Christ's sake [fə kraɪsts 'seɪk]	um Gottes willen!	
wonder ['wʌndə]	Wunder	*It's no **wonder** (that) he won the award. I'm not surprised about it.*
little ['lɪtl]	wenig	
less, least [les, liːst]	weniger, am wenigsten	

MERKE: **Little/a little**   I slept very **little** last night.   May I have **a little** of that cake?
             I've got **little** money left.   There is still **a little** wine in the bottle.
             (*wenig*)   (*ein bisschen, ein wenig*)

  Few/a few   **Few** people live to the age of 100.   Only **a few** people came to the party.
                  (*wenige*)   (*ein paar*)

MERKE: **Wortbildung mit Nachsilben 1**

Durch **Nachsilben** lassen sich **Nomen**, Adjektive und Verben aus anderen Wortarten bilden.

Nomen:

		Diese Nomen bezeichnen oft
-ment	argu**ment**, equip**ment**	• einen **Vorgang** oder sein **Ergebnis**,
-ing	build**ing**, hous**ing**, ice-skat**ing**	
-al	arriv**al** (*Ankunft*)	
-ation, -tion, -sion	communic**ation**, sugges**tion**, televi**sion**	
-ance/-ence	entr**ance** (*Eingang*), independ**ence**	• eine **Eigenschaft** oder einen **Zustand**
-ness	ill**ness**, mean**ness**	

Unit 3

WP	**colony** ['kɒləni]	Kolonie	❯ a country that is ruled by another country
	equal ['i:kwəl]	gleich	❯❯ the same
	right [raɪt]	Recht	the **right** to do sth
	to **vote** [vəʊt]	wählen, Stimme abgeben für	
	slave [sleɪv]	Sklave, Sklavin	**Slaves** had no freedom because they belonged to their owner.
	plantation [plæn'teɪʃn]	Pflanzung, Plantage	
	civil war [ˌsɪvl 'wɔː]	Bürgerkrieg	❯ a war between different groups of people in the same country
	slavery ['sleɪvəri]	Sklaverei	
	to **abolish** [ə'bɒlɪʃ]	abschaffen	Slavery in America was **abolished** in 1865.
	chief [tʃiːf]	Häuptling	Sitting Bull was a Sioux **chief**.
	native ['neɪtɪv]	gebürtig; eingeboren; Eingeborene/r	**Native** Americans
	not … either [nɒt 'aɪðə]	auch nicht	Gerry can't come, and I can't come **either**.
	wide [waɪd]	groß, weit	
	moon [muːn]	Mond	
	standard of living [ˌstændəd əv 'lɪvɪŋ]	Lebensstandard	There is a higher **standard of living** in the North than in the South.
Sit1	**pilgrim** ['pɪlɡrɪm]	Pilger/in	
	at first [ət 'fɜːst]	zuerst	❯❮ later
	tradition [trə'dɪʃn]	Tradition, Brauch	
	dinner ['dɪnə]	Hauptmahlzeit	
	colonist ['kɒlənɪst]	Kolonist/in	
	to **explore** [ɪk'splɔː]	erforschen, erkunden	❯ to go to a place to learn about it

> **MERKE: Invent/discover/explore**
>
> Who **invented** the telephone?   America **was discovered** in 1492.   Dr Livingstone **explored** Africa.
>
> Man **erfindet** etwas, das es vorher nicht gab.   Wenn man etwas **entdeckt**, findet man etwas, das **bereits existiert**.   Wenn man etwas **erforscht**, **untersucht** man es genau.

	region ['riːdʒən]	Gebiet, Region	❯❯ area
	to **fish** [fɪʃ]	fischen, angeln	
	fishing boat ['fɪʃɪŋ bəʊt]	Fischerboot	
Sit2	to **get mad with** someone [ˌɡet 'mæd wɪð]	mit jemandem böse werden	❯❯ to get angry with someone
	fight [faɪt]	Kampf, Streit	
	government ['ɡʌvənmənt]	Regierung	❯ the group of people who rule a country
	less [les]	weniger	❯❮ more It took **less** time than I thought.
	gift [ɡɪft]	Geschenk	❯❯ present
T1	**mouth** [maʊθ]	Mündung (Fluss)	
	healthy ['helθi]	gesund	**healthy** children/food/air
	continent ['kɒntɪnənt]	Erdteil, Kontinent	Africa is a **continent**.

UNIT 3   Wörterverzeichnis

tribe [traɪb]	Stamm	
to **hunt** [hʌnt]	jagen	❯ to chase wild animals for food or sport
to **grow** [grəʊ]	anbauen; wachsen	The farmer **grows** potatoes in this field.
grew, grown [gruː, grəʊn]		A lot of flowers **grow** very quickly.
vegetable ['vedʒtəbl]	Gemüse	Potatoes and beans are **vegetables**.
to **trade** [treɪd]	Handel treiben, handeln	He **trades in** fruit. They **trade with** East Asia.
leader ['liːdə]	Führer/in, Anführer/in	
to **capture** ['kæptʃə]	gefangen nehmen	❯ to catch and hold someone or something
to **lay** [leɪ]	legen; verlegen	She **laid** the letter **on** the chair.
laid, laid [leɪd, leɪd]		Can you **lay** the table please? (Tisch decken)
tobacco [təˈbækəʊ]	Tabak	

MERKE: **Verb + to +Infinitive**

Bestimmte Verben können als Ergänzung ein weiteres Verb im Infinitiv haben:

The marriage **helped to bring** peace.

Weitere Beispiele:
- to **agree to do** sth
- to **refuse to do** sth
- to **decide to do** sth
- to **pretend to do** sth (vorgeben)
- to **intend to do** sth (beabsichtigen)
- to **expect to do** sth
- to **hate to do** sth

→ page 120

---

peace [piːs]	Friede	✗ war
sensation [senˈseɪʃn]	Aufsehen, Sensation	The band became a **sensation** overnight.

MERKE: **Unregelmäßige Verben**

to **fall, fell, fallen**	*fallen*	to **get, got, gotten** *AE*	*bekommen*
to **lead, led, led**	*führen*	to **ring, rang, rung**	*läuten, klingeln*
to **hide, hid, hidden**	*verstecken*	to **pay, paid, paid**	*bezahlen*
to **catch, caught, caught**	*fangen*	to **wake, woke, woken**	*aufwecken, aufwachen*

Alle unregelmäßigen Verben findest du auf den Seiten 138–139.

---

	doll [dɒl]	Puppe	
	purse [pɜːs] *AE*	Handtasche	❯❯ handbag *BE*
	skin [skɪn]	Haut, Fell	
	offensive [əˈfensɪv]	beleidigend, kränkend	
Ex7	**buffalo** ['bʌfələʊ]	Bison, Büffel	
	pl **buffalo, buffaloes** ['bʌfələʊs]		

	prairie ['preəri]	Prärie, Grassteppe	
	reservation [ˌrezəˈveɪʃn]	Reservat; Reservierung	an Indian **reservation** I made a **reservation** for a flight to Washington.
Sit3	**themselves** [ðəmˈselvz]	sich; selbst	
	to **escape** [ɪˈskeɪp]	flüchten, entkommen	The budgie **escaped** from the cage.
	to **punish** ['pʌnɪʃ]	bestrafen	He was **punished** for his crimes.

128   one hundred and twenty-eight

Wörterverzeichnis UNIT 3

himself [hɪmˈself]	sich; selbst	
to **hang** [hæŋ] **hanged, hanged** [hæŋd, hæŋd]	aufhängen; erhängen	Nur *to hang* in der Bedeutung „erhängen = töten" bildet die regelmäßigen Formen *hanged/hanged*.

yourself [jɔːˈself]	dich, dir; selbst	
myself [maɪˈself]	mich, mir; selbst	
herself [hɜːˈself]	sich; selbst	
itself [ɪtˈself]	sich; selbst	
ourselves [ɑːˈselvz]	uns; selbst	
yourselves [jɔːˈselvz]	euch; selbst	

She's teaching herself Japanese.   *Taro is teaching her Japanese.*

Ex8	to **express** [ɪkˈspres]	ausdrücken	≫ *to say* › *to show a feeling, an opinion*
	to **fix** [fɪks]	reparieren	≫ *to repair*
Sit4	**railroad** [ˈreɪlrəʊd] *AE*	Eisenbahn	≫ *railway BE*
	organization [ˌɔːɡənaɪˈzeɪʃn]	Organisation	
	danger [ˈdeɪndʒə]	Gefahr	
	enjoy yourself! [ɪnˈdʒɔɪ jəself]	Viel Spaß!	≫ *Have a good time!*
Sit5	**independent (of/from)** [ˌɪndɪˈpendənt]	unabhängig	≫ *free* *The South wanted to be **independent from** the North.*
	each other [iːtʃ ˈʌðə]	einander, gegenseitig	*They couldn't see **each other** in the crowded room.*
	mirror [ˈmɪrə]	Spiegel	*They could see themselves in the **mirror**.*
T2	**segregation** [ˌseɡrɪˈɡeɪʃn]	Trennung	*racial **segregation*** (Rassentrennung)
	to **protest** [prəʊˈtest]	protestieren	*More than 100 people **protested** against segregation.*
	to **lynch** [lɪntʃ]	lynchen	*The man was **lynched** by the angry crowd.*
	to **go on** [ˌɡəʊ ˈɒn] **went, gone** [went, ɡɒn]	weitermachen, weitergehen	
	civil rights [ˌsɪvl ˈraɪts]	Bürgerrechte	› *the rights that every person in a country has*
	to **give up** [ˌɡɪv ˈʌp] **gave, given** [ɡeɪv, ˈɡɪvn]	aufgeben, verzichten auf	
	court [kɔːt]	Gericht, Gerichtshof	
	aisle [aɪl]	Mittelgang, Gang	
	to **fill** [fɪl]	füllen	*She **filled** two glasses with water.*
	to **let** [let] **let, let** [let, let]	lassen	*Will your father **let** you go to America alone?*

MERKE: **Let**   **Help**

Don't **let** the fire go out.   Rosa Park's action **helped** (to) start the civil rights movement.

Nach **let** folgt immer der   Nach **help** kann sowohl der **infinitive with to** oder der **infinitive**
infinitive without to.   **without to** folgen.

---

to **be tired of** doing sth [bi ˈtaɪəd əv]	es satt haben, etwas zu tun	*They were soon **tired of** watching tennis.*

one hundred and twenty-nine   **129**

UNIT 3   Wörterverzeichnis

to **give in** [ˌgɪv 'ɪn]	nachgeben	
gave, given [geɪv, 'gɪvn]		
to **be under arrest** [bi ˌʌndər ə'rest]	verhaftet sein	❯ to be a prisoner of the police
to **pick up** [ˌpɪk 'ʌp]	aufheben, aufsammeln	
squad car ['skwɒd kɑː]	Streifenwagen	❯❯ police car
to **fine** [faɪn]	Bußgeld verhängen	The police **fined** him for driving too fast.
boycott ['bɔɪkɒt]	Boykott	

MERKE: **Verb + Infinitive with to**   **Verb + Verb-*ing***

He **stopped to eat** an ice-cream.   Last year her father **stopped smoking**.
(… blieb stehen, um ein Eis zu essen)   (hörte auf, zu rauchen)

Remember to buy her a birthday present.   I **don't remember seeing** John at the party.
(Denk dran/Vergiss nicht, ihr … zu kaufen.)   (… erinnere mich nicht, … gesehen zu haben)

→ page 117, 120

---

	campaign [kæm'peɪn]	Kampagne, Aktion	❯❯ drive anti-smoking **campaign**
	Supreme Court [suːˌpriːm 'kɔːt] *AE*	Oberster Gerichtshof	
	victory ['vɪktəri]	Sieg	
	discrimination [dɪˌskrɪmɪ'neɪʃn]	Diskriminierung	**Discrimination against** black people is against the law.
	housing ['haʊzɪŋ]	Unterbringung, Wohnungen	poor **housing** conditions
Ex16	**translation** [træns'leɪʃn]	Übersetzung	
Com	**interviewer** ['ɪntəvjuːə]	Interviewer/in	
TYE	**wagon** ['wægən]	Wagen, Planwagen	
	halfway [ˌhɑːf'weɪ]	auf halbem Weg; die halbe Strecke	

	track [træk] *AE*	Gleisstrecke	
	westward ['westwəd]	westwärts, nach Westen	
	workman ['wɜːkmən]	Handwerker	
	pl **workmen** ['wɜːkmən]		
	wooden ['wʊdn]	hölzern, aus Holz	
	eastward ['iːstwəd]	ostwärts, nach Osten	
	to **employ** [ɪm'plɔɪ]	beschäftigen	❯ to give work to somebody
TYE1	**engineer** [ˌendʒɪ'nɪə]	Ingenieur/in	
TYE3	**rider** ['raɪdə]	Reiter/in; Radfahrer/in	
	hunter ['hʌntə]	Jäger/in	❯ someone who hunts wild animals
Read	**trail** [treɪl]	Weg, Pfad; Spur	
	destination [ˌdestɪ'neɪʃn]	Bestimmungsort, Ziel	❯ the place that you are traveling (*AE*) to
	attack [ə'tæk]	Angriff	❯❮ defense
	to **hire** ['haɪə]	mieten; jdn anstellen	❯ to pay someone to work for you

130   one hundred and thirty

Wörterverzeichnis UNIT 3

major ['meɪdʒə]	Major	
stove [stəʊv]	Ofen, Herd	
ox [ɒks]	Ochse	
pl **oxen** ['ɒksn]		

MERKE: Irregular plurals

one child	two child**ren**	a potato	some potat**oes**	a knife	two kni**ves**
one man	three m**e**n	a tomato	three tomat**oes**	a wife	two wi**ves**
a woman	two wom**en**	a hero	two her**oes**	one life	two li**ves**
a foot	two f**ee**t			a shelf	three shel**ves**
a tooth	some t**ee**th	one sheep	two **sheep**	a thief	two thie**ves**
a mouse	three m**i**ce	one deer	some **deer**		
a penny	50 pen**ce**	one fish	two **fish**	a person	some **people**
	(*Geldsumme*)				
	two pennies				
	(*2 Einpennymünzen*)				

---

firewood ['faɪəwʊd]	Brennholz	
buffalo chips ['bʌfələʊ tʃɪps]	getrockneter Büffelmist	
to **bite** [baɪt]	beißen	*Don't worry, the dog never **bites**.*
bit, bitten [bɪt, 'bɪtn]		
rattlesnake ['rætlsneɪk]	Klapperschlange	
sick [sɪk]	krank	

MERKE: Sick | **Ill**

I was at home because I was **sick**.   He can't go to school today. He's **ill**.
She looked after her **sick** mother.

ill kann nicht vor einem Nomen stehen!

---

to **pray** [preɪ]	beten	
to **rest** [rest]	ausruhen	≫ to relax
thunder ['θʌndə]	Donner	
shower ['ʃaʊə]	Regenschauer; Dusche	*Yesterday it was sunny with one or two **showers**.* *I'm going to have a **shower** before breakfast.*
fever ['fi:və]	Fieber	*Has she got a **fever**? – Yes, 39.3°C.*
to **bury** ['beri]	begraben	*Pocahontas is **buried** in Gravesend, England.*
to **carve** [kɑ:v]	schnitzen	*He **carved** his name in a tree with a knife.*
snowstorm ['snəʊstɔ:m]	Schneesturm	
heat [hi:t]	Hitze	*The **heat** of the fire will make the room warmer.*
to **cover** ['kʌvə]	bedecken	
pretty ['prɪti]	hübsch	≫ lovely
to **plant** [plɑ:nt]	pflanzen	≻ to put flowers, vegetables, etc in the ground to grow
crop [krɒp]	Feldfrüchte; Ernte	

one hundred and thirty-one **131**

UNIT 3   Wörterverzeichnis

> **MERKE:** **Wortbildung mit Nachsilben 2**
>
> Durch **Nachsilben** lassen sich Nomen, **Adjektive** und Verben aus anderen Wortarten bilden.
>
> **Adjektive:**
>
> | | | Diese Adjektive drücken aus, dass |
> |---|---|---|
> | **-ful** | beaut**iful**, care**ful**, use**ful** | • etwas **vorhanden** ist. |
> | **-y** | sunn**y**, storm**y**, nois**y**, hungr**y**, thirst**y** | |
> | **-less** | home**less**, end**less**, hope**less** | • eine **Eigenschaft fehlt**. |
> | **-ic** | electr**ic**, fantast**ic** | • etwas **zu tun hat mit** … . |
> | **-al** | internation**al**, centr**al**, soci**al** | |
> | **-able, -ible** | uncomfort**able**, read**able**, vis**ible** (*sichtbar*) | • etwas **machbar**, **durchführbar** oder **möglich** ist. |
> | **-ing** | interest**ing**, bor**ing**, excit**ing** | • die **Tendenz** vorhanden ist, etwas zu **bewirken**. |

Unit 4

WP	**stripe** [straɪp]	Streifen	
	border ['bɔːdə]	Grenze	❯ the line between two countries or areas
	atlas ['ætləs]	Atlas	❯ a book of maps
	motor ['məʊtə]	Motor; Auto-	
	to **produce** [prə'djuːs]	erzeugen, produzieren, herstellen	❯❯ to make This factory **produces** cars.

	cliff [klɪf]	Kliff, Klippe	
	scenery ['siːnəri]	(schöne) Landschaft	
	average ['ævərɪdʒ]	Durchschnitt(s-)	**on** average = **im** Durchschnitt
	temperature ['temprətʃə]	Temperatur	
	minus ['maɪnəs]	minus	❯❮ plus
	degree [dɪ'griː]	Grad	
	Celsius/°C ['selsiəs]	Celsius	
	oil [ɔɪl]	Öl	the **oil** industry, **oil** exporting countries
	to **defend** [dɪ'fend]	verteidigen	❯❮ to attack
Sit1	**sunshine** ['sʌnʃaɪn]	Sonnenschein	
	someplace ['sʌmpleɪs] *AE*	irgendwo, irgendwohin	❯❯ somewhere
	mountain bike ['maʊntən baɪk]	Mountainbike	
	to **kid** [kɪd]	Spaß machen, jdn aufziehen	I didn't mean it. **I was only kidding**. (Das Verb *to kid* wird normalerweise nur in der *progressive form* verwendet.)
	windsurfing ['wɪndsɜːfɪŋ]	Windsurfen	
Sit2	**zone** [zəʊn]	Zone, Bereich	❯❯ area
	would [wʊd]	würde	He said he **would** come tomorrow.

132   one hundred and thirty-two

Wörterverzeichnis **UNIT 4**

	to **put together** [ˌpʊt təˈgeðə] **put, put** [pʊt, pʊt]	zusammensetzen, zusammenlegen
Ex3	**charity** [ˈtʃærəti]	Wohltätigkeit, wohltätige Organisation
	to **promote** [prəˈməʊt]	werben (für); fördern
T1	**alligator** [ˈælɪgeɪtə]	Alligator
	golf [gɒlf]	Golf
	rocket [ˈrɒkɪt]	Rakete
	to **launch** [lɔ:ntʃ]	abschießen (Rakete); vom Stapel lassen (Schiff)
	to **experience** [ɪkˈspɪəriəns]	erleben, erfahren
	excitement [ɪkˈsaɪtmənt]	Aufregung
	theme park [ˈθi:m pɑ:k]	Freizeitpark
	plenty of [ˈplenti əv]	eine Menge, viel
	close (to) [kləʊs]	nahe, in der Nähe von
	shark [ʃɑ:k]	Hai
	trendy [ˈtrendi]	modisch, schick
	earth [ɜ:θ]	Erde
	to **photograph** [ˈfəʊtəgrɑ:f]	fotografieren
	pink [pɪŋk]	rosarot
	writer [ˈraɪtə]	Schriftsteller/in
	sunset [ˈsʌnset]	Sonnenuntergang
	to **be interested in** do**ing** sth [bi ˈɪntrəstɪd ɪn]	interessiert daran sein, etwas zu tun

lauching a rocket   *launching a ship*

She **experienced** some problems at work.
He **experienced** some pain in his arm.

Disneyland and Disney World are **theme parks**.
›› *a lot of*
›› *near*

› *to take a photo of someone/something*

Did you watch 'The **Pink** Panther' last night?
Someone who writes books is a **writer**.

Would you **be interested in** go**ing** to Florida with me this summer?

MERKE: **Interesting and interested**

This book on dinosaurs is very **interest**ing. (*interessant*)	Zoe is very **interest**ed in learning about dinosaurs. (*interessiert an*)
Die Adjektive auf *-ing* beschreiben, wie Dinge sind.	Die Adjektive auf *-ed* beschreiben, welches Gefühl sie bei Menschen auslösen.

Weitere Beispiele:

That's an **amaz**ing story. (*erstaunlich*)	I was **amaz**ed when I heard the story. (*erstaunt*)
The two-hour wait at the airport was **annoy**ing. (*ärgerlich*)	We were **annoy**ed about the wait. (*verärgert*)
I didn't enjoy the movie. It was **bor**ing. (*langweilig*)	I saw the movie but I felt **bor**ed. (*gelangweilt*)
The weather is so **depress**ing. (*deprimierend*)	This weather makes me so **depress**ed. (*niedergeschlagen*)
The quiz was **excit**ing. (*aufregend*)	The audience were **excit**ed. (*begeistert*)
The race was very **exhaust**ing. (*anstrengend*)	I was really **exhaust**ed after the race. (*erschöpft*)
This murder was a **shock**ing crime. (*schockierend*)	We were all **shock**ed when we heard about it. (*bestürzt*)
The football results were very **surpris**ing. (*überraschend*)	He was **surpris**ed at the results. (*überrascht*)

one hundred and thirty-three **133**

UNIT 4 Wörterverzeichnis

	clown [klaʊn]	Clown	
	fact [fækt]	Tatsache, Faktum	
	mostly ['məʊstli]	hauptsächlich	›› *mainly*
	hurricane ['hʌrɪkən]	Wirbelsturm	› *a violent storm with strong winds*
	crate [kreɪt]	Kiste	
	liter ['liːtə] *AE*	Liter	›› *litre BE*
Ex7	**fort** [fɔːt]	Festung, Fort	
	speedway (track) ['spiːdweɪ ˌtræk]	Speedway-, Aschenrennbahn	
	motorbike ['məʊtəbaɪk]	Motorrad	
	roller coaster ['rəʊlə ˌkəʊstə]	Achterbahn	
Sit3	**motel** [məʊ'tel]	Motel	› *a hotel where people traveling (AE) by car can stay*
	to resist [rɪ'zɪst]	widerstehen; sich widersetzen	*I can't* **resist** *chocolate cake.*
Sit4	**cellphone** ['selfəʊn] *AE*	Handy, Mobiltelefon	›› *mobile (phone) BE*
	tragedy ['trædʒədi]	Tragödie	*It was a* **tragedy** *that she died so young.*
Ex11	**aspirin** ['æsprɪn]	Aspirin	*He took some* **aspirin** *for his headache.*
T2	**to rent** [rent]	mieten; vermieten	*We* **rent** *the house from my aunt.* *They* **rent** *rooms to students.*
	oasis [əʊ'eɪsɪs]	Oase	› *a place with water and trees in a desert*
	wind [wɪnd]	Wind	
	air conditioning ['eə kənˌdɪʃnɪŋ]	Klimaanlage	*The hotel room was very hot because it had no* **air conditioning**.
	advice *no pl* [əd'vaɪs]	Rat	*I need some* **advice** *on what to wear for the party.*

> ⚠ Meint man einen konkreten Ratschlag, so sagt man **a piece of advice**:
> My friend gave me **a** good **piece of** advice.

	to get used to [ˌget 'juːst tə]	sich gewöhnen an	*She soon* **got used to** *living in Los Angeles.*
	climate ['klaɪmət]	Klima	*Italy has a wonderful* **climate**.
	dirt [dɜːt]	Schmutz, Dreck	*The farmer came back from the field with* **dirt** *on his shoes.*
	formation [fɔː'meɪʃn]	Bildung; Formation	
	arch [ɑːtʃ]	Bogen (Gebäude)	
	to take off [ˌteɪk 'ɒf] **took, taken** [tʊk, 'teɪkən]	abnehmen, ausziehen	*Please* **take off** *your dirty shoes.*
	pool [puːl]	Teich; Pfütze, Lache	
	stick [stɪk]	Stecken, Stock	› *a long, thin piece of wood*
	to hiss [hɪs]	zischen; fauchen	*The snake* **hissed** *at them.*
	bank [bæŋk]	Ufer	*We walked along the river* **bank**.

bank	=	Ufer (Fluss, See); Bank (Geld)
Bank	=	**bench**

	rattler ['rætlə]	Klapperschlange	
	to yell [jel]	brüllen, laut schreien	› *to shout something very loudly*
	to scratch [skrætʃ]	kratzen	*Did the cat* **scratch** *you?*
	sand [sænd]	Sand	
	to whisper ['wɪspə]	flüstern	*She* **whispered** *something in my ear.*
	lip [lɪp]	Lippe	

134 one hundred and thirty-four

Wörterverzeichnis UNIT 4

	to **put on** [ˌpʊt ˈɒn]	anziehen	❯❮ *take off*
	put, put [pʊt, pʊt]		
	to **frighten** [ˈfraɪtn]	jdn erschrecken	❯ *to make someone feel afraid*
	poisonous [ˈpɔɪzənəs]	giftig	***poisonous** snakes/plants*
	what if … ? [ˈwɒt ɪf]	was ist, wenn … ?	***What if** someone gets hurt during the tour?*
	on top of [ɒn ˈtɒp əv]	auf, über, obendrauf	
	over and over (again)	immer wieder	❯❯ *many times*
	[ˌəʊvər ənd ˈəʊvə]		
Ex15	to **impress** [ɪmˈpres]	beeindrucken	
Ex16	**difference** [ˈdɪfrəns]	Unterschied	

> **Beachte** die Betonung auf der ersten Silbe:
> **acc**ent – **arg**ument – **con**cert – **dif**ference – **hos**pital – **mo**dern – **ob**ject – **pro**gram(me) – **uni**form

	by [baɪ]	mit	**by** car/bus/train/plane but **on** foot

> **MERKE:** English 'by'
> America was discovered **by** Columbus. (… *von Kolumbus*)
> They went to a camp site **by** the river. (… *am Fluss*)
> Pat and Fiona got there **by** train. (… *mit dem Zug*)
>
> Deutsch „bei"
> I was **at** the baker's. (… *beim Bäcker*)
> Have you got money **on** you? (… *Geld bei dir?*)
> You can stay **with** us. (… *bei uns wohnen*)

Ex17	**blind** [blaɪnd]	blind	He's **blind**; he can't see you.
	electronic [ˌɪlekˈtrɒnɪk]	elektronisch	
Com	**request** [rɪˈkwest]	Aufforderung, Bitte	*'Please open the window' is a **request**.*
	biker [ˈbaɪkə]	Radfahrer/in	
TYE	**manatee** [ˈmænətiː]	Seekuh	
	flipper [ˈflɪpə]	Flosse, Schwimmflosse	
	tail [teɪl]	Schwanz	
	plant [plɑːnt]	Pflanze	
	human [ˈhjuːmən]	Menschen-; menschlich	
	propeller [prəˈpelə]	Schiffsschraube; Propeller	

	to **protect** [prəˈtekt]	beschützen	❯ *to keep something/someone safe from danger*
TYE1	**swimmer** [ˈswɪmə]	Schwimmer/in	❯ *someone who is swimming*
Read	**blizzard** [ˈblɪzəd]	Schneesturm	❯ *a snowstorm with strong winds*
	corn [kɔːn] *AE*	Mais	
	to **snow** [snəʊ]	schneien	*It often **snows** in Alaska in winter.*
	route [ruːt]	Route, Strecke	❯ *the way from one place to another*
	snowflake [ˈsnəʊfleɪk]	Schneeflocke	
	windshield [ˈwɪndʃiːld] *AE*	Windschutzscheibe	❯❯ *windscreen BE*
	deep [diːp]	tief	❯ *(going) a long way down*
	to **freeze** [friːz]	frieren, gefrieren	*Water **freezes** at 0 °C.*
	froze, frozen [frəʊz, ˈfrəʊzn]		
	farmhouse [ˈfɑːmhaʊs]	Bauernhaus	
	to **blow** [bləʊ]	blasen, wehen	*The strong wind **blew** her hat off.*
	blew, blown [bluː, bləʊn]		
	to **bend** [bend]	biegen; sich bücken	*She **bent** down to pick up a piece of paper.*
	bent, bent [bent, bent]		

one hundred and thirty-five **135**

UNIT 4
Proj/Rev

Wörterverzeichnis

	gentle ['dʒentl]	sanft	
	stuck [stʌk]	stecken geblieben	*The car was **stuck** in the deep snow.*
	power cut ['pauə kʌt]	Stromsperre, Stromausfall	
	tractor ['træktə]	Traktor, Zugmaschine	
	grateful ['greɪtfl]	dankbar	*I'm **grateful** to you for your help.*
	atmosphere ['ætməsfɪə]	Atmosphäre	*a happy **atmosphere***
	style [staɪl]	Stil	*I don't like his **style** of painting.*
Proj1	**earthquake** ['ɜ:θkweɪk]	Erdbeben	
Proj2	**auto** ['ɔ:təʊ]	Auto	*the **auto** industry*
	guidance counselor [ˌgaɪdns 'kaʊnsələ]	Schulberater/in	
	principal ['prɪnsəpl]	Rektor/in	❭ *the head of a college or school*
	sophomore ['sɒfəmɔ:] *AE*	Student/in im zweiten Studienjahr	
	social ['səʊʃl]	sozial; Sozial-	***social** problems*
	freshman ['freʃmən] *AE* *pl* **freshmen** ['freʃmən]	Student/in im ersten Studienjahr	
	wall chart ['wɔ:l tʃɑ:t]	Wandkarte	
	to **exchange** [ɪks'tʃeɪndʒ]	austauschen	*to **exchange** ideas*
Proj4	**link** [lɪŋk]	Link, Verknüpfung im Internet	
	presentation [ˌprezn'teɪʃn]	Präsentation, Vorstellung	
Proj5	**task** [tɑ:sk]	Aufgabe	❭❭ *job*
	offensive [ə'fensɪv]	offensiv; Angriff(s-)	
	defensive [dɪ'fensɪv]	defensiv; Verteidigungs-	
Rev1	**airfield** ['eəfi:ld]	Flugplatz	❭ *a place where planes can land or take off*
	successful [sək'sesfl]	erfolgreich	*Bill Gates is a **successful** businessman.*
	headlights ['hedlaɪts]	Scheinwerfer (Auto)	
Rev3	**powerful** ['pauəfl]	stark; mächtig	❭❭ *very strong*
	typewriter ['taɪpraɪtə]	Schreibmaschine	
	program ['prəʊgræm]	Computerprogramm	Betonung: *program* ● ●

MERKE:	**programme** *BE*	←	Fernseh-/Radiosendung	→	**program** *AE*
	program *BE*	←	Computerprogramm	→	**program** *AE*

---

	user ['ju:zə]	Benutzer/in	
Rev4	**trek** [trek]	anstrengende Wanderung	❭ *a very long walk in the mountains*
	unfortunately [ʌn'fɔ:tʃənətli]	unglücklicherweise	***Unfortunately,** we had to leave early.*
	foreign language [ˌfɒrən 'læŋgwɪdʒ]	Fremdsprache	
Rev8	**best-selling** [ˌbest'selɪŋ]	verkauft sich am besten	
	novel ['nɒvl]	Roman	
	to **direct** [də'rekt]	Regie führen	❭ *to tell the actors in a film what they have to do*
	suburb ['sʌbɜ:b]	Vorort	*Wimbledon is a **suburb** of London.*
	university [ˌju:nɪ'vɜ:səti]	Universität	
	to **study** ['stʌdi]	studieren; sich genau ansehen	*She's **studying** to be a doctor.*

136 one hundred and thirty-six

Wörterverzeichnis Proj/Rev

	medical [ˈmedɪkl]	medizinisch
	best-known [ˌbestˈnəʊn]	bekannteste(r, s)
Rev9	**noon** [nuːn]	Mittag
Rev10	**man-eater** [ˈmæniːtə]	Menschenfresser
	bat [bæt]	Fledermaus
Rev11	**vintage car** [ˌvɪntɪdʒ ˈkɑː]	Oldtimer
	limousine [ˈlɪməziːn]	Limousine
	sports car [ˈspɔːts kɑː]	Sportwagen
	engine [ˈendʒɪn]	Motor
Rev12	**envelope** [ˈenvələʊp]	Briefumschlag, Kuvert
Rev14	**necessary** [ˈnesəsəri]	notwendig
Rev15	**comedian** [kəˈmiːdiən]	Komiker, Witzbold
	disaster [dɪˈzɑːstə]	Katastrophe
	captain [ˈkæptɪn]	Kapitän
Lit	to **found** [faʊnd]	(be)gründen
	frontier [ˈfrʌntɪə]	Grenze, Grenzgebiet
	further [ˈfɜːðə]	weiter
	cruel [ˈkruːəl]	grausam
	well-known [ˌwelˈnəʊn]	berühmt
	poem [ˈpəʊɪm]	Gedicht
	descendant [dɪˈsendənt]	Nachfahre, Abkömmling
	strict [strɪkt]	streng
	to **be based on** [bɪ ˈbeɪst ɒn]	sich stützen auf, basieren auf
	reason [ˈriːzn]	Grund, Begründung

› *12 o'clock in the day*

engine

› *sth that is needed for a purpose*
A **comedian** makes people laugh.
Fires, hurricanes and earthquakes are **disasters**.

› *to start to build a town or business*
›› *border* (hier: Grenzgebiet zwischen Indianergebiet und Siedlungsgebiet der Weißen)
Two miles **further** on we came to a train station.

›› *famous*
A limerick is a sort of **poem**.

Most teachers here are very **strict**.

What is the **reason** for your success?

MERKE: Der **infinitive with to** steht nicht nur nach bestimmten Verben, sondern auch …

… nach **Nomen**: z.B. reason, right, chance job, plan, way, time, …
It's **time to go** to bed now.
I have every **reason to feel** angry.

… nach **Adjektiven**, z.B. glad, easy, difficult dangerous, ready, afraid, too good, …
Her parents were **glad to see** her again.
This story is too **good to be** true.

---

depth [depθ]	Tiefe	
to **measure** [ˈmeʒə]	messen	
struggle [ˈstrʌgl]	Kampf, Auseinandersetzung	›› *a hard fight*

MERKE: **Wortbildung mit Nachsilben 3**

Durch Nachsilben lassen sich Nomen, Adjektive und **Verben** aus anderen Wortarten bilden.

Verben: Diese Verben drücken aus,

- **-ize/ise**   modern**ize** (*modernisieren*), colon**ize**, central**ize**   • dass sich ein **Zustand verändert**.
- **-en**   black**en** (*schwärzen*), dark**en** (*verdunkeln*)
- **-ify**   simpl**ify** (*vereinfachen*), electr**ify** (*elektrifizieren*)

one hundred and thirty-seven **137**

Irregular verbs   Unregelmäßige Verben

INFINITIVE	SIMPLE PAST	PAST PARTICIPLE	
to be	was/were	been	sein
to beat	beat	beaten	schlagen
to become	became	become	werden
to begin	began	begun	anfangen, beginnen
to bend	bent	bent	biegen
to bite	bit	bitten	beißen
to blow	blew	blown	blasen
to break	broke	broken	brechen
to bring	brought	brought	bringen
to build	built	built	bauen
to burn	burnt/burned	burnt/burned	(ver)brennen
to buy	bought	bought	kaufen
to catch	caught	caught	fangen
to choose	chose	chosen	wählen
to come	came	come	kommen
to cost	cost	cost	kosten
to cut	cut	cut	schneiden
to dig	dug	dug	graben
to do	did	done	tun, machen
to draw	drew	drawn	ziehen, zeichnen
to drink	drank	drunk	trinken
to drive	drove	driven	fahren
to eat	ate	eaten	essen
to fall	fell	fallen	fallen
to feed	fed	fed	füttern
to feel	felt	felt	fühlen
to fight	fought	fought	kämpfen
to find	found	found	finden
to fly	flew	flown	fliegen
to forbid	forbade	forbidden	verbieten, untersagen
to forget	forgot	forgotten	vergessen
to freeze	froze	frozen	(ge)frieren
to get	got	got	bekommen
to give	gave	given	geben
to go	went	gone	gehen
to hang	hung	hung	hängen
to hang	hanged	hanged	erhängen (töten)
to have	had	had	haben
to hear	heard	heard	hören
to hide	hid	hidden	(sich) verstecken
to hit	hit	hit	treffen, schlagen
to hold	held	held	halten
to hurt	hurt	hurt	verletzen
to keep	kept	kept	halten, behalten
to know	knew	known	wissen, kennen
to lay	laid	laid	legen
to lead	led	led	führen
to learn	learnt/learned	learnt/learned	lernen

138   one hundred and thirty-eight

Unregelmäßige Verben

INFINITIVE	SIMPLE PAST	PAST PARTICIPLE	
to leave	left	left	verlassen
to lend	lent	lent	leihen, borgen
to let	let	let	lassen, zulassen
to lie	lay	lain	liegen
to light	lit	lit	anzünden
to lose	lost	lost	verlieren
to make	made	made	machen
to mean	meant	meant	bedeuten, meinen
to meet	met	met	treffen, begegnen
to pay	paid	paid	bezahlen
to put	put	put	setzen, stellen
to quit	quit	quit	verlassen
to read	read	read	lesen
to ride	rode	ridden	reiten; fahren
to ring	rang	rung	klingeln, anrufen
to rise	rose	risen	ansteigen, aufgehen
to run	ran	run	laufen
to say	said	said	sagen
to see	saw	seen	sehen
to sell	sold	sold	verkaufen
to send	sent	sent	schicken, senden
to shine	shone	shone	scheinen
to shoot	shot	shot	schießen
to show	showed	shown /showed	zeigen
to shut	shut	shut	schließen
to sing	sang	sung	singen
to sink	sank	sunk	sinken, untergehen
to sit	sat	sat	sitzen
to sleep	slept	slept	schlafen
to speak	spoke	spoken	sprechen
to spend	spent	spent	ausgeben, verbringen
to spill	spilt/spilled	spilt/spilled	verschütten
to split	split	split	spalten, teilen
to spread	spread	spread	verbreiten
to stand	stood	stood	stehen
to steal	stole	stolen	stehlen
to stick	stuck	stuck	kleben, stecken bleiben
to swim	swam	swum	schwimmen
to swing	swung	swung	schwingen
to take	took	taken	nehmen
to teach	taught	taught	unterrichten, lehren
to tell	told	told	erzählen
to think	thought	thought	denken, glauben
to throw	threw	thrown	werfen
to understand	understood	understood	verstehen
to wake	woke	woken	aufwecken, aufwachen
to wear	wore	worn	tragen
to win	won	won	gewinnen
to write	wrote	written	schreiben

List of names Liste der Eigennamen

Boys/Men

A
Adam ['ædəm]
Andrew ['ændru:]
Andy ['ændi]
Antonio [æn'təʊniəʊ]

B
Bill [bɪl]
Brandon ['brændən]
Brian ['braɪən]

C
Carlos ['kɑ:lɒs]
Christopher
  ['krɪstəfə]
Collier ['kɒliə]
Craig [kreɪg]

E
Eric [erɪk]

F
Frank [fræŋk]

G
Geoffrey ['dʒefri]
Gray [greɪ]

H
Herbert ['hɜ:bət]

J
James [dʒeɪmz]
Jason ['dʒeɪsn]
Jim [dʒɪm]
Joseph ['dʒəʊzɪf]
Juan [xu'an]
Justin ['dʒʌstɪn]

K
Kevin ['kevɪn]

M
Matthew ['mæθju:]
Michael ['maɪkl]
Mike [maɪk]

N
Nathan ['neɪθən]
Neil [ni:l]

R
Randy ['rændi]
Ray [reɪ]
Rob [rɒb]
Robert ['rɒbət]
Ronald ['rɒnld]
Ryan ['raɪən]

S
Samuel ['sæmjuəl]

T
Thomas ['tɒməs]
Tom [tɒm]

Girls/Women

A
Alice ['ælɪs]
Alicia [ə'lɪʃə]
Allison ['ælɪsən]
Amber ['æmbə]
Amy ['eɪmi]
Angela ['ændʒələ]
Anna ['ænə]
Annie ['æni]
Ashley ['æʃli]

B
Barbara ['bɑ:brə]
Betty ['beti]
Brittany ['brɪtəni]

C
Careen [kə'ri:n]
Courtney ['kɔ:tni]

D
Danielle [ˌdæni'el]
Deanne [di'æn]
Della ['delə]
Dilcey ['dɪlsi]

E
Erica ['erɪkə]
Evelyn ['i:vlɪn]

F
Fiona [fi'əʊnə]

H
Helen ['helən]

J
Jane [dʒeɪn]
Janet ['dʒænɪt]
Jasmine ['dʒæzmɪn]
Jennifer ['dʒenɪfə]
Jessica ['dʒesɪkə]

K
Katie ['keɪti]
Kayla ['keɪlə]
Kirsty ['kɜ:sti]

L
Laura ['lɔ:rə]
Lauren ['lɔ:rən]
Lindsey ['lɪndzi]
Lisa ['li:sə]

M
Margaret ['mɑ:grət]
Marlene ['mɑ:li:n]
Megan ['megən]
Melanie ['meləni]
Melissa [mə'lɪsə]
Mia ['mi:ə]

N
Natasha [nə'tæʃə]
Nicole [nɪ'kəʊl]

P
Polly ['pɒli]

R
Rachel ['reɪtʃl]
Rebecca [rɪ'bekə]

S
Sally ['sæli]
Sarah ['seərə]
Shelly ['ʃeli]
Suellen [ˌsu:'elən]
Susan ['su:zn]
Sylvia ['sɪlviə]

T
Teresa [tə'ri:zə]
Tiffany ['tɪfəni]
Tina ['ti:nə]

V
Victoria [vɪk'tɔ:riə]

W
Whitney ['wɪtni]

Family names

B
Baxter ['bækstə]
Blake [bleɪk]
Brown [braʊn]

D
Davis ['deɪvɪs]
Delgado [del'gɑ:dəʊ]
Dunlap ['dʌnlæp]

E
Evans ['evənz]

F
Ferris ['ferɪs]
Frinton ['frɪntən]

G
Gordon ['gɔ:dn]
Graham ['greɪəm]

H
Hamilton ['hæmltən]
Hansen ['hænsn]
Howard ['haʊəd]

J
James [dʒeɪmz]
Joad [dʒəʊd]
Johnson ['dʒɒnsn]

K
Klasnov ['klæznɒv]
Kline [klaɪn]

L
Lesemann
  ['leɪzəmæn]
Long [lɒŋ]

M
Miller ['mɪlə]
Morrisson
  ['mɒrɪsən]

Q
Quinn [kwɪn]

R
Rodriguez
  [rɒ'dri:gez]

S
Sage [seɪdʒ]
Shoemaker
  ['ʃu:meɪkə]
Shulman ['ʃu:lmən]
Stephans ['sti:vnz]
Stoltzfus ['stɒltsfu:s]
Sudd [sʌd]

T
Trump [trʌmp]

W
White [waɪt]
Williams ['wɪljəmz]

Z
Zimmer ['zɪmə]

140 one hundred and forty

List of names

Famous people

B

Harriet Beecher-Stowe [ˌhærɪət ˌbiːtʃəˈstəʊ] am. Schriftstellerin (1811 – 1896)

Bill Bryson [bɪl ˈbraɪsn] am. Autor (*1951)

Buffalo Bill [ˈbʌfələʊ bɪl] berühmter Büffeljäger im am. Westen, ging später mit einer „Wild West Show" auf Tournee

C

Charlie Chaplin [ˌtʃɑːli ˈtʃæplɪn] engl. Schauspieler (1886 – 1977)

William Clark [ˌwɪljəm ˈklɑːk] erforschte 1804/5 den Westen der USA

Samuel L. Clemens [ˌsæmjuəl el ˈklemənz] am. Autor und Humorist (1835 – 1910)

Christopher Columbus [ˌkrɪstəfə kəˈlʌmbəs] gilt als Entdecker Amerikas (1451 – 1506)

James Fenimore Cooper [dʒeɪmz ˌfenɪmɔː ˈkuːpə] am. Schriftsteller (1789 – 1851)

Michael Crichton [ˌmaɪkl ˈkraɪtn] am. Autor (*1942)

Tom Cruise [tɒm ˈkruːz] am. Schauspieler (*1962)

D

Leonardo DiCaprio [ˌliːəʊˈnɑːdəʊ dɪˈkæprɪəʊ] am. Schauspieler (*1974)

John Dillinger [dʒɒn ˈdɪlɪndʒə] berüchtigter am. Bankräuber und Gangster (1903 – 1934)

Grenville Dodge [ˌgrenvɪl ˈdɒdʒ] Chefingenieur der Union Pacific Railroad

F

Henry Flagler [ˌhenri ˈflæglə] Freund J.D. Rockefellers, wichtige Figur in der Entwicklung Floridas

Harrison Ford [ˌhærɪsən ˈfɔːd] am. Schauspieler (*1942)

G

Clark Gable [ˌklɑːk ˈgeɪbl] am. Schauspieler (1901 – 1960)

Geronimo [dʒəˈrɒnɪməʊ] Häuptling der Chiricahua-Apachen (1829 – 1909)

H

King Harold [ˌkɪŋ ˈhærəld] (ca. 1020 – 1066)

Nathaniel Hawthorne [nəˌθæniəl ˈhɔːθɔːn] am. Schriftsteller (1804 – 1864)

Ernest Hemingway [ˌɜːnɪst ˈhemɪŋweɪ] am. Schriftsteller (1899 – 1961)

John Edgar Hoover [dʒɒn ˌedgə ˈhuːvə] Chef des FBI von 1924 – 1972

J

James I [ˌdʒeɪmz ðə ˈfɜːst] engl. König (1566 – 1625)

K

John F. Kennedy [ˌdʒɒn ef ˈkenədi] 35. am. Präsident (1917 – 1963)

Martin Luther King [ˌmɑːtɪn ˌluːθə ˈkɪŋ] am. Bürgerrechtsführer (1929 – 1968)

L

Vivien Leigh [ˌvɪviən ˈliː] am. Schauspielerin (1913 – 1967)

Meriwether Lewis [ˌmeriweðə ˈluːɪs] erforschte 1804/5 den Westen der USA

Abraham Lincoln [ˌeɪbrəhæm ˈlɪŋkən] 16. am. Präsident (1809 – 1865)

Charles A. Lindbergh [ˌtʃɑːlz eɪ ˈlɪndbɜːg] am. Flugpionier (1902 – 1974)

Jack London [ˌdʒæk ˈlʌndən] am. Schriftsteller (1876 – 1916)

M

Paul McCartney [ˌpɔːl məˈkɑːtni] Mitglied der Beatles (*1942)

Herman Melville [ˌhɜːmən ˈmelvɪl] am. Schriftsteller (1819 – 1891)

Margaret Mitchell [ˌmɑːgrət ˈmɪtʃəl] am. Autorin (1900 – 1949)

'Baby Face' Nelson [ˌbeɪbi feɪs ˈnelsn] am. Gangster (1908 – 1934)

P

Rosa Parks [ˌrəʊzə ˈpɑːks] Afro-amerikanerin, die 1955 den Busboykott in Montgomery, Alabama, auslöste (*1913)

Pocahontas [ˌpɒkəˈhɒntəs] Tochter von Powhatan (ca. 1595 – 1617)

Edgar Allan Poe [ˌedgə ˌælən ˈpəʊ] am. Schriftsteller (1809 – 1849)

Harry Potter [ˌhæri ˈpɒtə] Figur in den Romanen von J.K. Rowling

Powhatan [ˈpaʊətæn] Häuptling des gleichnamigen Indianerstamms (ca. 1550 – 1618)

R

John Rolfe [ˌdʒɒn ˈrəʊf] Ehemann von Pocahontas

J.K. Rowling [ˌdʒeɪ keɪ ˈrəʊlɪŋ] britische Autorin (*1965)

S

John Smith [ˌdʒɒn ˈsmɪθ] Anführer der englischen Jamestown-Kolonie (ca. 1579 – 1631)

Joseph Späh [ˌdʒəʊzɪf ˈspæː] Komödiant, überlebte das Hindenburg-Unglück

Britney Spears [ˌbrɪtni ˈspɪəz] am. Sängerin (*1981)

Spice Girls [ˈspaɪs gɜːlz] brit. Popgruppe

Squanto [ˈskwɒntəʊ] Indianer, der den Pilgrims zu überleben half (†1622)

John Steinbeck [ˌdʒɒn ˈstaɪnbek] am. Schriftsteller (1902 – 1968)

Levi Strauss [ˌlevi ˈstraʊs] Begründer der gleichnamigen Jeansfirma (1829 – 1902)

T

Harriet Tubman [ˌhærɪət ˈtʌbmən] Fluchthelferin für Sklaven aus den Südstaaten (1821 – 1913)

Nat Turner [næt ˈtɜːnə] Anführer eines Sklavenaufstands in Virginia

Mark Twain [ˌmɑːk ˈtweɪn] am. Schriftsteller (1835 – 1810), siehe S. L. Clemens

W

George Washington [ˌdʒɔːdʒ ˈwɒʃɪŋtən] 1. Präsident der USA (1732 – 1799)

Stevie Wonder [ˌstiːvi ˈwʌndə] am. Soul- und Rock-Sänger (*1950)

one hundred and forty-one 141

List of names

Other names

A

African ['æfrɪkən] Afrikaner/in; afrikanisch

Amish ['ɑːmɪʃ] christlich-religiöse Gruppe v.a. in Pennsylvania, Ohio und Indiana

Amtrak ['æmtræk] *American Railroad Company*

Apache [ə'pætʃi] Indianerstamm

B

Ben Hur [ben 'hɜː] Titel eines Filmes

Rhett Butler [ret 'bʌtlə] Figur im Roman *Gone With the Wind*

C

The Call of the Wild [ðə ˌkɔːl əv ðə 'waɪld] Roman von Jack London

Central Pacific Railroad [ˌsentrəl pəˌsɪfɪk 'reɪlrəʊd] amerikanische Eisenbahngesellschaft

Cherokee ['tʃerəkiː] Indianerstamm

Chicago [ʃɪ'kɑːgəʊ] Musical

CNN [ˌsiː en 'en] am. Fernsehanstalt

Comanche [kə'mæntʃi] Indianerstamm

Cuban ['kjuːbən] kubanisch; Kubaner/in

D

Dakota [də'kəʊtə] Indianerstamm

F

The Fall of the House of Usher [ðə ˌfɔːl əv ðə haʊs əv 'ʌʃə] Geschichte von Edgar Allan Poe

A Farewell to Arms [ə feəˌwel tu 'ɑːmz] Roman von Ernest Hemingway

For Whom the Bell Tolls [fə ˌhuːm ðə ˌbel 'təʊlz] Roman von Ernest Hemingway

42nd Street [ˌfɔːti'sekənd striːt] Musical

G

the Giants [ðə 'dʒaɪənts] Footballteam

Gone with the Wind [ˌgɒn wɪð ðə 'wɪnd] Roman von Margaret Mitchell

The Grapes of Wrath [ðə ˌgreɪps əv 'rɒθ] Roman von John Steinbeck

H

Hindenburg ['hɪndənbɜːg] Name eines Luftschiffes

Hurricane Andrew [ˌhʌrɪkən 'ændruː] Hurrikan, der 1992 in Florida wütete

K

Keiko ['keɪkəʊ] Name des Wals im Film *Free Willy*

L

The Last of the Mohicans [ðə ˌlɑːst əv ðə məʊ'hiːkənz] Roman von James F. Cooper

Latin American [ˌlætɪn ə'merɪkən] lateinamerikanisch; Lateinamerikaner/in

Leatherstocking Tales ['leðəstɒkɪŋ teɪlz] Romanreihe von James F. Cooper

M

Mayflower ['meɪflaʊə] Schiff der Pilgrims

MGM [ˌem dʒiː 'em] Filmstudio

Miccosukee [ˌmɪkəʊ'suːkiː] Indianerstamm in Florida

Moby Dick [ˌməʊbi 'dɪk] Roman von Herman Melville

Motown ['məʊtaʊn] umgangssprachlich für Detroit (*motor town*); Motown Records ist eine berühmte Plattenfirma in Detroit

The Murders in the Rue Morgue [ðə ˌmɜːdəz ɪn ðə ˌruː 'mɔːg] Geschichte von Edgar Allan Poe

N

Navaho ['nævəhəʊ] Indianerstamm

NBC [ˌen biː 'siː] am. Fernsehanstalt

New York Yankees [ˌnjuː jɔːk 'jæŋkiːz] Name einer Baseballmannschaft

NFL [ˌen ef 'el] National Football League

O

Scarlett O'Hara [ˌskɑːlət əʊ'hɑːrə] Figur im Roman *Gone With the Wind*

The Old Man and the Sea [ði əʊld ˌmæn ən ðə 'siː] Geschichte von Ernest Hemingway

P

Pony Express [ˌpəʊni ɪk'spres] Postreiterdienst im Wilden Westen

The Prairie [ðə 'preəri] Roman von James F. Cooper

R

The Raven [ðə 'reɪvn] Gedicht von Edgar Allan Poe

S

The Scarlet Letter [ðə ˌskɑːlət 'letə] Roman von Nathaniel Hawthorne

The Sea-Wolf [ðə 'siːwʊlf] Roman von Jack London

Shawnee [ˌʃɔː'niː] Indianerstamm

Sioux [suː] Indianerstamm

The Sun Also Rises [ðə ˌsʌn ˌɔːlsəʊ 'raɪzɪz] Roman von Ernest Hemingway

T

Tara ['tɑːrə] Baumwollplantage, Schauplatz von *Gone With the Wind*

Tom Sawyer and Huckleberry Finn [tɒm 'sɔːjə ənd ˌhʌklbəri 'fɪn] Roman von Mark Twain

U

Uncle Tom's Cabin [ˌʌŋkl tɒmz 'kæbɪn] Roman von Harriet Beecher Stowe

Union Pacific Railroad [ˌjuːniən pəˌsɪfɪk 'reɪlrəʊd] Eisenbahngesellschaft in den USA

Universal Orlando [juːnɪˌvɜːsl ɔː'lændəʊ] Filmstudio mit Themenpark bei Orlando, Florida

Universal Studios [juːnɪˌvɜːsl 'stjuːdiəʊz] Filmstudios in Hollywood

W

Wampanoag [ˌwɒmpə'nəʊəg] Indianerstamm, der im Osten der USA lebte

West Side Story [ˌwest saɪd 'stɔːri] Musical

White Fang [ˌwaɪt 'fæŋ] Roman von Jack London

Place names

A

Africa ['æfrɪkə] Afrika
Alabama [ˌælə'bæmə] am. Bundesstaat
Alaska [ə'læskə] am. Bundesstaat
Amana Colonies [ə'mɑːnə 'kɒləniz] Siedlung in Iowa
American Falls [ə'merɪkən fɔːlz] Teil der Niagara Wasserfälle
American Museum of Natural History [əˌmerɪkən mjuˌziːəm əv ˌnætʃrəl 'hɪstri] Naturkundliches Museum in New York
Annapurna [ˌænə'pɜːnə] Berg im Himalaya
Arizona [ˌærɪ'zəʊnə] am. Bundesstaat
Asia ['eɪʃə] Asien
Austria ['ɒstriə] Österreich

B

Baltimore ['bɔːltɪmɔː] größte Stadt im Bundesstaat Maryland
Barry ['bæri] Stadt in den USA
Battery Park ['bætri pɑːk] Park am südlichen Ende von Manhattan
Bavaria [bə'veəriə] Bayern
Bavarian [bə'veəriən] bayerisch; Bayer/in
Belgium ['beldʒəm] Belgien
Berlin ['bɜːrlɪn] Stadt in den USA
Biograph Theater [ˌbaɪəgræf 'θɪətə] Kino in Chicago
Bismarck ['bɪzmɑːk] Stadt in den USA
Boston ['bɒstən] Hauptstadt von Massachusetts
Broadway ['brɔːdweɪ] berühmte Straße in Manhattan
the Bronx [ðə 'brɒŋks] Stadtteil von New York City
Brooklyn ['brʊklɪn] Stadtteil von New York City
Busch Gardens [ˌbʌʃ 'gɑːdnz] Freizeitpark und Zoo bei Tampa, Florida

C

California [ˌkælə'fɔːniə] am. Bundesstaat
Canada ['kænədə] Kanada
Canyonlands National Park ['kænjənlændz ˌnæʃnəl 'pɑːk] Nationalpark in Utah
Carlsbad ['kɑːlzbæd] Stadt in den USA
Cascade Mountains [kæˌskeɪd 'maʊntɪnz] Gebirge im Westen der USA
Central Park ['sentrəl pɑːk] Stadtpark in Manhattan
Charleston ['tʃɑːlstən] Stadt in South Carolina
Chicago [ʃɪ'kɑːgəʊ] Stadt in Illinois
China ['tʃaɪnə] China
Chinatown ['tʃaɪnətaʊn] Stadtteil von San Francisco, New York, London mit chinesischer Bevölkerung

Chrysler Building ['kraɪslə bɪldɪŋ] berühmtes Gebäude in Manhattan
Colorado [ˌkɒlə'rɑːdəʊ] am. Bundesstaat
Conyers ['kɒnjəz] Stadt in Georgia
Cuba ['kjuːbə] Kuba
Cypress Gardens [ˌsaɪprəs 'gɑːdnz] Park bei Orlando, Florida

D

Dallas ['dæləs] Stadt in Texas
Daytona Beach [deɪˌtəʊnə 'biːtʃ] Ort in Florida
Des Moines [də 'mɔɪn] Stadt in Iowa
Detroit [dɪ'trɔɪt] Stadt in Michigan
Disney World ['dɪzni wɜːld] Vergnügungspark in Florida

E

El Barrio [el 'bæriəʊ] hispanisches Viertel von New York
Ellis Island [ˌelɪs 'aɪlənd] Einwanderungsmuseum im Hafen von New York
Empire State Building [ˌempaɪə 'steɪt bɪldɪŋ] berühmtes Gebäude in Manhattan
Everglades National Park ['evəgleɪdz ˌnæʃnəl 'pɑːk] Nationalpark in Florida

F

Fifth Avenue [ˌfɪfθ 'ævənjuː] vornehme Einkaufsstraße in New York
Flint [flɪnt] Stadt in Michigan
Florida ['flɒrɪdə] am. Bundesstaat
Fort Sumter [ˌfɔːt 'sʌmtə] Fort in South Carolina, an dem am 12. April 1861 der Bürgerkrieg begann
France [frɑːns] Frankreich
Frankenmuth ['fræŋkənmuːt] Stadt in den USA
Frankfort ['fræŋkfət] Stadt in den USA
Fredericksburg ['fredrɪksbɜːg] Stadt in den USA

G

Georgia ['dʒɔːdʒə] am. Bundesstaat
Golden Gate Bridge [ˌgəʊldən geɪt 'brɪdʒ] Brücke in San Francisco
Grand Canyon [ˌgrænd 'kænjən] Naturwunder in Arizona
Great Lakes [ˌgreɪt 'leɪks] Gruppe von fünf großen Seen an der nordöstlichen Grenze zu Kanada
Great Smoky Mountains [ˌgreɪt ˌsməʊki 'maʊntɪnz] Bergkette an der Ostküste der USA
Green River [griːn 'rɪvə] Fluss in Utah
Guggenheim Museum [ˌgʊgənhaɪm mju'ziːəm] Museum für moderne Kunst in New York

H

Hannibal ['hænɪbl] Stadt in Missouri
Hard Rock Café [ˌhɑːd rɒk 'kæfeɪ] Fastfoodkette mit Niederlassungen auf der ganzen Welt
Harlem ['hɑːləm] Stadtteil im Nordosten Manhattans, in dem hauptsächlich Afroamerikaner leben
Harrisburg ['hærɪsbɜːg] Hauptstadt des Bundesstaates Pennsylvania
Harvard University [ˌhɑːvəd juːnɪ'vɜːsəti] älteste am. Universität in Cambridge, Massachusetts
Hawaii [hə'waɪi] am. Bundesstaat
Henry Ford Museum [ˌhenri fɔːd mju'ziːəm] Automuseum in Detroit
Hollywood ['hɒliwʊd] Stadtteil von Los Angeles
Horseshoe Falls/Canadian Falls ['hɔːsʃuː fɔːlz, kə'neɪdiən fɔːlz] Teil der Niagara Wasserfälle
Houston ['hjuːstən] Stadt in Texas
Hudson River [ˌhʌdsn 'rɪvə] Fluss im Bundesstaat New York
Hull [hʌl] Stadt in den USA

I

Idaho ['aɪdəhəʊ] am. Bundesstaat
Illinois [ˌɪlə'nɔɪ] am. Bundesstaat
Independence [ˌɪndɪ'pendəns] Stadt in Missouri
Indiana [ˌɪndi'ænə] am. Bundesstaat
Intercourse ['ɪntəkɔːs] Stadt in Pennsylvania
Iowa ['aɪəʊə] am. Bundesstaat

J

Jacksonville ['dʒæksənvɪl] Stadt in den USA
James River ['dʒeɪmz rɪvə] Fluss in Virginia
Jamestown ['dʒeɪmztaʊn] Stadt in Virginia

K

Kansas ['kænzəs] am. Bundesstaat
Kennedy Space Center [ˌkenədi 'speɪs sentə] Weltraumbahnhof in Florida
Kentucky [ken'tʌki] am. Bundesstaat
Key West [ˌkiː 'west] Insel vor Florida

L

Lakehurst ['leɪkhɜːst] Flughafen in New Jersey
Lancaster County ['læŋkəstə kaʊnti] Gegend in Pennsylvania
Las Vegas [læs 'veɪgəs] Stadt in Nevada
Le Bourget [lə bʊə'ʒeɪ] Flughafen bei Paris
Leavenworth ['levnwɜːθ] Stadt in den USA
Leeds [liːdz] Stadt in England

List of names

Liberty Island [ˌlɪbəti ˈaɪlənd] Insel im Hafen von New York, auf der die Freiheitsstatue steht
Little Havana [ˌlɪtl həˈvænə] hispanisches Viertel von Florida
Little India [ˌlɪtl ˈɪndiə] indisches Viertel von New York
Little Italy [ˌlɪtl ˈɪtəli] italienisches Viertel von New York
Little Korea [ˌlɪtl kəˈrɪə] koreanisches Viertel von New York
Littleton [ˈlɪtltən] Stadt in Colorado
Los Angeles [lɒs ˈændʒəliːz] Stadt in Kalifornien
Lower East Side [ˌləʊə iːst ˈsaɪd] ärmliches Viertel von New York

M

Mallory Square [ˈmæləri skweə] Platz in Key West, Florida
Manhattan [mænˈhætn] Stadtteil von New York
Massachusetts [ˌmæsəˈtʃuːsɪts] am. Bundesstaat
Mexico [ˈmeksɪkəʊ] Staat in Mittelamerika
Miami [maɪˈæmi] Stadt in Florida
Minnesota [ˌmɪnɪˈsəʊtə] am. Bundesstaat
Mississippi [ˌmɪsɪˈsɪpi] Fluss im Süden der USA
Missouri [mɪˈsʊəri] am. Bundesstaat
Moab [ˈməʊæb] Stadt in Utah
Montana [mɒnˈtænə] am. Bundesstaat
Montgomery [məntˈɡʌməri] Stadt in Alabama
Mount Hood [maʊnt ˈhʊd] Berg in Oregon

N

Nebraska [nəˈbræskə] am. Bundesstaat
Nepal [nɪˈpɔːl] Nepal
the Netherlands [ðə ˈneðələndz] die Niederlande
New Jersey [ˌnjuː ˈdʒɜːzi] am. Bundesstaat
New Mexico [ˌnjuː ˈmeksɪkəʊ] am. Bundesstaat
New Orleans [ˌnjuː ɔːˈliːəns] Stadt in Louisiana
New York (City) [ˌnjuː jɔːk ˈsɪti] größte Stadt in den USA
New York State [ˌnjuː jɔːk ˈsteɪt] am. Bundesstaat
Newfoundland [ˈnjuːfndlənd] Neufundland (kanadische Provinz)
Niagara (Falls) [naɪˌægərə ˈfɔːlz] Wasserfälle an der Grenze zu Kanada
Nob Hill [ˈnɒb hɪl] Hügel in San Francisco

O

Ohio [əʊˈhaɪəʊ] am. Bundesstaat
Oklahoma [ˌəʊkləˈhəʊmə] am. Bundesstaat
Oregon [ˈɒrɪɡən] am. Bundesstaat
Orlando [ɔːˈlændəʊ] Stadt in Florida
Oxville [ˈɒksvɪl] Stadt in den USA

P

Pennsylvania [ˌpensəlˈveɪniə] am. Bundesstaat
the People's Place [ˌðə ˈpiːpls pleɪs] Museum, das die Kultur der Amish zeigt
Philadelphia [ˌfɪləˈdelfiə] Stadt in den USA
Pittsburgh [ˈpɪtsbɜːɡ] Stadt in Pennsylvania
Pittsfield [ˈpɪtsfiːld] Stadt in den USA
Platte [plæt] Fluss in den USA
Plymouth [ˈplɪməθ] Ort in den USA
Poland [ˈpəʊlənd] Polen
Puerto Rico [ˌpwɜːtəʊ ˈriːkəʊ] Inselstaat mit eigener Regierung; Einwohner sind allerdings US-Bürger

Q

Queens [kwiːnz] Stadtteil von New York

R

Radio City (Music Hall) [ˈreɪdiəʊ sɪti ˈmjuːzɪk hɔːl] das größte Theater/Kino der Welt im Rockefeller Center
Richmond [ˈrɪtʃmənd] Stadt in den USA
Rockefeller Center [ˈrɒkəfelə sentə] Gebäudekomplex in Manhattan
Rocky Mountains [ˌrɒki ˈmaʊntɪnz] Bergmassiv im Osten der USA
Roslyn [ˈrɒzlɪn] Vorort von New York
Russia [ˈrʌʃə] Russland

S

Sacramento [ˌsækrəˈmentəʊ] Stadt in Kalifornien
Salt Lake City [ˌsɔːlt leɪk ˈsɪti] Hauptstadt von Utah
San Antonio [sæn ænˈtəʊniəʊ] Stadt in Texas
San Diego [ˌsæn diˈeɪɡəʊ] Stadt in Kalifornien
San Francisco [ˌsæn frənˈsɪskəʊ] Stadt in Kalifornien
Santee [sænˈtiː] Stadt in Kalifornien
Scandinavia [ˌskændɪˈneɪviə] Skandinavien
Seattle [siˈætl] Stadt in den USA
Smithsonian Museum of American History [smɪθˌsəʊniən mjuːˈziːəm əv əˌmerɪkən ˈhɪstri] historisches Museum in Washington, DC
Snake River [ˌsneɪk ˈrɪvə] Fluss in Idaho
South Carolina [ˌsaʊθ ˌkærəˈlaɪnə] am. Bundesstaat

South Dakota [ˌsaʊθ dəˈkəʊtə] am. Bundesstaat
Springfield [ˈsprɪŋfiːld] Stadt in den USA
St Augustine [sənt ɔːˈɡʌstɪn] Stadt in Florida
St Louis [sənt ˈluːɪs] Stadt in den USA
Staten Island [ˌstætn ˈaɪlənd] Stadtteil von New York
Switzerland [ˈswɪtsələnd] Schweiz

T

Texas [ˈteksəs] am. Bundesstaat
the Alamo [ði ˈæləməʊ] Missionsgebäude, das 1836 von Amerikanern gegen eine Übermacht von 4000 Mexikanern verteidigt wurde.
the Atlantic (Ocean) [ði ətˌlæntɪk ˈəʊʃn] der Atlantik
The Dalles [ðə ˈdælz] Siedlung in Idaho
The Intrepid Sea/Air/Space Museum [ði ɪnˈtrepɪd siː, eə, speɪs mjuːˈzɪːəm] Museum in New York
3 Com Park [θri ˈkɒm paːk] Stadion der San Francisco Giants
Tillamook [ˈtɪləmɒk] Stadt in Oregon
Twentynine Palms [twentiˌnaɪn ˈpaːmz] Ort in Kalifornien

U

Utah [ˈjuːtɑː] am. Bundesstaat

V

Virginia [vəˈdʒɪniə] am. Bundesstaat

W

Wall Street [ˈwɔːl striːt] Straße in Manhattan, Finanzzentrum von New York
Washington [ˈwɒʃɪŋtən] am. Bundesstaat
Washington DC [ˈwɒʃɪŋtən ˌdiː ˈsiː] Hauptstadt der USA
Wichita [ˈwɪtʃɪtɔː] Stadt in Kansas
Williamsburg [ˈwɪljəmzbɜːɡ] Stadt in den USA
Wilmington [ˈwɪlmɪŋtən] Stadt in den USA
Wisconsin [wɪˈskɒnsɪn] am. Bundesstaat
World Trade Center [ˌwɜːld ˈtreɪd sentə] ehemaliges Handelszentrum in New York; die Zwillingstürme waren bis zum Terrorangriff vom 11. September 2001 die höchsten Gebäude Manhattans

Y

Yellowstone Lake [ˌjeləʊstəʊn ˈleɪk] See im Yellowstone Nationalpark in Wyoming
Yellowstone National Park [ˈjeləʊstəʊn ˌnæʃnəl ˈpaːk] Nationalpark in Wyoming
York [jɔːk] Stadt in den USA

INDEX

Aa

a, an ein, eine, ein **5-U0**, D
abbey Abtei, Kloster(kirche) **7-U4**, Ex7
able to, be können, in der Lage sein **8-U1**, Sit1
abolish abschaffen **8-U3**, WP
about ungefähr **5-U7**, T2
about über **5-U2**, T2
above oberhalb, über **6-U4**, T2
absolute absolut **7-U3**, T2
absolutely völlig **7-U3**, T1
accident Unfall **5-U6**, T1
across über, hinüber **6-U4**, T1
act spielen, aufführen **5-U6**, Ex9
  act out durchspielen, aufführen **7-U1**, Ex16
action Handlung **5-U6**, Ex6
activity Aktivität, Tätigkeit, Beschäftigung **5-U5**, Sit2
actor Schauspieler **6-U6**, WPB
actually tatsächlich, in Wirklichkeit **7-U3**, T1
add hinzufügen **5-U5**, Ex5
address Adresse **6-U3**, T1
admit zugeben, eingestehen **7-U2**, T2
adult Erwachsene/r; erwachsen **7-U5**, Ex6
adventure Abenteuer **7-U2**, T2
advertise Werbung machen (für) **8-U2**, T2
advertisement Reklame **6-U1**, Ex14
advice Rat **8-U4**, T2
affair Affäre; Angelegenheit **7-U4**, T2
afraid, be Angst haben **6-U2**, Sit4
  afraid, I'm ich fürchte, leider **7-U1**, Com
  afraid of doing sth, be Angst davor haben, etwas zu tun **8-U1**, T1
after nach, hinter, danach **5-U5**, WPA
afternoon Nachmittag **5-U1**, Sit6
afterwards danach **7-U2**, Sit3
again wieder, noch einmal **5-U5**, T1
against gegen **6-U2**, Ex10
age Alter **5-U1**, PYE6
aged im Alter von **7-U3**, T2
agent Agent/in, Detektiv/in **8-U1**, Read
ago vor **6-U2**, T1
agree zustimmen, einwilligen **7-U3**, T1
ahead (of) voraus, vor **6-U4**, T2
aid Hilfe **7-U5**, WP
aim Ziel **8-U2**, Ex12
air Luft **6-U2**, WPB
  air conditioning Klimaanlage **8-U4**, T2
  air force Luftwaffe **7-U3**, Read
airfield Flugplatz **8-Rev1**
airport Flughafen **5-U7**, Sit5
aisle Mittelgang, Gang **8-U3**, T2
alarm Alarm **8-U1**, Read
alcohol Alkohol **8-U1**, T2
alive lebendig, am Leben **7-U5**, Rev
all alle **5-U4**, WPB
  all over überall in, auf **7-U3**, WP

all right in Ordnung **5-U3**, T2
alligator Alligator **8-U4**, T1
allowed to do sth, be etwas tun dürfen **8-U1**, Sit3
almost beinahe **6-U6**, T1
alone, be allein sein **7-U3**, TYE
along entlang **6-U2**, T1
  along with zusammen mit **7-U5**, Read
alphabet Alphabet **5-U7**, Ex5
already schon **6-U4**, Sit3
also auch **5-U4**, Sit5
although obwohl **7-U4**, Read
altogether insgesamt, im Ganzen **8-U2**, Sit1
always immer **5-U1**, T2
A.M./a.m./am vor 12 Uhr **8-U1**, Ex10
amazed erstaunt **7-U3**, Sit4
ambassador Botschafter/in **7-U1**, TYE
ambulance Krankenwagen **6-U2**, T2
American Amerikaner/in; amerikanisch **5-U0**, A
among zwischen, unter **8-U2**, T2
amount Betrag; Menge **8-U2**, Sit3
amusement park Vergnügungspark **8-U2**, Read
and und **5-U0**, A
  and so on und so weiter **6-U3**, T1
Angles, the die Angeln **7-U2**, WP
angry wütend, verärgert **5-U6**, T2
animal Tier **6-U2**, WPA
annoying ärgerlich **7-U3**, T1
annual jährlich; Jahres- **8-U2**, T1
another ein(e) andere(r, s), noch ein(e, es) **6-U4**, WPC
answer Antwort **5-U2**, Sit2
answer (be)antworten **7-U1**, Ex10
any (irgend)eine(r, s) **6-U4**, Sit4
anybody irgendeine(r) **7-U5**, Ex12
anyone irgendeine(r) **7-U5**, Ex12
anything irgendetwas **7-U1**, Read
anyway jedenfalls **7-U5**, Sit2
anywhere irgendwo **7-U5**, Ex12
apartment Wohnung **8-U1**, WP
appear erscheinen, scheinen **7-U3**, T2
appetite Appetit **6-U4**, T2
apple Apfel **5-U0**, D
April April **5-U4**, Sit5
apron Schürze **7-U5**, Sket2
arcade Spielhalle, Arkade **5-U7**, WPA
arcade Einkaufspassage **7-U5**, Ex13
arch Bogen (Gebäude) **8-U4**, T2
archery Bogenschießen **7-U2**, T1
area Gebiet; Bereich **8-U1**, Ex7
argue streiten, argumentieren **7-U5**, T2
argument Streit **6-U1**, T1
arm Arm **5-U5**, T1
armour Rüstung **7-U2**, T2
army Armee **7-U4**, WP
around herum, umher **5-U3**, WPA
arrange vereinbaren; anordnen **8-U1**, Ex16
  arrange to do sth vereinbaren, etwas zu tun **8-U1**, Ex16

arrest festnehmen **7-U1**, T2
arrival Ankunft **8-U1**, Ex10
arrive ankommen **6-U5**, T1
arrow Pfeil **7-U4**, T1
art Kunst, Kunsterziehung **7-U3**, TYE
article Artikel, Beitrag **8-U2**, Ex2
as als, während **6-U6**, T1
  as ... as so … wie **6-U1**, Sit5
Asian asiatisch; Asiate, Asiatin **7-U5**, TYE
ask fragen; bitten **5-U2**, T2
aspirin Aspirin **8-U4**, Ex11
at an, auf, in **5-U1**, WPB
  at first zuerst **8-U3**, Sit1
  at last endlich **5-U7**, T1
  at least zumindest, mindestens **7-U3**, WP
  at (nine o'clock) um (neun Uhr) **5-U1**, Ex10
  at school in der Schule **5-U1**, WPB
  at the moment im Augenblick **5-U4**, Sit1
athlete (Leicht)athlet/in, Sportler/in **7-U3**, Read
atlas Atlas **8-U4**, WP
atmosphere Atmosphäre, Stimmung **8-U4**, Read
attack Angriff **8-U3**, Read
attack angreifen **7-U4**, T1
attention Aufmerksamkeit **7-U3**, TYE
attraction Attraktion, Anziehung **7-U4**, Ex10
audience Zuschauer, Publikum **7-U3**, Sit1
August August **5-U4**, Sit5
aunt Tante **6-U1**, Sit1
auntie Tante **5-U1**, Song
auto Auto **8-Proj2**
automobile Auto, Automobil **8-U2**, TYE
autumn Herbst **6-U4**, WPB
avenue Boulevard, breite Straße, Allee **8-U1**, Ex7
average Durchschnitt(s-) **8-U4**, WP
awake wach **7-U5**, T2
award Auszeichnung, Preis **7-U5**, WP
away weg, fort **5-U1**, Sit6
awful schrecklich **5-U1**, Sit2
axe Axt **7-U4**, T1

Bb

baby Baby **5-U3**, Sit3
back zurück **5-U3**, T2
back Rücken **6-U2**, T2
back Rückseite **5-U6**, Ex4
backpack Rucksack **7-U5**, T1
backwards rückwärts **8-U2**, Ex12
backyard Hinterhof, Garten **7-U1**, Read
bad schlecht **5-U2**, Ex17
  bad language Kraftausdrücke, unanständige Ausdrücke **7-U3**, Sit3

one hundred and forty-five **145**

Index

badger Dachs **6-U2**, T1
bag Tasche **5-U0**, D
ball Ball **5-U6**, T1
banana Banane **5-U6**, Sit4
band Band, Musikgruppe **5-U2**, T2
bang peng! **6-U4**, T2
bank Bank(haus) **5-U2**, T1
bank Ufer **8-U4**, T2
barbecue Grillparty; Grillgericht **6-U7**, T1
bareback ohne Sattel **7-U1**, Read
bar mitzvah Bar-Mizwa **7-U3**, T2
barrel Fass **6-U4**, T1
baseball Baseball **5-U6**, Sit3
based on, be sich stützen auf, basieren auf **8-Lit**
basket Korb **5-U6**, Ex4
basketball Basketball **5-U2**, Ex12
bat Fledermaus **8-Rev10**
bath Bad **7-U2**, WP
bathroom Badezimmer **5-U1**, T2
batter Schlagmann **6-U7**, Sit3
battle Schlacht **7-U2**, T1
battlefield Schlachtfeld **7-U4**, T1
be sein **5-U0**, F
beach Strand **5-U7**, WPA
bean Bohne **6-U5**, Sit2
beard Bart **7-U4**, Com
beat schlagen; klopfen **8-U2**, Sit4
beautiful schön, hübsch **7-U2**, T1
because weil **5-U7**, Sit4
  because of wegen **8-U2**, T2
become werden **6-U6**, WPC
bed Bett **5-U1**, Sit6
bedroom Schlafzimmer **5-U2**, WPB
beer Bier **7-U1**, Read
before vor, vorher, bevor **5-U5**, Sit2
begin anfangen **7-U4**, WP
  begin to do sth anfangen, etwas zu tun **7-U4**, WP
beginner Anfänger/in **8-U2**, Ex18
beginning Anfang, Beginn **7-U3**, Ex1
behind hinter **5-U2**, WPA
believe (in) glauben (an) **7-U2**, Sit2
bell Glocke, Klingel **6-U1**, WPA
belong to gehören **5-U5**, T2
below unten, unterhalb **6-U7**, Song
bend Kurve, Biegung **8-U2**, Read
bend biegen; sich bücken **8-U4**, Read
berry Beere **7-U4**, T1
best beste(r, s) **5-U3**, PYE3
best-known bekannteste(r, s) **8-Rev8**
best-selling verkauft sich am besten **8-Rev8**
better besser **6-U1**, Sit4
between zwischen **6-U6**, T1
big groß **5-U5**, T2
  big time, hit/be the groß rauskommen, ganz oben sein **7-U3**
bike Rad **5-U2**, Sit3
biker Radfahrer/in **8-U4**, Com
bin Mülleimer, Abfalleimer **7-U3**, T1
biology Biologie **8-U2**, Sit2

bird Vogel **6-U2**, WPB
birthday Geburtstag **5-U0**, G
biscuit Keks **5-U4**, WPA
bit, a etwas, ein wenig **6-U4**, WPB
bite beißen **8-U3**, Read
black schwarz **5-U0**, C
blind blind **8-U4**, Ex17
blister Blase **7-U5**, T1
blizzard Schneesturm **8-U4**, Read
block Häuser-, Wohnblock **8-U1**, Ex7
blow blasen, wehen **8-U4**, Read
  blow up in die Luft jagen, explodieren **6-U4**, WPA
blue blau **5-U0**, C
board (Wand-)Tafel **5-U0**, D
board Kommission, Gremium, Aufsichtsrat **7-U1**, WP
boat Boot, Schiff **5-U7**, WPD
body Leiche; Körper **7-U4**, T1
bomb Bombe **8-U2**, Ex10
bonfire Freudenfeuer **6-U4**, WPA
book Buch **5-U0**, D
book buchen **8-U1**, Sit2
bookshop Buchhandlung **5-U6**, WPB
border Grenze **8-U4**, WP
bored gelangweilt **6-U2**, T2
boring langweilig **6-U1**, Sit5
born, be geboren werden **7-U1**, TYE
borough (Stadt)Bezirk **8-U1**, WP
borrow sich ausleihen **5-U7**, Ex14
both beide **6-U2**, Sit5
bottle Flasche **5-U5**, PYE4
bottom Boden, Fuß (Berg) **5-U7**, T2
bounce aufprallen lassen **8-U2**, Ex12
bowling Bowling, Kegeln **6-U7**, T1
box Kiste, Schachtel **5-U5**, T2
boxing Boxen, Box- **8-U2**, T1
boy Junge **5-U1**, WPA
boycott Boykott **8-U3**, T2
boyfriend fester Freund **5-U1**, WPC
bracket Klammer **7-U1**, TYE4
bread Brot **6-U5**, Sit2
break (zer)brechen **7-U1**, T1
  break in einbrechen **7-U1**, T1
break Chance **7-U3**, T1
break-dancing Breakdancing **8-U1**, T2
breakfast Frühstück **5-U4**, WPB
break-in Einbruch **7-U1**, T2
breeze Brise **8-U2**, Sit1
brick Ziegelstein **6-U1**, Song
bridge Brücke **6-U1**, WPA
bright hell; strahlend, klar **8-U1**, T2
bring bringen **5-U4**, Ex6
  bring out herausbringen **7-U1**, Sit5
British britisch **7-U3**, TYE
Briton Brite, Britin **7-U2**, WP
broken zerbrochen, kaputt **6-U5**, T2
bronze Bronze **7-U5**, WP
brooch Brosche **7-U5**, Sket1
broomstick Besen(stiel) **7-U2**, Read
brother Bruder **5-U0**, I
brown braun **5-U4**, Ex16
brush bürsten, putzen **8-U2**, Read

budgie Wellensittich **5-U3**, WPB
buffalo Bison, Büffel **8-U3**, Ex7
  buffalo chips getrockneter Büffelmist **8-U3**, Read
build bauen **6-U1**, Song
building Gebäude **6-U7**, T2
burger Hamburger **6-U7**, T1
burn verbrennen, brennen **6-U4**, WPA
  burn down niederbrennen **7-U3**, TYE
bury begraben **8-U3**, Read
bus Bus **5-U0**, D
  bus service Busverbindung **8-U1**, Ex10
  bus station Busbahnhof **5-U6**, WPA
bush Busch, Strauch **5-U3**, T1
business Geschäft; Betrieb **8-U1**, Ex7
bus-stop Bushaltestelle **5-U3**, Sit3
busy beschäftigt, belebt **6-U1**, T1
but aber **5-U1**, Sit2
butter Butter **6-U5**, Sit2
buy kaufen **5-U4**, WPA
by an, bei, neben **6-U1**, WPA
by mit **8-U4**, Ex16
bye Tschüss **5-U0**, B

Cc

cable car Straßenbahn (in San Francisco) **6-U7**, T2
café Imbiss, Café **5-U6**, WPA
cafeteria Cafeteria **8-U2**, T1
cage Käfig **5-U3**, WPA
cake Kuchen **5-U4**, WPC
calculate rechnen **7-U5**, Read
calendar Kalender **8-U2**, WP
call Ruf, Anruf **7-U1**, T2
call rufen, anrufen **7-U2**, T1
called, be heißen **5-U3**, WPA
camera Fotoapparat, Kamera **5-U2**, WPC
camp Lager **5-U7**, WPD
camp zelten **5-U7**, Ex14
camping Camping, Zelten **6-U7**, T1
camp site Campingplatz **5-U7**, WPD
campaign Kampagne, Aktion **8-U3**, T2
can Dose **7-U1**, Read
can können **5-U0**, F
canal Kanal **5-U6**, Ex16
candle Kerze **6-U4**, WPB
cap Mütze **6-U7**, T1
capital Hauptstadt **8-U1**, Sit1
captain Kapitän **8-Rev15**
capture gefangen nehmen **8-U3**, T1
car Auto **5-U1**, Sit6
  car park Parkplatz, -haus **5-U5**, T2
caravan Wohnwagen **5-U7**, WPB
card Karte **6-U3**, Ex4
careful vorsichtig, sorgfältig **5-U5**, T1
carnival Volksfest; Karneval, Fasching **8-U2**, WP
carry tragen **6-U2**, T2
cart Wagen, Karren **7-U5**, Sket2
cartoon Zeichentrickfilm **6-U6**, WPA
carve schnitzen **8-U3**, Read
case Koffer **5-U7**, T1

146 one hundred and forty-six

Index

cassette Kassette **6-U5**, T2
castle Schloss, Burg **6-U4**, T2
cat Katze **5-U0**, E
catch fangen **5-U3**, T2
   catch a bus einen Bus erreichen **6-U2**, Ex9
catcher Fänger/in **6-U7**, T1
cathedral Dom, Kathedrale **7-U5**, Ex13
Catholic katholisch; Katholik/in **6-U4**, T1
cattle Vieh, Rinder **7-U5**, Sket2
CD CD **5-U2**, T2
   CD player CD-Spieler **7-U1**, Sit5
céilí irische Tanzveranstaltung **7-U1**, T1
celebrate feiern **8-U2**, WP
cellar Keller **6-U4**, T1
cellphone Handy, Mobiltelefon **8-U4**, Sit4
Celsius/C Celsius **8-U4**, WP
Celt Kelte, Keltin **7-U2**, WP
cent Cent **8-U2**, T1
central zentral **6-U1**, WPB
centre Zentrum **6-U1**, WPA
century Jahrhundert **7-U4**, WP
certain sicher **8-U1**, Sit2
certainly sicherlich **8-U1**, Sit2
chain-link fence Maschendrahtzaun **8-U2**, Read
chair Stuhl **5-U0**, D
chalk Kreide **7-U2**, WP
chamber of horrors Gruselkabinett **6-U1**, T1
championship Meisterschaft (Sport) **8-U2**, T2
chance Chance **7-U3**, Sit1
change umsteigen **8-U1**, T1
change ändern, verändern **7-U1**, WP
channel Programm, Kanal **6-U6**, T2
character Figur, Charakter **6-U6**, WPA
charge anstürmen, angreifen **7-U4**, T1
charity Wohltätigkeit, wohltätige Organisation **8-U4**, Ex3
charming charmant, bezaubernd **8-U1**, Read
chat room Chatroom **8-U2**, Ex2
cheap billig **6-U1**, Sit2
check überprüfen **5-U5**, Ex17
cheeky frech **7-U3**, T2
cheer zujubeln, bejubeln, anfeuern **7-U3**, T1
cheerleader Cheerleader **8-U2**, T1
cheese Käse **5-U4**, WPB
chess Schach **5-U5**, WPB
chief Häuptling **8-U3**, WP
child Kind **5-U3**, Sit3
chimney Schornstein **7-U5**, Sit1
Chinese chinesisch; Chinese, Chinesin **8-U1**, WP
chips Pommes frites **5-U4**, WPA
chocolate Schokolade **5-U4**, Song
choose wählen **7-U2**, Proj
Christmas Weihnachten **5-U4**, Sit5
church Kirche **7-U2**, WP
cinema Kino **5-U3**, PYE3

circle Kreis **6-U1**, WPB
city Stadt, Großstadt **6-U1**, WPA
civil rights Bürgerrechte **8-U3**, T2
civil war Bürgerkrieg **8-U3**, WP
class Klasse; Unterrichtsstunde **5-U1**, WPB
classmate Klassenkamerad/in **8-U1**, T2
classroom Klassenzimmer **5-U0**, D
clay Lehm **6-U1**, Song
clean sauber **6-U5**, WPB
clean sauber machen **8-U1**, Ex13
clear klar **7-U3**, T2
clever klug **7-U2**, T1
click on anklicken **6-U3**, WPB
cliff Kliff, Klippe **8-U4**, WP
climate Klima **8-U4**, T2
climb klettern **7-U5**, T1
close schließen **5-U0**, F
close knapp **8-U2**, T2
close (to) nahe, in der Nähe von **8-U4**, T1
clothes Kleidung **6-U5**, WPB
clothing Bekleidung, Kleidung **8-U1**, Sit1
cloud Wolke **5-U7**, WP
cloudy wolkig, bewölkt **7-U5**, T1
clown Clown **8-U4**, T1
club Club **5-U5**, WPB
coast Küste **6-U2**, T1
coat Mantel **6-U5**, Sit2
code Code, Chiffre **7-U2**, Read
coffee Kaffee **5-U4**, WPA
cola Cola **5-U4**, WPC
cold kalt **5-U7**, WPD
collect sammeln, einsammeln **7-U5**, Rev
college College **7-U1**, T1
colonist Kolonist/in **8-U3**, Sit1
colony Kolonie **8-U3**, WP
colour Farbe **5-U0**, C
come kommen **5-U0**, F
   Come on Komm schon! **5-U4**, Sit1
comedian Komiker **8-Rev15**
comedy Komödie **6-U6**, WPA
comic Comic **6-U4**, Sit4
commercial Werbespot **8-U2**, T2
communication Kommunikation, Verständigung **5-U1**, Com
community Bevölkerungsgruppe; Gemeinde **7-U1**, T1
community centre Gemeindezentrum **7-U1**, T1
company Firma **5-U2**, T1
compare vergleichen **7-U5**, Rev
complain sich beschweren **7-U3**, T2
complete vollständig **7-U5**, Read
complete vervollständigen **5-U5**, Ex1
computer Computer **5-U1**, Sit7
concert Konzert **6-U4**, Ex13
concrete Beton **7-U5**, TYE
condition Bedingung, Verhältnisse, Zustand **8-U1**, WP
confident zuversichtlich, selbstsicher **8-U2**, T2
confuse verwechseln, durcheinanderbringen **7-U5**, Read

conquer erobern **7-U2**, WP
continent Erdteil, Kontinent **8-U3**, T1
contract Vertrag **7-U3**, Sit1
control Kontrolle **5-U7**, Sit5
conversation Gespräch **6-U2**, Ex13
cook kochen **7-U5**, T1
cool kühl **6-U2**, T1
copper Kupfer; kupfern **8-U1**, T1
copy kopieren, abschreiben **6-U4**, Ex17
cork Kork(en) **8-U2**, Read
corn Mais **8-U4**, Read
corner Ecke **8-U1**, T1
cornflakes Cornflakes **5-U1**, Sit2
correct richtig **5-U5**, Ex15
correct verbessern, korrigieren **8-U1**, T2
corrupt bestechlich, korrupt **8-U2**, TYE4
cost Kosten **8-U2**, Sit5
cost kosten **5-U5**, Sit4
costume Kostüm **7-U2**, Sit4
cottage Hütte **6-U2**, WPA
could könnte **8-U2**, Com
could konnte **8-U1**, Sit1
count zählen **7-U5**, Sket1
counter Ladentisch, Tresen **8-U2**, Sit1
country Land **6-U2**, WPA
country Land, Staat **7-U1**, WP
county Verwaltungsbezirk, Grafschaft **7-U1**, T1
couple Paar, Ehepaar **7-U4**, WP
   couple of, a ein paar **7-U4**, WP
courage Mut **8-U1**, T1
course Kurs, Lehrgang **7-U3**, Ex11
court Gericht, Gerichtshof **8-U3**, T2
cousin Cousin, Cousine **6-U1**, Sit1
cover bedecken **8-U3**, Read
cow Kuh **6-U2**, WPA
cowboy Cowboy **7-U1**, Read
cowgirl Cowgirl **7-U1**, Read
crane Kran **7-U4**, TYE
crash Krach(en) **7-U1**, T2
crate Kiste **8-U4**, T1
crazy verrückt; wütend **7-U1**, Read
creaking knarrend **7-U4**, Read
create (er)schaffen, hervorbringen; verursachen **8-U1**, Ex16
cricket Cricket **7-U1**, TYE
crime Verbrechen, Kriminalität **7-U5**, TYE
criminal Verbrecher/in **6-U1**, T2
crisps Kartoffelchips **5-U4**, T2
crop Feldfrüchte; Ernte **8-U3**, Read
cross überqueren **8-U3**, Sit3
crossroads Kreuzung **7-U5**, Com
crowd Menge **7-U2**, T2
crowded voll, überfüllt **8-U1**, T1
crown Krone **8-U1**, T1
cruel grausam **8-Lit**
cry weinen; schreien **7-U2**, Read
cup Tasse; Pokal **6-U4**, Sit1
cupboard Schrank **6-U5**, T2
cut (zer)schneiden **7-U4**, Sit5

one hundred and forty-seven   **147**

Index

cut off abschneiden **7-U4**, Sit5
cut out ausschneiden **8-U2**, Ex8
cycle Rad fahren **7-U5**, WP

Dd

dad Vati, Papa **5-U1**, WPC
daily täglich; Tages- **8-U2**, Sit5
damn verflucht, verdammt **6-U5**, T1
dance Tanzen; Tanz(veranstaltung) **8-U2**, T1
dance tanzen **5-U4**, Ex2
danger Gefahr **8-U3**, Sit4
dangerous gefährlich **5-U5**, T1
dark dunkel **6-U2**, T1
date Datum **5-U4**, Ex13
daughter Tochter **6-U1**, Sit1
day Tag **5-U1**, Sit4
day-dream Tagtraum **6-U2**, Sit2
dead tot **7-U4**, T1
dead end Sackgasse **6-U6**, T1
dear lieber, liebe, liebes **5-U4**, Sit4
death Tod **6-U4**, T1
December Dezember **5-U4**, Sit5
decide entscheiden, beschließen
 6-U6, WPC
 decide to do sich entschließen, etwas
 zu tun **7-U2**, WP
decorate schmücken; tapezieren
 8-U2, T1
deep tief **8-U4**, Read
deer Reh, Hirsch **6-U2**, WPB
defeat (völlig) besiegen, eine Niederlage
 zufügen **7-U4**, WP
defend verteidigen **8-U4**, WP
defense Verteidigung **8-U2**, T2
defensive defensiv; Verteidigungs-
 8-Proj5
definition Definition **7-U4**, Ex11
degree Grad **8-U4**, WP
deliver (aus)liefern, austragen **6-U5**, WPA
demo tape Demoband, Musterband **7-U3**, T1
deny bestreiten, leugnen **8-U2**, T2
departure Abfahrt, Abreise **8-U1**, Ex10
depth Tiefe **8-Lit**
descendant Nachfahre **8-Lit**
describe beschreiben **6-U6**, Com
desert Wüste **6-U7**, WPA
desk Schülertisch, Schreibtisch **5-U0**, D
desk clerk Empfangschef/in **8-U1**, Ex8
destination Bestimmungsort, Ziel
 8-U3, Read
detail Einzelheit, Detail **8-U1**, Ex15
detective Detektiv/in **7-U2**, Com
develop (sich) entwickeln **8-U2**, T2
dial wählen (Telefonnummer) **6-U6**, T2
dialogue Dialog **5-U5**, Ex8
diary Tagebuch **6-U2**, Sit2
die sterben **7-U2**, T1
difference Unterschied **8-U4**, Ex16
different verschieden, anders **5-U6**, Ex16
difficult schwierig **5-U7**, T1
dig graben **6-U4**, T1
dining-room Esszimmer **5-U2**, WPB

dinner Hauptmahlzeit **8-U3**, Sit1
dinosaur Dinosaurier **6-U6**, WPB
direct Regie führen **8-Rev8**
direction Richtung **8-U1**, T1
dirt Schmutz, Dreck **8-U4**, T2
dirty schmutzig **6-U5**, WPB
disabled behindert **7-U5**, Sit1
disappear verschwinden **7-U5**, Read
disaster Katastrophe **8-Rev15**
disc Disk, Diskette **6-U3**, WPB
disco Disco **5-U1**, Ex16
discover entdecken **8-U2**, WP
discrimination Diskriminierung **8-U3**, T2
discuss besprechen, diskutieren **8-U1**, T2
disease Krankheit **7-U1**, Read
disk drive Diskettenlaufwerk **7-U5**, Read
display Ausstellung, Vorführung
 7-U1, Proj
distance Entfernung **7-U4**, T1
district Gebiet, Bezirk, Stadtviertel
 8-U1, Ex7
disturb stören **7-U4**, Read
divide teilen, aufteilen; trennen **8-U1**, Ex7
divorce sich scheiden lassen **7-U4**, T2
DJ Discjockey **8-U2**, T2
do tun **5-U1**, Sit6
doctor Arzt, Ärztin **6-U4**, T2
documentary Dokumentarfilm **6-U6**, WPB
dog Hund **5-U1**, WPA
doll Puppe **8-U3**, T1
dollar Dollar **8-U1**, Sit1
dome Kuppel **6-U1**, WPA
door Tür **5-U0**, D
doorway Eingang **7-U4**, Read
double doppelt **5-U1**, PYE6
dough Teig **7-U5**, Read
doughnut Berliner, Krapfen **5-U4**, WPA
down unten, nach unten **5-U0**, F
download herunterladen **6-U3**, T1
downtown (im/ins) Stadtzentrum
 8-U1, Ex7
dozen, a (ein) Dutzend **7-U5**, Read
drama Schauspiel **5-U5**, Sit2
draw zeichnen **5-U4**, Sit2
dream Traum **6-U6**, Ex2
dress Kleid **5-U0**, C
drink trinken **5-U4**, WPB
drink Getränk **6-U5**, T2
drive Aktion, Kampagne **8-U2**, T1
drive fahren **5-U1**, Sit7
driver Fahrer/in **6-U5**, WPC
drop fallen lassen, fallen **6-U4**, T1
drug Droge; Medikament **7-U1**, Read
Druid Druide **7-U2**, TYE
drums Schlagzeug **7-U3**, T1
duck Ente **6-U4**, Ex18
duke Herzog **7-U2**, T1
during während **7-U5**, T2
Dutch holländisch, niederländisch
 8-U2, TYE
DVD DVD **6-U3**, WPB

Ee

each jeder, jede, jedes **5-U5**, Ex18
 each other einander, gegenseitig
 8-U3, Sit5
ear Ohr **6-U6**, Com
early früh **7-U4**, WP
earn verdienen **6-U5**, WPB
earth Erde **8-U4**, T1
earthquake Erdbeben **8-Proj1**
east Osten **6-U1**, WPA
Easter Ostern **5-U4**, Sit5
eastern östlich, Ost- **8-U1**, TYE
eastward ostwärts, nach Osten
 8-U3, TYE
easy einfach, leicht **5-U6**, T1
eat essen **5-U3**, WPA
eight acht **5-U0**, G
eighteen achtzehn **5-U0**, G
eighty achtzig **5-U4**, WPA
electric elektrisch **8-U1**, Read
electronic elektronisch **8-U4**, Ex17
elephant Elefant **6-U3**, WPA
elevator Aufzug, Lift **8-U1**, T1
eleven elf **5-U0**, G
else sonst **7-U1**, T1
e-mail E-Mail **6-U3**, WPC
emperor Kaiser **7-U2**, WP
empire Reich, Imperium **8-U1**, WP
employ beschäftigen **8-U3**, TYE
empty leer **6-U4**, T1
encyclopedia Lexikon, Enzyklopädie
 6-U4, PYE4
end Ende **5-U1**, Song
end beenden **6-U2**, Ex6
ending Endung, Ende **8-U1**, Ex14
endless endlos **6-U7**, Song
enemy Feind/in **7-U2**, Proj
engine Motor **8-Rev11**
engineer Ingenieur/in **8-U3**, TYE1
English englisch; Engländer/in **5-U0**, A
enjoy gern haben, genießen **5-U7**, WPC
 enjoy doing sth gerne etwas tun
 7-U2, T2
 enjoy yourself! Viel Spaß! **8-U3**, Sit4
enough genug **6-U4**, Ex11
enter eintreten (in) **8-U1**, Ex9
entertainment Unterhaltung **8-U2**, T2
entrance Eingang **6-U4**, T2
envelope Briefumschlag **8-Rev12**
equal gleich **8-U3**, WP
equipment Ausrüstung **6-U7**, T1
escape flüchten, entkommen **8-U3**, Sit3
especially besonders **7-U3**, T1
etc usw. **6-U5**, Ex12
European europäisch; Europäer/in
 8-U2, WP
even sogar **7-U4**, TYE
 even though obwohl **8-U1**, T2
evening Abend **5-U1**, Sit6
event Ereignis, Veranstaltung **8-U2**, Sit3
ever jemals **6-U5**, Sit4
every jeder, jede, jedes **5-U1**, Sit6
everybody jede(r), alle **7-U3**, Com

Index

everyone jede(r), alle **6-U2**, Sit2
everything alles **6-U3**, WPC
everywhere überall **6-U2**, Song
exact genau **6-U7**, T2
examine untersuchen **8-U1**, TYE
example (of) Beispiel (für) **8-U2**, Ex17
except außer **7-U1**, WP
exchange austauschen **8-Proj2**
excited aufgeregt, begeistert **7-U2**, T2
excitement Aufregung **8-U4**, T1
exciting spannend, aufregend
   6-U1, WPA
excuse Entschuldigung **7-U2**, Ex3
excuse me Entschuldigung **5-U6**, WPB
execute hinrichten, exekutieren **7-U4**, T2
exercise Übung **5-U1**, Ex1
   exercise book Schulheft **5-U0**, D
exhausted erschöpft **7-U5**, T1
exist existieren, vorhanden sein **6-U5**, T1
expect erwarten **6-U6**, Sit1
expedition Expedition, Forschungsreise
   7-U5, WP
expensive teuer **5-U7**, WPA
experience erleben, erfahren **8-U4**, T1
expert Experte, Expertin **7-U5**, Sket1
explain erklären **6-U2**, T2
explanation Erklärung **6-U7**, Com
explore erforschen, erkunden **8-U3**, Sit1
export ausführen, exportieren **7-U1**, WP
express ausdrücken **8-U3**, Ex8
expressway Autobahn **8-U2**, Read
extra zusätzlich **6-U5**, WPB
eye Auge **6-U6**, Com

Ff

face Gesicht **6-U6**, Com
fact Tatsache, Faktum **8-U4**, T1
factory Fabrik **6-U5**, WPA
fail scheitern, keinen Erfolg haben
   7-U3, Read
fair fair, gerecht **6-U5**, T1
fair schön, liebreizend **6-U1**, Song
fair(-haired) blond **7-U4**, Com
fairground Rummelplatz **7-U5**, Sit1
fake unecht; Fälschung **8-U1**, Read
fall fallen **5-U5**, T1
   fall in love (with) sich verlieben (in)
      7-U2, T1
   fall off herunterfallen **6-U2**, T2
   fall over hinfallen, umkippen
      8-U1, Sit1
false falsch, unrichtig **8-U1**, Ex12
family Familie **5-U1**, WPA
famous berühmt **6-U1**, WPA
fan Anhänger/in, Fan **5-U2**, T2
fancy mögen **6-U3**, T2
fantastic wundervoll **5-U2**, T1
far weit **5-U5**, T1
farm Bauernhof **6-U2**, WPA
farmer Bauer, Bäuerin **5-U3**, Song
farmhouse Bauernhaus **8-U4**, Read
fashion Mode **7-U3**, T1
fast schnell **5-U5**, WPA

fat dick, fett **7-U4**, T2
father Vater **5-U2**, Sit4
fault Fehler **6-U6**, T2
favour Gefallen **6-U6**, T2
favourite Lieblings- **5-U1**, Sit2
February Februar **5-U4**, Sit5
Federal Bureau of Investigation/FBI FBI
   8-U1, Read
fed up, be die Nase voll haben **6-U1**, T2
feed füttern **5-U3**, WPA
feel (sich) fühlen **6-U2**, T1
feeling Gefühl **7-U2**, T2
female weiblich **7-U3**, Read
fence Zaun **5-U3**, T1
festival Fest, Festival **6-U4**, WPB
fetch holen **7-U5**, T2
fever Fieber **8-U3**, Read
few, a ein paar **6-U4**, Sit2
field Feld **7-U1**, WP
fifteen fünfzehn **5-U0**, G
fifty fünfzig **5-U1**, Sit5
fight Kampf, Streit **8-U3**, Sit2
fight kämpfen **7-U2**, WP
fill füllen **8-U3**, T2
film Film **5-U1**, Sit1
filthy dreckig **7-U5**, T1
final letzte(r,s), endgültig **7-U4**, T2
finally schließlich **7-U4**, T2
find finden **5-U0**, J
   find out herausfinden **6-U3**
fine gut, schön **5-U0**, B
fine Bußgeld verhängen **8-U3**, T2
finish beenden **5-U4**, WPA
fire Feuer **6-U4**, WPA
fire feuern, schießen **6-U4**, T2
fire-eater Feuerschlucker **6-U1**, WPA
firewood Brennholz **8-U3**, Read
fireworks Feuerwerk **6-U4**, WPA
first erste, erster, erstes **5-U1**, Sit3
   first aid erste Hilfe **7-U5**, WP
fish Fisch **7-U5**, Ex6
fish fischen, angeln **8-U3**, Sit1
fishing boat Fischerboot **8-U3**, Sit1
fit fit, geeignet, gesund **7-U5**, Rev
fix befestigen **6-U5**, T2
fix reparieren **8-U3**, Ex8
flag Flagge **8-U2**, WP
flashing blinkend, blitzend **8-U1**, T2
flat flach **8-U2**, Read
flat Wohnung **5-U2**, WPA
fleet Flotte **7-U4**, TYE
flight Flug **5-U7**, Ex2
flipper Flosse, Schwimmflosse **8-U4**, TYE
floor (Fuß)Boden **5-U5**, Sit1
floor Stockwerk, Etage **8-U1**, T1
flower Blume **6-U2**, WPB
flute Flöte **7-U3**, Ex11
fly fliegen **5-U1**, Sit8
follow folgen **6-U6**, T1
food Essen, Lebensmittel **5-U4**, WPC
fool Narr, Dummkopf **6-U4**, WPD
fool zum Narren halten **8-U1**, Read

foot Fuß **5-U5**, T1
football Fußball **5-U1**, Ex10
footballer Fußballspieler/in **6-U1**, Ex2
for für **5-U1**, WPB
   for Christ's sake um Gottes willen!
      8-U2, Read
   for example zum Beispiel **7-U4**, T2
   for sale zu verkaufen **7-U4**, Read
for seit **7-U1**, Sit4
forbid verbieten, untersagen **7-U1**, Read
forecast Vorhersage **6-U3**, Sit1
foreign language Fremdsprache **8-Rev4**
foreleg Vorderbein **7-U1**, Read
forest Wald, Forst **6-U2**, Sit3
forget vergessen **5-U4**, T2
form Form **6-U1**, Ex4
form formen, bilden **8-U1**, Read
formal Tanzveranstaltung **8-U2**, T1
formation Bildung; Formation **8-U4**, T2
Formula One Formel 1 **5-U2**, T1
fort Festung, Fort **8-U4**, Ex7
forty vierzig **5-U1**, Sit5
forward(s) vorwärts **7-U1**, Ex3
found (be)gründen **8-Lit**
foundation Stiftung; Gründung **7-U3**, Read
four vier **5-U0**, G
fourteen vierzehn **5-U0**, G
free kostenlos, frei **5-U7**, Sit1
freedom Freiheit **8-U1**, Sit3
freeway (gebührenfreie) Autobahn **8-U2**,
   Read
freeze frieren, gefrieren **8-U4**, Read
freezing kalt, frierend **7-U5**, T1
French Französisch; französisch
   5-U1, Sit3
french fries Pommes frites **6-U7**, Ex1
fresh frisch **7-U1**, Read
freshman Student/in im ersten
   Studienjahr **8-Proj2**
Friday Freitag **5-U1**, Sit4
friend Freund/in **5-U1**,
friendly freundlich **6-U7**, T2
frighten jdn erschrecken **8-U4**, T2
from von, aus **5-U0**, A
front Vorderseite **6-U2**, T1
frontier Grenze, Grenzgebiet **8-Lit**
frozen gefroren, tiefgefroren **7-U5**, T1
full voll **5-U7**, T2
fun Spaß **6-U4**, WPD
funny witzig, komisch, seltsam **5-U7**, T2
furious wütend **7-U4**, T2
further weiter **8-Lit**
future Zukunft **6-U5**, Sit1

Gg

Gaeltacht Gebiet, in dem Gälisch
   gesprochen wird **7-U1**, T1
game Spiel **5-U1**, Sit7
gang Bande, Gang **8-U1**, Read
gangster Gangster, Verbrecher
   8-U1, T2
garage Garage **5-U2**, WPA
garbage Müll, Abfall **6-U7**, Sit4

Index

garden Garten **5-U2**, WPA
gas Benzin **6-U7**, Ex1
gate Tor **6-U5**, T2
gentle sanft **8-U4**, Read
genuine echt, unverfälscht **7-U4**, Ex10
geography Geografie **8-U2**, Read
German Deutsch; deutsch; Deutsche/r **5-U0**, A
get holen **5-U3**, T1
get bekommen, werden **6-U3**, T2
   get clean sauber machen, sauber bringen **6-U5**, WPB
   get home heimkommen **5-U2**, T1
   get in einsteigen (in) **5-U1**, T2
   get mad with someone mit jemandem böse werden **8-U3**, Sit2
   get on with auskommen mit **7-U3**, T2
   get out (of) aussteigen, herauskommen **7-U1**, T2
   get ready vorbereiten **6-U5**, Sit2
   get to gehen zu, kommen zu **6-U6**, T1
   get up aufstehen **5-U1**, Sit6
   get used to sich gewöhnen an **8-U4**, T2
ghetto Getto, abgesondertes Wohnviertel **7-U1**, Read
ghost Geist, Gespenst **6-U6**, WPA
gift Geschenk **8-U3**, Sit2
gig Konzert, Auftritt **7-U3**, Sit1
girl Mädchen **5-U1**, WPA
girlfriend (feste) Freundin **5-U1**, Song
give geben **5-U3**, Sit1
   give away abgeben, verschenken **8-U2**, T2
   give in nachgeben **8-U3**, T2
   give somebody a lift jemanden im Auto mitnehmen **7-U4**, Sit3
   give up aufgeben, verzichten auf **8-U3**, T2
glad froh **6-U4**, T2
glass Glas **6-U3**, Ex14
glasses Brille **7-U4**, Com
go gehen **5-U0**, A
   go on weitermachen, weitergehen **8-U3**, T2
goal Tor **7-U3**, Read
goalkeeper Torwart **8-U2**, Ex12
God Gott **6-U4**, T1
going to, be werden **6-U3**, Sit1
go-kart Gokart **5-U7**, Sit4
gold Gold **7-U5**, WP
golden golden, aus Gold **6-U7**,
golf Golf **8-U4**, T1
good gut **5-U1**, Sit2
   good at doing sth, be gut sein in, etwas gut können **8-U2**, TYE
goodbye auf Wiedersehen **5-U0**, B
government Regierung **8-U3**, Sit2
gown Robe, Talar **7-U2**, TYE
graduate die Abschlussprüfung bestehen **8-U2**, T1
graffiti Graffiti **8-U1**, T1
grandad Opa **5-U5**, Sit3

grandma Oma **6-U3**, Sit1
grandparents Großeltern **6-U2**, WPA
grandson Enkel(sohn) **7-U3**, T2
grass Gras **5-U3**, WPA
grateful dankbar **8-U4**, Read
great großartig **5-U1**, Sit2
great-grandfather Urgroßvater **8-U1**, TYE3
green grün **5-U0**, C
grey grau **7-U4**, Com
grizzly bear Grizzlybär **5-U0**, Song
grocery (store) Lebensmittelgeschäft **8-U1**, Read
ground Grund, Boden **6-U2**, WPB
   ground floor Erdgeschoss **5-U2**, WPB
group Gruppe **5-U1**, Ex4
grow anbauen; wachsen **8-U3**, T1
guard Polizist/in (in Irland) **7-U1**, T2
guess raten, schätzen **6-U2**, Ex7
guest Gast **6-U6**, WPA
   guest house Gästehaus, Pension **7-U1**, Sit1
guidance counselor Schulberater/in **8-Proj2**
guide Führer/in **6-U2**, T1
guitar Gitarre **5-U0**, E
gulf Golf **6-U7**, Song
gun Schusswaffe **5-U3**, Song
gunpowder Schießpulver **6-U4**, T1
guy Typ, Bursche **6-U4**, WPA

Hh

hair Haar **6-U2**, Sit2
half halb **5-U1**, Sit5
   half past (ten) halb (elf) **5-U1**, Sit5
half-term Schulferien **5-U4**, Sit5
halfway auf halbem Weg; die halbe Strecke **8-U3**, TYE
hall Flur **5-U2**, WPB
ham Schinken **7-U5**, T1
hamburger Hamburger **5-U4**, WPA
hamster Hamster **5-U3**, WPA
hand Hand **5-U6**, T1
handsome gut aussehend **8-U1**, Read
hang aufhängen; erhängen **8-U3**, Sit3
   hang around herumlungern, herumhängen **7-U1**, Read
happen passieren **6-U2**, Ex3
happy glücklich, froh **5-U0**, G
   Happy birthday! Herzlichen Glückwunsch zum Geburtstag! **5-U0**, G
hard hart, schwer, schwierig **5-U6**, T1
hardly kaum **5-U6**, T1
hate hassen, gar nicht mögen **5-U5**, Sit2
haunted Spuk- **7-U4**, Read
have got haben, besitzen **5-U0**, E
have to müssen **6-U6**, T1
he er **5-U1**, WPA
head Kopf, Oberhaupt **6-U2**, Ex7
headache Kopfschmerzen **7-U1**, Ex14
heading Überschrift **8-U2**, Ex14
headlights Scheinwerfer (Auto) **8-Rev1**
headline Schlagzeile **8-U2**, Ex11

healthy gesund **8-U3**, T1
hear hören **5-U7**, T1
heat Hitze **8-U3**, Read
heavy schwer **7-U2**, TYE
   heavy metal Heavy Metal **8-U1**, Sit1
hedge Hecke **6-U6**, T1
hello hallo **5-U0**, A
help helfen **5-U3**, Com
help Hilfe **6-U5**, Sit2
hen Henne, Huhn **6-U2**, WPA
her ihr, ihre, ihr **5-U1**, T1
her sie; ihr **5-U2**, Sit5
here hier; hierher **5-U0**, F
hero Held **7-U3**, Proj
hers ihr(e, s) **6-U3**, Sit2
herself sich; selbst **8-U3**, Sit3
hey hey! **5-U7**, T1
hi hallo **5-U0**, A
hide (sich) verstecken **7-U1**, Read
high hoch **5-U7**, T2
   high school Oberschule **6-U3**, T2
highway Hauptverkehrsstraße **6-U7**, Song
hill Hügel **6-U7**, WPA
him ihn, ihm **5-U2**, Sit5
himself sich; selbst **8-U3**, Sit3
Hindu Hindu **6-U4**, WPB
hip hop Hip-Hop **8-U1**, T2
hire mieten; jdn anstellen **8-U3**, Read
his sein, seine, sein **5-U1**, WPB
Hispanic hispanisch; Hispanoamerikaner/in **8-U1**, WP
hiss zischen; fauchen **8-U4**, T2
history Geschichte **6-U3**, WPE
hit schlagen, treffen **6-U7**, Sit3
hit Hit **7-U3**, T1
hockey Hockey **5-U5**, Sit2
hold halten **5-U4**, T1
hold enthalten, fassen **8-U1**, T1
hole Loch **5-U3**, T1
holiday Ferien, Urlaub **5-U4**, Sit5
home Heim, Zuhause **5-U1**, Sit6
homeless obdachlos **7-U5**, TYE
homework Hausaufgaben **5-U1**, Sit6
honey Honig **6-U5**, WPA
hoot hupen (Auto): rufen (Eule) **7-U2**, Read
hope hoffen **5-U2**, T2
   hope to do sth hoffen, etwas zu tun **7-U2**, TYE6
hopeful optimistisch, voller Hoffnung **7-U3**, T2
hopeless hoffnungslos **6-U1**, T1
horrible fürchterlich, schrecklich **6-U1**, T2
horror Horror **7-U4**, T1
horse Pferd **6-U2**, WPA
hospital Krankenhaus **5-U6**, WPA
host Gastgeber/in; Moderator/in **8-U2**, T2
hot heiß **5-U7**, WPD
hot-air balloon Heißluftballon **7-U5**, Rev
hotel Hotel **5-U7**, WPD

Index

hour Stunde **5-U5**, Sit3
house Haus **5-U0**, G
housing Unterbringung, Wohnungen **8-U3**, T2
how wie **5-U0**, B
  how about …? wie wär's mit …? **8-U2**, Ex9
  how many … ? wie viele …? **5-U0**, H
  how much … ? wie viel … ? **5-U6**, Sit3
however jedoch **8-U2**, T2
huge riesig **6-U7**, WPA
human Menschen-; menschlich **8-U4**, TYE
hundred hundert **5-U4**, WPA
hungry hungrig **5-U4**, WPA
hunt jagen **8-U3**, T1
hunter Jäger/in **8-U3**, TYE3
hurricane Wirbelsturm **8-U4**, T1
hurry Eile **7-U1**, T2
hurry eilen, sich beeilen **5-U1**, Sit6
  hurry (up) sich beeilen **5-U1**, T2
hurt schmerzen, weh tun **5-U6**, T1
husband Ehemann **6-U1**, Sit1
hutch Kaninchenstall **5-U3**, WPA

Ii

I ich **5-U0**, A
iceberg Eisberg **7-U3**, WP
ice-cream (Speise)Eis **5-U4**, WPA
ice-rink Eisbahn **7-U5**, TYE
idea Idee **5-U4**, T2
idiot Dummkopf, Idiot **5-U6**, T2
if ob **7-U2**, T1
if wenn, falls **6-U1**, Sit2
ill krank **6-U2**, Ex1
imagine sich vorstellen **5-U7**, WPD
immigrant Einwanderer/Einwanderin **8-U1**, TYE
immigration Einwanderung **8-U1**, TYE
important wichtig, bedeutend **7-U2**, T1
impress beeindrucken **8-U4**, Ex15
in in **5-U0**, A
  in a hurry in Eile **7-U1**, T2
  in a mess durcheinander, in Unordnung **7-U5**, T2
  in fact eigentlich, tatsächlich **8-U1**, T2
  in front of vor **5-U2**, WPA
  in trouble in Schwierigkeiten **7-U3**, Sit1
inch Inch, Zoll **7-U5**, Read
include einschließen, beinhalten **7-U5**, Read
increase zunehmen, anwachsen **8-U2**, Sit5
independence Unabhängigkeit **8-U2**, WP
independent (of/from) unabhängig **8-U3**, Sit5
Indian Indianer/in; Inder/in **8-U2**, Ex7
individual einzeln, individuell **8-U2**, Sit5
information Information(en) **5-U7**, Ex3
injure verletzen **8-U2**, Sit2
in-line skates Inlineskates, Rollerblades **5-U5**, WPA
inn Gasthaus **7-U2**, T2
inside innen, drinnen **6-U6**, T1

instead of anstatt **8-U1**, Ex1
interest Interesse **7-U2**, Com
interested in, be interessiert sein (an) **6-U3**, T2
  interested in doing sth, be interessiert daran sein, etwas zu tun **8-U4**, T1
interesting interessant **6-U1**, WPA
international international **7-U5**, TYE
internet Internet **6-U3**, WPC
interpreter Dolmetscher/in **8-U1**, TYE2
inter-school zwischen Schulen **8-U2**, Sit3
intersection Kreuzung, Autobahnkreuz **8-U2**, Read
interview interviewen **6-U2**, Ex9
interviewer Interviewer/in **8-U3**, Com
into hinein, in **6-U2**, T1
introduction Einführung **5-U1**, Intro
invade einmarschieren in, eindringen in **7-U4**, WP
invader Eindringling, Angreifer/in **7-U4**, WP
invent erfinden **8-U2**, TYE
invention Erfindung **8-U2**, TYE
invisible unsichtbar **7-U5**, Read
invitation Einladung **7-U1**, Com
invite einladen **6-U6**, WPC
Irish irisch **7-U1**, WP
iron Eisen **7-U4**, T1
island Insel **6-U7**, Song
it es **5-U0**, W
  it's fun es macht Spaß **6-U4**, WPD
  It's my turn. Ich bin dran. **5-U1**, T2
Italian italienisch; Italiener/in **8-U1**, TYE4
italics Kursivdruck **7-U1**, Ex6
its sein, seine, sein; ihr, ihre, ihr **5-U3**, Sit1
itself sich; selbst **8-U3**, Sit3

Jj

jacket Jacke, Jackett **5-U4**, Ex16
jail Gefängnis **8-U1**, Read
jam Marmelade, Konfitüre **6-U5**, WPA
January Januar **5-U4**, Sit5
jeans Jeans **6-U6**, Com
jet lag Jetlag **6-U7**, T1
Jew Jude, Jüdin **8-U1**, WP
jewelry Schmuck, Juwelen **8-U2**, TYE
job Job, Arbeitsplatz **5-U2**, T1
jockey Jockey **7-U1**, Read
join verbinden, sich anschließen **7-U2**, Sit4
joke Witz, Scherz **6-U1**, Sit4
journey Reise **5-U7**, WPC
judo Judo **5-U5**, WPB
juggler Jongleur/in **6-U1**, WPA
July Juli **5-U4**, Sit5
jump springen **5-U5**, WPA
junction Straßenkreuzung, Verkehrsknotenpunkt **8-U2**, Read
June Juni **5-U4**, Sit5
junior Student/in im vorletzten Studienjahr **8-U2**, T1

just genau, gerade **6-U4**, Sit3
just nur, bloß **5-U4**, T1

Kk

keep halten, behalten **6-U5**, WPC
  keep back zurückbleiben, zurückhalten **6-U2**, T2
  keep out fernhalten, nicht hereinlassen **7-U2**, WP
key Schlüssel **7-U2**, Read
keyboard Keyboard (Musikinstrument) **7-U3**, T2
kick (mit dem Fuß) treten **7-U1**, T2
kid Kind **5-U5**, WPB
kid Spaß machen, jdn aufziehen **8-U4**, Sit1
kill töten, umbringen **7-U2**, T1
killer Mörder/in **8-U1**, Read
king König **6-U1**, T2
kingdom Königreich **7-U1**, WP
kiss Kuss **6-U7**, T2
kitchen Küche **5-U2**, T1
knee Knie **5-U5**, T1
knife Messer **7-U2**, T2
knight Ritter **7-U2**, WP
knock klopfen **7-U4**, Read
know wissen, kennen **5-U2**, Sit2

Ll

label Etikett, Schildchen **6-U5**, Ex17
lady Dame **6-U1**, Song
lake See **5-U7**, T2
land Land, Boden **6-U7**, Song
land landen **6-U2**, T2
landlord Wirt; Vermieter **7-U4**, Read
lane Feldweg, Gasse **7-U1**, T2
language Sprache **7-U3**, Sit3
large groß **5-U4**, Sit4
last letzte(r, s) **6-U2**, Sit2
late spät **5-U1**, Sit1
later später **5-U7**, T1
laugh (at) lachen (über) **6-U4**, T2
launch abschießen (Rakete); vom Stapel lassen (Schiff) **8-U4**, T1
law Gesetz, Recht **7-U1**, Read
lay legen; verlegen **8-U3**, T1
  lay the table den Tisch decken **6-U4**, Sit3
lead führen, leiten **8-U2**, T1
leader (An)führer/in **8-U3**, T1
league Bündnis, Liga **6-U3**, T1
learn lernen, erfahren **5-U1**, Sit8
  learn to do sth lernen, etwas zu tun **7-U3**, Ex11
leave verlassen, weggehen, abfahren **5-U1**, Sit6
leave lassen, liegen lassen **5-U5**, Sit1
left links **5-U6**, WPB
left, be übrig sein **7-U3**, Sit1
leg Bein **5-U5**, T1
lemonade Zitronenlimonade **6-U5**, T2
lend leihen **6-U4**, Sit4
less weniger **8-U3**, Sit2

Index

lesson Unterrichtsstunde **5-U1**, Ex4
let lassen **8-U3**, T2
   let out hinauslassen, herauslassen **5-U3**, WPA
   let's Lass(t) uns **5-U0**, A
letter Brief **5-U6**, Sit1
letter Buchstabe **6-U1**, Ex19
liberty Freiheit **8-U1**, WP
library Bibliothek, Bücherei **5-U5**, T2
license Erlaubnis; Führerschein **8-U1**, Sit3
lie Lüge **7-U5**, Read
lie liegen **6-U2**, WPB
life Leben **5-U6**, T1
lift Mitfahrgelegenheit **7-U4**, Sit3
lift hochheben **6-U2**, T2
light Licht **6-U2**, T1
light anzünden **6-U4**, WPA
like wie **5-U7**, WPD
like mögen **5-U1**, Sit7
   like doing sth etwas gerne tun **7-U1**, Sit1
   like to do sth etwas gerne tun **8-U1**, Sit2
limousine Limousine **8-Rev11**
line Linie, Zeile **6-U1**, WPB
line Reihe, Schlange **8-U1**, T1
link Link, Verknüpfung im Internet **8-Proj4**
lion Löwe **7-U1**, TYE
lip Lippe **8-U4**, T2
list Liste **5-U5**, PYE6
listen (to) zuhören **5-U1**, Sit8
liter Liter **8-U4**, T1
litter Abfall **8-U1**, T1
little klein **5-U0**, Song
little wenig **8-U2**, Read
live leben, wohnen **5-U0**, A
lively lebendig, rege, lebhaft **6-U1**, WPA
living-room Wohnzimmer **5-U2**, WPB
load laden, beladen **6-U4**, PYE2
local örtlich, am Ort, Lokal- **8-U2**, Sit3
locked verschlossen **7-U2**, T2
Londoner Londoner, Bewohner Londons **7-U5**, TYE3
long lang **5-U1**, T2
look schauen **5-U2**, Sit5
   look after sich kümmern um **6-U1**, T1
   look for suchen **5-U6**, WPB
   look forward to sich freuen auf **6-U1**, Ex5
   look, have a etwas ansehen **8-U1**, T1
   Look out! Pass auf! **5-U5**, T1
   look round sich umschauen **6-U3**, Sit1
look aussehen **6-U1**, T2
Lord Lord **6-U4**, T1
lorry LKW **6-U7**, Ex1
lose verlieren **6-U4**, Sit1
lost, get sich verlaufen **6-U6**, T1
lot of, a eine Menge, viel **6-U1**, Sit2
lots of viel **6-U7**, Sit2
loud laut **8-U1**, Sit1
love herzliche Grüße **5-U4**, T2
love Liebe **5-U5**, PYE4
love lieben **6-U2**, T1

lovely schön, hübsch **6-U2**, WPB
luck Glück **6-U7**, T2
lucky Glück haben **5-U1**, T1
lunch Mittagessen **5-U3**, WPA
lunchtime Mittagsstunde **5-U3**, WPA
lynch lynchen **8-U3**, T2

Mm

machine Maschine **6-U5**, WPD
madam meine Dame, gnädige Frau **5-U7**, Sit5
magazine Zeitschrift **5-U5**, WPB
magic Magie, Zauberkunst **7-U2**, T1
magician Zauberer, Magier **7-U2**, T1
magnificent prächtig, großartig **7-U5**, Read
mail schicken, aufgeben **6-U7**, Ex1
main Haupt-, hauptsächlich **6-U6**, T1
major Major **8-U3**, Read
major größer, bedeutend **6-U3**, T1
make machen **5-U4**, Sit1
   make a mess of verkorksen, verpfuschen, Mist bauen **7-U3**, T2
   make sure sicherstellen, sorgen für **7-U4**, WP
man Mann **5-U3**, Sit3
manager Geschäftsführer, Manager, Filialleiter/in **6-U5**, WPA
manatee Seekuh **8-U4**, TYE
man-eater Menschenfresser **8-Rev10**
many viele **5-U7**, Sit4
map Landkarte **5-U7**, T1
March März **5-U4**, Sit5
Mardi Gras Mardi Gras (Karneval) **8-U2**, WP
market Markt **6-U5**, WPB
marmalade Marmelade aus Zitrusfrüchten **6-U5**, WPA
marriage Ehe, Hochzeit **7-U4**, T2
marry heiraten **7-U2**, T1
marvellous fabelhaft **7-U2**, T2
master Meister, Herr **7-U5**, Read
match passend zusammenfügen, zusammenpassen **7-U4**, Ex5
math Mathematik *AE* **8-U1**, Ex11
maths Mathematik *BE* **5-U1**, Ex4
matter Angelegenheit **6-U4**, T1
May Mai **5-U4**, Sit5
may I? darf ich? **5-U7**, Sit5
maybe vielleicht **5-U7**, T2
maze Labyrinth **6-U6**, T1
me mich; mir **5-U2**, Sit5
meal Mahlzeit **5-U4**, WPB
mean meinen, sagen wollen **5-U6**, T2
mean bedeuten **7-U1**, T1
mean gemein, geizig **6-U6**, T2
meaning Bedeutung **7-U5**, Ex4
meanwhile inzwischen **6-U7**, T1
measure messen **8-Lit**
meat Fleisch **7-U5**, Sket2
media Medien **7-U3**, TYE
medical medizinisch **8-Rev8**
medium mittelgroß **5-U4**, Sit4

meeow Miau **7-U4**, Read
meet treffen **6-U6**, WPA
member Mitglied **6-U3**, T1
memory Erinnerung, Gedächtnis; Arbeitsspeicher **7-U5**, Read
mention erwähnen **8-U2**, TYE1
menu Speisekarte **5-U4**, WPA
mess Durcheinander **7-U5**, T2
message Mitteilung, Nachricht, Botschaft **6-U3**, WPC
metal Metall **8-U1**, Sit1
metre Meter **5-U7**, T2
microwave Mikrowelle **7-U5**, Read
middle Mitte **6-U6**, T1
midnight Mitternacht **8-U1**, T2
midtown Manhattan Stadtteil von Manhattan zwischen der 42. und 59. Straße **8-U1**, T1
might könnte (vielleicht) **7-U3**, T1
mile Meile **5-U1**, Sit6
milk Milch **5-U4**, WPA
milk melken **8-U2**, Ex1
millennium Jahrtausend, Millennium **6-U1**, WPA
million Million **6-U3**, WPC
millionaire Millionär **6-U6**, WPC
mine meine(r, s) **6-U3**, Sit2
minibus Kleinbus **7-U5**, T1
mini-golf Minigolf **5-U2**, Sit1
minister Minister/in **7-U4**, T2
minus minus **8-U4**, WP
minute Minute **5-U1**, Sit1
mirror Spiegel **8-U3**, Sit5
miss verpassen **6-U6**, T1
missing fehlend, nicht vorhanden **6-U1**, Ex8
mission Mission, Auftrag; Missionsstation **6-U7**, WPA
mistake Fehler **7-U3**, Ex12
mixture Mischung, Gemisch **7-U1**, Proj
mobile (phone) Handy **6-U2**, T2
model Modell; Fotomodell **6-U1**, Ex20
modern modern **7-U5**, TYE
mom Mama **6-U7**, T1
moment Moment **6-U2**, T1
Monday Montag **5-U1**, Sit4
money Geld **5-U4**, Sit3
monster Ungeheuer, Scheusal, Monster **7-U4**, T2
month Monat **5-U4**, Sit5
moon Mond **8-U3**, WP
more mehr **6-U1**, Com
morning Morgen **5-U1**, Sit6
most meiste(r, s) **5-U6**, T2
mostly hauptsächlich **8-U4**, T1
motel Motel **8-U4**, Sit3
mother Mutter **5-U2**, Sit2
motor Motor, Auto- **8-U4**, WP
motorbike Motorrad **8-U4**, Ex7
motor-racing Autorennen **7-U3**, Read
mountain Berg **5-U2**, Song
   mountain bike Mountainbike **8-U4**, Sit1
mouse Maus **5-U3**, WPB

Index

mouth Mund **6-U6**, Com
mouth Mündung (Fluss) **8-U3**, T1
move (sich) bewegen, umziehen **5-U5**, T2
movement Bewegung **8-U1**, TYE
movie Film **6-U7**, WPA
Mr Herr **5-U0**, F
Mrs Frau **5-U0**, B
much viel **5-U5**, Sit3
mug überfallen und ausrauben **8-U1**, Read
mum Mutti, Mama **5-U1**, WPC
murder Mord **8-U2**, TYE4
museum Museum **6-U1**, Sit2
music Musik **5-U1**, Sit3
musical Musical **7-U1**, T1
   musical instrument Musikinstrument
     6-U6, Ex2
must müssen **5-U6**, Sit1
mustn't nicht dürfen **7-U5**, Sit3
my mein, meine, mein **5-U0**, A
myself mich, mir; selbst **8-U3**, Sit3

Nn
nachos Nachos **8-U1**, T2
name Name **5-U0**, A
name nennen **7-U1**, TYE1
national national, National- **6-U7**, WPA
native gebürtig; eingeboren; Einge-
   borene/r **8-U3**, WP
natural history Naturkunde,
   Naturgeschichte **8-U1**, Ex7
near nah **5-U1**, Sit6
neat ordentlich, sauber, gepflegt
   7-U5, Read
necessary notwendig **8-Rev14**
need brauchen **5-U4**, Sit1
   need to do sth etwas tun müssen
     7-U1, Com
   needn't nicht müssen, nicht brauchen
     7-U5, Sit3
needle Nadel **7-U1**, Read
negative negativ **7-U2**, Sit1
neighbour Nachbar/in **5-U3**, Sit1
nephew Neffe **8-U1**, Read
nervous nervös **6-U6**, Ex9
network Sendenetz (TV, Radio) **8-U2**, T2
never niemals **5-U5**, Sit2
   never mind macht nichts, vergiss es
     6-U1, T2
new neu **5-U0**, E
news Neuigkeit(en), Nachricht(en)
   6-U3, WPC
newspaper Tageszeitung **6-U3**, WPD
next nächste(r, s) **5-U3**, T1
   next time (the) das nächste Mal
     7-U5, TYE4
nice nett, schön, hübsch **5-U1**, Sit2
night Nacht **5-U7**, Sit1
nine neun **5-U0**, G
nineteen neunzehn **5-U0**, G
ninety neunzig **5-U4**, WPA
no nein **5-U0**, B
no kein(e) **6-U1**, T1
   no one niemand **7-U1**, T2

nobody niemand **7-U2**, Read
noise Lärm **6-U2**, T1
non-white farbig; Farbige/r **7-U5**, TYE
noon Mittag **8-Rev9**
Norman normannisch; Normanne,
   Normannin **7-U4**, WP
north Norden **5-U7**, T1
northern nördlich, Nord- **7-U1**, WP
nose Nase **6-U6**, Com
not nicht **5-U0**, B
   not ... either auch nicht **8-U3**, WP
note Notiz **7-U3**, Ex14
   note down notieren, aufschreiben
     8-U1, Ex11
nothing nichts **6-U2**, T2
notice bemerken **7-U2**, T2
notice Zettel, Notiz **7-U5**, Sket1
November November **5-U4**, Sit5
novel Roman, **8-Rev8**
now jetzt **5-U0**, F
nowhere nirgendwo **7-U3**, T2
nuisance Ärgernis, Quälgeist **7-U3**, Sit2
number Zahl **5-U0**, G

Oo
oasis Oase **8-U4**, T2
observatory Sternwarte, Observatorium
   7-U2, TYE
obsolete veraltet **7-U5**, Read
occur geschehen **7-U3**, Ex1
ocean Meer, Ozean **6-U7**, WPB
o'clock Uhr **5-U1**, Sit5
October Oktober **5-U4**, Sit5
odd word out Wort, das anders ist
   6-U2, Ex16
of von **5-U1**, Sit2
   of course natürlich **5-U1**, Sit8
off von ... herunter, weg **6-U2**, T2
offensive beleidigend, kränkend **8-U3**, T1
offensive offensiv; Angriff(s-) **8-Proj5**
offer anbieten **7-U3**, T2
office Büro **6-U5**, WPD
   office block Bürogebäude, Büro-
     komplex **7-U1**, WP
officer Beamte, Beamtin **5-U7**, Sit5
often häufig, oft **5-U3**, PYE3
oil Öl **8-U4**, WP
OK O.K. **5-U0**, B
old alt **5-U0**, G
on auf **5-U1**, T2
   on foot zu Fuß **7-U5**, Sit3
   on (Monday) am (Montag) **5-U1**, Sit4
   on time pünktlich **5-U1**, Sit6
   on top of auf, über, obendrauf **8-U4**, T2
   on your own (ganz) allein **6-U1**, T2
once einmal **6-U5**, Sit4
one eins **5-U0**, G
only nur, bloß **5-U5**, Sit3
onto auf ...(hinauf) **6-U3**, Ex7
open offen, geöffnet **7-U1**, TYE
open öffnen **5-U0**, F
opinion Meinung **7-U3**, T2
opportunity Gelegenheit, Chance
   8-U1, Sit1

opportunity to do sth Gelegenheit,
   Chance, etwas zu tun **8-U1**, Sit1
opposite Gegenteil **5-U5**, Ex16
or oder **5-U0**, I
   or so ungefähr **7-U4**, Read
orange Orange, Apfelsine **5-U6**, Sit4
   orange juice Orangensaft
     5-U4, WPA
order Reihenfolge **5-U7**, Ex9
ordinary normal, gewöhnlich
   7-U3, WP
organization Organisation **8-U3**, Sit4
organize organisieren **7-U3**, Sit1
origin Ursprung, Herkunft
   7-U5, TYE
other andere(r, s) **5-U4**, Ex6
ought to sollte **7-U4**, T1
our unser, unsere, unser **5-U3**, Sit1
ours unsere(r, s) **6-U3**, Sit3
ourselves uns; selbst **8-U3**, Sit3
outlaw Gesetzlose/r **7-U5**, Sket2
out (of) hinaus **5-U1**, Sit7
outside draußen **6-U1**, Sit4
outside außerhalb **7-U2**, Ex6
over zu Ende **7-U1**, T2
   over über **5-U3**, T1
   over über, mehr als **7-U1**, TYE
   over and over (again) immer wieder **8-U4**, T2
   over there dort drüben **6-U1**, T2
overnight über Nacht, ganz plötzlich **7-U3**, Sit1
owl Eule **7-U2**, Read
own eigen **5-U2**, WPB
owner Besitzer/in, Eigentümer/in **7-U5**, Rev
ox Ochse **8-U3**, Read

Pp
pack (ver)packen, einpacken **7-U5**, T2
packet Paket **5-U5**, PYE4
page Seite **5-U1**, Ex1
pain Schmerz **7-U5**, T1
paint malen, streichen **6-U5**, T2
painter Maler **7-U4**, TYE4
pair Paar **6-U4**, Ex1
palace Palast **6-U1**, WPA
paper Papier **6-U5**, T2
parade Umzug, Festzug, Parade **8-U2**, WP
paragliding Drachenfliegen, Paragliding
   7-U5, WP
paragraph Absatz, Abschnitt **6-U6**, Ex8
paramedic Rettungsassistent/in **6-U2**, T2
pardon? Verzeihung? **7-U5**, T2
parents Eltern **5-U2**, T2
park Park **5-U2**, Sit3
park parken **8-U1**, T1
parliament Parlament **6-U1**, WPA
part Teil **6-U1**, T1
part Rolle **7-U2**, Sit4
partner Partner/in **5-U5**, WPB
party Party, Feier **5-U4**, WPC
pass bestehen (Prüfung) **8-U1**, Sit3

one hundred and fifty-three   **153**

Index

passenger Fahrgast, Passagier/in
8-U1, TYE
passport Reisepass **5-U7**, Sit3
past Vergangenheit **6-U2**, Sit2
past nach **5-U1**, Sit5
path Fußweg, Pfad **5-U5**, T1
pattern Muster **8-U1**, Ex7
pavement Gehsteig **8-U1**, Ex15
pay zahlen **6-U5**, T2
peace Friede **8-U3**, T1
pen Füllfederhalter, Füller **5-U0**, D
  pen pal Brieffreund/in **8-U2**, T1
pencil Bleistift **5-U0**, D
penny Penny **5-U4**, WPA
people Leute **5-U3**, Sit3
perform spielen, vorführen **7-U3**, Sit3
perhaps vielleicht **7-U2**, Sit2
period (Unterrichts-)Stunde **8-U2**, Sit2
person Person **5-U1**, T1
pet Haustier **5-U3**, WPA
  pet shop Tierhandlung **5-U6**, WPB
petrol Benzin **6-U7**, Ex1
  petrol station Tankstelle **5-U2**, T1
phone telefonieren **5-U5**, PYE4
photo Foto **5-U1**, Sit2
photocopy fotokopieren **7-U4**, Proj
photograph fotografieren **8-U4**, T1
phrase Ausdruck, Satzglied **6-U3**, WPC
physics Physik **8-U2**, Sit2
piano Klavier **5-U1**, Sit8
pick pflücken, auswählen **7-U4**, T1
  pick up aufheben, -sammeln **8-U3**, T2
picnic Picknick **7-U5**, Ex6
picture Bild **5-U1**, WP
pie Pastete, Obstkuchen **7-U5**, Read
piece Stück, Teil **6-U5**, T2
pig Schwein **6-U1**, Ex19
pilgrim Pilger/in **8-U3**, Sit1
pink rosarot **8-U4**, T1
pitcher Werfer **6-U7**, Sit3
pity, it's a schade **6-U5**, Com
pizza Pizza **5-U4**, WPA
place Ort, Platz **5-U6**, WPA
plan Plan **5-U2**, WPB
plan planen **8-U1**, Sit2
  plan to do sth planen, etwas zu tun
  8-U1, Sit2
plane Flugzeug **5-U7**, WPC
plant Pflanze **8-U4**, TYE
plant pflanzen **8-U3**, Read
plantation Pflanzung, Plantage **8-U3**, WP
plastic Plastik, Kunststoff **7-U4**, Com
plate Teller **5-U4**, WPA
play (Schau-)Spiel **7-U2**, Com
play spielen **5-U1**, Sit7
player Spieler/in **6-U7**, T1
playground Spielplatz **5-U6**, Sit2
play-off Entscheidungsspiel **8-U2**, T2
please bitte **5-U0**, F
plenty of eine Menge, viel **8-U4**, T1
plot Komplott, Verschwörung **6-U4**, T1
plotter Verschwörer/in **6-U4**, T1
plug Stecker, Stöpsel **7-U1**, Sit5

P.M./p.m./pm nach 12 Uhr **8-U1**, T1
pocket Tasche **6-U1**, T1
poem Gedicht **8-Lit**
point Punkt **8-U2**, T2
point zeigen **7-U5**, Sket1
poisonous giftig **8-U4**, Ex3
police Polizei **7-U1**, T2
policeman Polizist **5-U5**, T1
polite höflich **6-U1**, Com
polo Polo **7-U1**, TYE
pony Pony **6-U2**, WPA
pool Teich; Pfütze, Lache **8-U4**, T2
poor arm **5-U3**, T1
pop (music) Popmusik **5-U1**, Sit7
pope Papst **7-U4**, WP
popular beliebt **6-U1**, Sit2
population Bevölkerung **8-U2**, WP
posh chic, vornehm, nobel **7-U3**, WP
position Stellung, Lage **6-U7**, T1
positive positiv **7-U2**, Sit1
possible möglich **7-U5**, WP
post zur Post bringen **5-U6**, Sit1
  post office Postamt **5-U6**, WPA
postcard Postkarte **5-U7**, WPD
poster Poster **5-U0**, D
postman Postbote **5-U2**, T1
potato Kartoffel **6-U5**, T1
pound Pfund **5-U4**, WPA
pour gießen, sich ergießen **7-U5**, Sit1
power cut Stromsperre, Stromausfall
  8-U4, Read
powerful stark; mächtig **8-Rev3**
practice Training, Übung **7-U5**, T1
practise üben **5-U1**, PYE
  practise doing sth üben, etwas zu tun
  8-U1, Ex16
prairie Prärie, Grassteppe **8-U3**, Ex7
pray beten **8-U3**, Read
premier bedeutendste(r) **7-U5**, Read
present Geschenk **5-U3**, Sit5
present Gegenwart **6-U5**, Ex6
presentation Präsentation **8-Proj4**
presenter Moderator/in **6-U1**, T2
president Präsident/in **6-U1**, T2
pretty ziemlich **7-U5**, Read
pretty hübsch **8-U3**, Read
price Preis **6-U5**, T1
priest Priester/in **7-U2**, TYE
prince Prinz; Fürst **7-U3**, T1
princess Prinzessin **6-U1**, T2
principal Rektor/in **8-Proj2**
print (out) (aus)drucken **6-U3**, WPB
prison Gefängnis **6-U1**, WPA
prisoner Gefangene(r), Häftling **7-U4**, Sit5
prize Preis, Gewinn **6-U4**, Ex3
probably wahrscheinlich **6-U6**, T1
problem Problem **5-U1**, T2
produce erzeugen, herstellen **8-U4**, WP
product Produkt **8-U2**, Sit1
production Herstellung, Produktion
  8-U2, T1
professional Berufs-, Fach-, **8-U2**, T2
program Computerprogramm **8-Rev3**

programme Sendung **6-U6**, WPA
project Projekt **6-U2**, Sit2
promote werben (für); fördern **8-U4**, Ex3
propeller Schiffsschraube; Propeller
  8-U4, TYE
proper hinreichend, gebührend, richtig
  7-U1, Read
protect beschützen **8-U4**, TYE
protest protestieren **8-U3**, T2
proud (of) stolz (auf) **7-U1**, Read
pub Kneipe, Pub **7-U3**, Read
public öffentlich **5-U5**, T1
pull ziehen **7-U2**, T1
  pull down (ab-), einreißen **7-U5**, TYE
punish bestrafen **8-U3**, Sit3
pupil Schüler/in **5-U1**, WPB
purpose Zweck, Ziel, Absicht
  8-U1, Ex6
purse Geldbeutel **6-U5**, Sit2
purse Handtasche **8-U3**, T1
push schieben, anrempeln **5-U6**, T1
put setzen, stellen, legen **5-U3**, T1
  put in einstecken, einlegen **7-U1**, Sit5
  put on anziehen **8-U4**, T2
  put on anmachen, auflegen **7-U1**, Sit5
  put together zusammensetzen,
  zusammenlegen **8-U4**, Sit2
puzzle Rätsel, Geduldsspiel **6-U5**, Ex2

Qq

quarter Viertel **5-U1**, Sit5
queen Königin **6-U1**, WPA
question Frage **5-U2**, Sit2
questionnaire Fragebogen **7-U5**, Sket1
queue Warteschlange **6-U1**, Sit2
quick schnell **5-U3**, T1
quiet ruhig, still **5-U1**, T2
quite ziemlich **7-U4**, Com
quiz Quiz **5-U5**, Sit3

Rr

rabbit Kaninchen **5-U3**, WPA
race Rennen **5-U5**, T2
racket Tennisschläger **5-U2**, WPC
radio Radio **5-U1**, T2
railroad Eisenbahn **8-U3**, Sit4
rain regnen **5-U4**, Sit1
rain Regen **6-U1**, Ex13
ramp Rampe **7-U2**, TYE
rap Rap **8-U1**, T2
rattler Klapperschlange **8-U4**, T2
rattlesnake Klapperschlange **8-U3**, Read
raven Rabe **7-U1**, Sit2
reach erreichen **8-U1**, T1
read lesen **5-U1**, Sit7
ready fertig, bereit **5-U1**, T1
real echt **5-U3**, Sit4
realize erkennen, begreifen, klar werden
  8-U2, Read
really wirklich **5-U5**, Sit3
reason Grund, Begründung **8-Lit**
recognize erkennen, anerkennen
  8-U1, Read

Index

record aufnehmen **6-U6**, T2
recycle wieder verwerten **6-U7**, Sit4
red rot **5-U0**, C
redwood Redwood **6-U7**, WPA
refuse sich weigern **8-U2**, TYE
region Gebiet, Region **8-U3**, Sit1
relative Verwandte/r **5-U7**, WPC
relax sich erholen **7-U1**, T1
religion Religion **8-U1**, TYE
remember sich erinnern **5-U6**, Ex6
remind erinnern **7-U3**, T1
rent mieten, vermieten **8-U4**, T2
repair reparieren **7-U5**, Rev
repeat wiederholen **5-U5**, Ex17
report Bericht **6-U3**, T1
reporter Reporter/in **7-U2**, Ex3
republic Republik **7-U1**, WP
request Aufforderung, Bitte **8-U4**, Com
reservation Reservat; Reservierung
   8-U3, Ex7
residence Residenz, Amtssitz **7-U1**, TYE
resist widerstehen; sich widersetzen
   8-U4, Sit3
resolution Vorsatz, Beschluss **6-U3**, Ex2
resort Ferienort **6-U7**, WPA
rest Rest **6-U6**, Ex14
rest Ruhe **7-U4**, T1
rest ausruhen **8-U3**, Read
result Ergebnis **6-U3**, WPC
return zurückkehren **8-U1**, T2
revolt Aufstand, Aufruhr, Revolte
   6-U3, Sit3
rewrite umschreiben, neu schreiben
   7-U1, Ex6
rhyme (sich) reimen **7-U3**, T1
rich reich **6-U6**, WPC
ride Karussell, Fahrt **5-U7**, Sit4
rider Reiter/in; Radfahrer/in **8-U3**, TYE3
ridge Bergkamm, Grat **6-U7**, WPA
riding accident Reitunfall **5-U6**, T1
right Recht **8-U3**, WP
right rechts **5-U6**, WPB
right richtig **5-U1**, T1
right genau **7-U5**, T2
ring anrufen **6-U2**, Ex2
river Fluss, Strom **6-U1**, WPA
road Straße **5-U1**, Sit6
rob berauben, ausrauben **8-U1**, Read
robber Räuber/in **8-U1**, Read
robot Roboter **6-U5**, Sit1
rocket Rakete **8-U4**, T1
roll Brötchen **7-U5**, T1
roll rollen **7-U5**, T2
  roll up zusammenrollen **7-U5**, T2
roller coaster Achterbahn **8-U4**, Ex7
Roman römisch; Römer/in **7-U2**, WP
room Zimmer **5-U1**, Ex4
rope Seil, Tau **7-U2**, TYE
rough uneben; rau **5-U5**, T2
round rund **7-U2**, T2
round Runde **6-U6**, WPC
round umher, um … herum **5-U2**, Song
route Route, Strecke **8-U4**, Read

royal königlich **6-U1**, T2
rubbish Abfall, Müll **6-U5**, T2
ruin Ruine **7-U2**, Sit1
rule Regel **6-U1**, Ex10
ruler Lineal **5-U0**, D
run laufen **5-U3**, WPA
run leiten, führen **7-U1**, Sit1

Ss

sad traurig **6-U2**, T2
safari Safari **6-U6**, WPA
safe sicher **7-U2**, T1
sail segeln **7-U4**, Sit1
salad Salat **5-U4**, WPA
sale Verkauf, Ausverkauf **6-U5**, T2
same gleich **5-U1**, Sit6
sample Kostprobe, Muster **8-U2**, Sit1
sand Sand **8-U4**, T2
sandwich Sandwich, belegtes Brot **5-U1**, T2
Saturday Samstag, Sonnabend **5-U1**, Sit4
sausage Wurst **5-U4**, WPA
save retten **7-U1**, Read
save sparen **6-U5**, T1
Saxon sächsisch; Sachse, Sächsin
   7-U2, WP
say sagen **5-U2**, Sit2
scared (of), to be Angst haben (vor)
   7-U4, T1
scene Szene **6-U1**, T2
scenery (schöne) Landschaft **8-U4**, WP
schedule Stundenplan, Zeitplan **8-U2**, T1
school Schule **5-U1**, WPB
science (Natur-)Wissenschaft **6-U6**, WPA
score erzielen **7-U3**, Read
scratch kratzen **8-U4**, T2
screen Bildschirm, Leinwand **6-U3**, WPB
sea Meer, die See **6-U2**, Sit3
seafood Meeresfrüchte **8-U2**, T1
search (for) suchen (nach) **6-U3**, WPC
seaside Meeresküste **5-U7**, WPA
season Jahreszeit; Saison **8-U2**, T1
  season ticket Dauerkarte **8-U2**, Sit5
seat Sitz, Sitzplatz **5-U7**, T2
secret geheim **7-U1**, T2
see sehen **5-U0**, B
  see you bis dann!, tschüss! **5-U0**, B
seem scheinen **7-U3**, T2
  seem to do etwas zu tun scheinen
   7-U3, T2
segregation Trennung **8-U3**, T2
sell verkaufen **6-U5**, WPB
seller Verkäufer **7-U5**, Rev
send schicken **6-U3**, WPC
senior Student/in im letzten Studienjahr
   8-U2, T1
sensation Aufsehen **8-U3**, T1
sentence Satz **5-U5**, Ex1
separate getrennt **7-U1**, WP
September September **5-U4**, Sit5
series Serie **6-U6**, WPA
serious ernst **6-U3**, T2
serve servieren, bedienen **8-U2**, Sit1
service Dienst **8-U1**, Ex10

settle sich ansiedeln, niederlassen **8-U2**,
   TYE
settler Siedler/in **8-U2**, WP
seven sieben **5-U0**, G
seventeen siebzehn **5-U0**, G
seventy siebzig **5-U4**, WPA
several mehrere, einige **7-U4**, T2
sew nähen **7-U5**, Read
share (sich) teilen, gemeinsam haben **7-
   U5**, T2
shark Hai **8-U4**, T1
she sie **5-U1**, Sit2
shed Schuppen, Stall **5-U3**, T2
sheep Schaf **6-U2**, WPA
shelf Regal, Ablage **5-U5**, Sit1
sheriff Sheriff **7-U5**, Sket2
shield (Schutz-)Schild **7-U2**, Sit5
ship Schiff **7-U3**, WP
shirt Hemd **5-U0**, C
shock Schock **6-U2**, T2
shoe Schuh **5-U3**, Sit2
shoot schießen **7-U1**, Read
shop Geschäft **5-U4**, Sit1
shop einkaufen (gehen), Einkäufe
   machen **8-U1**, Sit2
shopping centre Einkaufszentrum
   5-U6, WPB
shore Strand, Ufer **7-U4**, TYE
short kurz **6-U1**, Ex3
shot Schuss **8-U1**, Read
should sollte **6-U6**, T2
shout schreien, rufen **5-U6**, T2
show Sendung **5-U5**, Sit3
show zeigen **6-U1**, Ex21
shower Regenschauer; Dusche
   8-U3, Read
shut up den Mund halten **7-U1**, T1
shy schüchtern, scheu **7-U3**, TYE
sick krank **8-U3**, Read
side Seite **6-U2**, T1
sidewalk Gehsteig, Bürgersteig **8-U1**, T1
sight Sehenswürdigkeit **6-U1**, WPA
sightseeing Stadtbesichtigung
   6-U4, PYE6
sign Schild, Zeichen **5-U7**, T1
signal Signal **6-U4**, T2
silicon Silizium **6-U7**, WPA
silly albern **5-U1**, T1
silver Silber **7-U5**, WP
simple einfach, schlicht **6-U5**, Ex13
since seit **7-U1**, Sit4
sing singen **5-U1**, Ex13
singer Sänger/in **6-U1**, WPA
single einzeln, Einzel- **8-U1**, Com
sink sinken, untergehen **7-U3**, WP
sir mein Herr **5-U1**, Ex7
sister Schwester **5-U0**, I
sit sitzen; sich hinsetzen **5-U0**, F
site Stelle, Platz **5-U7**, WPD
situation Situation **5-U1**, Sit1
six sechs **5-U0**, G
sixteen sechzehn **5-U0**, G
sixty sechzig **5-U4**, WPA

one hundred and fifty-five 155

Index

size Größe **5-U4**, Sit4
skate Rollschuh laufen **5-U5**, WPA
    skate park Skatinggelände **5-U5**, T1
ski Ski fahren **6-U7**, WPA
skin Haut, Fell **8-U3**, T1
skirt Rock **6-U6**, Ex3
sky Himmel **5-U7**, T2
skyline Silhouette, Skyline **8-U1**, T
skyscraper Wolkenkratzer **8-U1**, T1
skyway Himmelsweg **6-U7**, Song
slave Sklave, Sklavin **8-U3**, WP
slavery Sklaverei **8-U3**, WP
sleep schlafen **6-U2**, Sit4
sleeping bag Schlafsack **7-U5**, T1
slogan Parole, Wahlspruch **6-U1**, Ex14
slope Gefälle, Hang **7-U4**, T1
slow langsam **5-U5**, Ex1
slums, the Elendsviertel **7-U1**, Read
small klein **5-U2**, WPA
smart schick, elegant, flott **7-U1**, WP
smell riechen **5-U3**, WPB
smile lächeln **6-U1**, T2
smoke Rauch **7-U5**, Sit1
smuggle (into) (ein)schmuggeln (in)
    8-U1, Read
snack Imbiss **5-U5**, PYE5
snake Schlange **7-U2**, Read
snow Schnee **8-U2**, T1
snow schneien **8-U4**, Read
snowflake Schneeflocke **8-U4**, Read
snowstorm Schneesturm **8-U3**, Read
so so **5-U7**, Sit4
    so that sodass, damit **8-U1**, Sit1
    so what? na und? **7-U3**, T1
soap opera Seifenoper **6-U6**, WPA
soccer Fußball **7-U3**, Read
social sozial; Sozial- **8-Proj2**
sock Socke **7-U2**, Ex9
soda Soda(Wasser) **8-U1**, T2
soft weich, zart **6-U4**, T2
softball Softball **6-U3**, T2
software Software **7-U1**, WP
soldier Soldat, Soldatin **6-U4**, T1
some etwas, ein wenig; einige, ein paar
    5-U4, Sit1
somebody jemand **7-U3**, Sit1
somehow irgendwie **8-U1**, T2
someone jemand **6-U2**, Sit2
someplace irgendwo, irgendwohin **8-U4**, Sit1
something etwas **5-U4**, Sit3
sometimes manchmal **5-U1**, T1
somewhere irgendwo **7-U1**, T1
son Sohn **6-U1**, Sit1
song Lied **5-U0**, J
soon bald **6-U5**, T1
sophomore Student/in im zweiten
    Studienjahr **8-Proj2**
sorry tut mir leid **5-U1**, Sit1
sound Klang, Laut **5-U5**, Ex17
sound klingen **6-U7**, T1
soup Suppe **7-U5**, T1
south Süden **6-U1**, WPA
southern südlich, Süd- **8-U1**, WP

souvenir Andenken, Souvenir **8-U2**, TYE
sow säen **7-U5**, Read
space Lücke, Raum, Platz **5-U5**, Ex18
spaceship Raumschiff **7-U2**, Ex3
spare time Freizeit **5-U5**, WPA
speak sprechen **5-U1**, Sit8
speaker Sprecher/in, Redner/in **7-U1**, Ex4
special spezial, besondere(r, s) **6-U4**
spectacular sensationell, atemberaubend
    8-U1, T1
speedway (track) Speedway-,
    Aschenrennbahn **8-U4**, Ex7
spell buchstabieren **5-U0**, J
spelling Rechtschreibung **6-U7**, Sit1
spend ausgeben (Geld) **7-U4**, T2
spider Spinne **6-U4**, WPD
spill verschütten, vergießen **7-U1**, Sit3
splash bespritzen, platschen **6-U7**, T2
sponsor finanziell unterstützen **6-U5**, Com
spoon Löffel **7-U5**, T2
sport Sport **5-U2**, Sit1
sporting Sport, sportlich; **7-U3**, Proj
sports car Sportwagen **8-Rev11**
spot Fleck(en) **5-U7**, Ex13
spray (be)sprühen **7-U4**, TYE
spring Frühling, Frühjahr **6-U4**, T1
squad car Streifenwagen **8-U3**, T2
square Platz **6-U7**, T2
stamp Briefmarke **5-U6**, Sit1
stamp stampfen **7-U3**, T2
stand stehen; sich hinstellen **5-U0**, F
standard of living Lebensstandard **8-U3**, WP
star Stern **7-U3**, Com
star (Film-)Star **5-U1**, Sit2
star (in) eine Hauptrolle spielen (in)
    7-U3, WP
start Start **7-U1**, Ex3
start anfangen **5-U4**, WPA
    start doing sth anfangen, etwas zu tun
    7-U1, WP
state (Bundes)Staat; Zustand **6-U7**, WP
station Bahnhof, Station **5-U7**, T2
statue Statue **8-U1**, WP
stay Aufenthalt **8-U1**, T2
stay bleiben; wohnen **5-U7**, Sit1
steal stehlen **6-U5**, T1
steep steil **6-U7**, WPA
step Stufe; Schritt **8-U1**, T1
step gehen, treten **7-U1**, Read
stepbrother Stiefbruder **7-U3**, T1
stereo Stereogerät **5-U2**, WPC
stew Eintopf **5-U3**, Song
stick Stecken, Stock **8-U4**, T2
still (immer) noch **7-U1**, WP
still ruhig **6-U2**, T2
stolen gestohlen **7-U1**, T2
stone Stein **6-U1**, Song
stop Halt(en), Haltestelle; Aufenthalt
    8-U1, T1
stop anhalten, aufhören **6-U2**, Sit2
store Laden, Geschäft **8-U1**, Sit1
storm Sturm **7-U4**, WP
story Geschichte **6-U2**, Ex5

stove Ofen, Herd **8-U3**, Read
straight gerade **7-U5**, Com
    straight ahead geradeaus **5-U6**, WPB
    straight on geradeaus **7-U5**, Com
strange merkwürdig **6-U2**, T2
stranger Fremder, Fremde **7-U4**, WP
strawberry Erdbeere **7-U1**, Sit3
stream Bach **6-U2**, WPB
street Straße **6-U1**, WPB
stretcher Tragbahre **6-U2**, T2
strict streng **8-Lit**
stripe Streifen **8-U4**, WP
strong stark **7-U2**, T1
struggle Kampf, Auseinandersetzung **8-Lit**
stuck stecken geblieben **8-U4**, Read
studio Studio **8-U1**, T2
study studieren; sich genau ansehen
    8-Rev8
stupid dumm, blöd **5-U3**, T2
style Stil **8-U4**, Read
subject Schulfach **5-U6**, T1
suburb Vorort **8-Rev8**
subway U-Bahn **8-U1**, T1
succeed (in) gelingen, Erfolg haben (mit)
    7-U3, Sit1
successful erfolgreich **8-Rev1**
suddenly plötzlich **6-U2**, T2
sugar Zucker **5-U4**, Sit1
suggestion Vorschlag **5-U5**, Ex18
summary Zusammenfassung **8-U1**, Ex5
summer Sommer **5-U4**, Sit5
sun Sonne **6-U2**, Sit3
Sunday Sonntag **5-U1**, Sit4
sunny sonnig **7-U5**, T1
sunset Sonnenuntergang **8-U4**, T1
sunshine Sonnenschein **8-U4**, Sit1
Super Bowl Super Bowl **8-U2**, T2
supermarket Supermarkt **5-U2**, Sit4
supermodel Supermodel **7-U3**, TYE
superstar Superstar **8-U2**, T2
support unterstützen **5-U2**, T1
Supreme Court Oberster Gerichtshof
    8-U3, T2
sure sicher **5-U1**, Sit3
surf surfen **7-U5**, Ex7
surfing Surfen **6-U7**, WPA
surprised überrascht **7-U3**, Sit4
surround umzingeln, umgeben **8-U1**, Read
survive überleben **8-U2**, WP
swallow Schwalbe **6-U2**, WPB
swap tauschen **5-U2**, Ex1
sweater Pullover **5-U0**, C
sweet talk Schmeicheleien, **7-U1**, Proj
sweet talk jmd schmeicheln **7-U1**, Proj
sweets Süßigkeiten **6-U4**, T2
swim schwimmen **5-U1**, Sit8
swimmer Schwimmer/in **8-U4**, TYE1
swimming-pool Schwimmbad **5-U6**, WPA
swing Schaukel **5-U3**, T1
swing schwingen **7-U4**, T1
switch on anschalten, einschalten **6-U3**, T2
sword Schwert **7-U2**, T1

156   one hundred and fifty-six

Index

Tt

table Tisch **5-U1**, T2
tackle angreifen **8-U2**, Ex12
tail Schwanz **8-U4**, TYE
take nehmen **5-U4**, WPA
  take a photo ein Foto machen **5-U5**, WPB
  take off abnehmen, ausziehen **8-U4**, T2
  take out herausnehmen, herausziehen **7-U1**, Sit5
  take part (in) teilnehmen (an) **8-U2**, T1
  take place stattfinden **8-U2**, T2
take dauern, Zeit in Anspruch nehmen **6-U5**, Ex2
talk reden **5-U2**, T2
tall groß **6-U6**, Com
tape Tonband, Videoband **6-U6**, T2
tapestry Wandbehang, -teppich **7-U4**, WP
task Aufgabe **8-Proj5**
taste schmecken **7-U5**, Sit1
taxi Taxi **5-U7**, Ex6
tea Abendessen **5-U3**, Sit1
tea Tee, Schwarzer Tee **5-U4**, WPA
teach unterrichten **6-U3**, T1
teacher Lehrer/in **5-U0**, D
team Team, Mannschaft **5-U1**, Ex17
technician Techniker/in **7-U1**, Sit1
technology Technik **6-U3**, T1
teenager Teenager **6-U6**, WPA
telephone Telefon **5-U1**, PYE6
(tele)phone box Telefonzelle **7-U1**, T2
television Fernsehen **5-U1**, Sit6
tell erzählen, mitteilen **5-U5**, WPB
temper Laune, Stimmung; Wesensart **7-U4**, T2
temperature Temperatur **8-U4**, WP
temple Tempel, Kultstätte **6-U4**, WPB
ten zehn **5-U0**, G
tennis Tennis **5-U2**, WPC
tension Anspannung, Spannung **8-U2**, T2
tent Zelt **7-U5**, T1
term Semester, Trimester **5-U4**, Sit5
terrible schrecklich **5-U6**, T2
test testen, ausprobieren **6-U6**, WPA
test Test **6-U5**, Com
text Text **5-U1**, T1
textbook Lehrbuch **5-U3**, Ex11
than als **6-U1**, Sit3
thanks danke **5-U0**, B
  thank you danke **5-U0**, B
Thanksgiving Erntedankfest **8-U2**, WP
that der, die, das (dort) **5-U0**, D
the der, die, das **5-U0**, D
theatre Theater **7-U4**, WP
their ihr, ihre, ihr **5-U1**, WPB
theirs ihre(r, s) **6-U3**, Sit3
them sie, ihnen **5-U2**, Sit5
theme Thema; Motto **8-U2**, T1
  theme park Freizeitpark **8-U4**, T1
themselves sich; selbst **8-U3**, Sit3
then dann **5-U1**, Sit7
then also, nun **5-U3**, Sit1

there dort **5-U1**, Ex4
  there is es gibt, ist vorhanden **5-U1**, WPA
these diese **5-U3**, Sit2
they sie **5-U1**, WPB
thick dick, dicht **7-U5**, Sit1
thief Dieb/in **7-U5**, T2
thin dünn **7-U4**, Com
thing Sache, Gegenstand **5-U4**, T2
think denken, meinen **5-U1**, T2
thirsty durstig **7-U5**, T1
thirteen dreizehn **5-U0**, G
thirty dreißig **5-U1**, Sit5
this dieser, diese, dieses, dies **5-U0**, D
those jene **5-U3**, Sit2
thousand tausend **5-U7**, T2
three drei **5-U0**, G
through durch **6-U2**, T1
throw werfen **5-U6**, Ex4
thunder Donner **8-U3**, Read
Thursday Donnerstag **5-U1**, Sit4
ticket Fahr-; Eintrittskarte, **6-U1**, T1
tidy ordentlich **7-U1**, Sit2
tidy aufräumen **5-U5**, Sit1
tiger Tiger **6-U3**, Ex3
till bis **8-U1**, Sit2
time Zeit **5-U0**, B
times mal **7-U2**, Ex7
timetable Stundenplan **5-U1**, PYE1
tin Büchse, Dose **6-U5**, Sit2
tip Tipp, nützlicher Hinweis **7-U3**, Sit1
tired müde **5-U6**, T1
  tired of doing sth, be es satt haben, etwas zu tun **8-U3**, T2
title Titel **7-U1**, Ex3
to zu **5-U0**, B
toast Toast **5-U4**, WPB
tobacco Tabak **8-U3**, T1
today heute **5-U0**, G
together zusammen **5-U5**, Ex6
tomato Tomate **7-U5**, T1
tomorrow morgen **6-U2**, Sit2
tonight heute Abend **6-U4**, Ex2
ton Tonne **7-U2**, TYE
too auch **5-U0**, G
too zu **5-U5**, Ex1
tooth Zahn **8-U2**, Read
top Spitze, Gipfel **5-U7**, T2
top Oberteil, Top **7-U1**, Sit1
torch Fackel **7-U2**, TYE
torture Folter, Qual **6-U1**, T2
total (End)Summe **8-U3**, T1
touch berühren **8-U2**, Ex12
touchdown Versuch **8-U2**, Ex12
tough robust, hart, zäh **6-U4**, T2
tour Rundfahrt, Führung **6-U1**, WPA
tourist Tourist/in **6-U1**, Sit2
tower Turm **6-U1**, WPA
town Stadt **5-U6**, WPA
  town hall Rathaus **7-U5**, Ex13
toy Spielzeug **6-U5**, T2
track Gleisstrecke **8-U3**, TYE
tractor Traktor, Zugmaschine **8-U4**, Read

trade Handel **8-U1**, Ex7
trade Handel treiben, handeln **8-U3**, T1
tradition Tradition, Brauch **8-U3**, Sit1
traditional traditionell **7-U1**, WP
traffic Verkehr **6-U6**, T2
tragedy Tragödie **8-U4**, Sit4
trail Weg, Pfad; Spur **8-U3**, Read
train Zug **5-U7**, WPA
tram Tram, Straßenbahn **7-U5**, Sit1
trampolining Trampolin springen **6-U5**, Sit4
translate übersetzen **7-U3**, TYE4
translation Übersetzung **8-U3**, Ex16
travel reisen **5-U7**, WPA
treat behandeln **8-U2**, Sit3
tree Baum **5-U3**, PYE2
trek anstrengende Wanderung **8-Rev4**
trendy modisch, schick **8-U4**, T1
tribe Stamm **8-U3**, T1
trip Reise **6-U4**, PYE6
trouble Mühe, Umstände **8-U1**, Sit2
truck LKW, Truck **6-U7**, Ex1
true wahr **7-U2**, Sit1
truth Wahrheit **7-U2**, Read
try versuchen **5-U5**, T1
T-shirt T-Shirt **5-U4**, Sit3
tube U-Bahn **6-U1**, WPB
Tuesday Dienstag **5-U1**, Sit4
tunnel Tunnel **6-U4**, T1
turkey Truthahn **8-U2**, WP
turn Kurve, Abzweigung **8-U2**, Read
turn einbiegen **5-U6**, WPB
turn drehen **6-U6**, T1
turning Abzweigung **6-U6**, T1
tutor Betreuungslehrer/in, Klassenlehrer/in **5-U1**, WPB
TV Fernsehen **5-U6**, Ex9
twelve zwölf **5-U0**, G
twenty zwanzig **5-U0**, G
twice zweimal **6-U5**, Sit4
twin Zwilling **6-U6**, WPA
two zwei **5-U0**, G
  two out of three zwei von dreien **7-U1**, Read
type Typ **7-U1**, T1
type (in) (ein)tippen **6-U3**, WPC
typewriter Schreibmaschine **8-Rev3**
typical (of) typisch (für) **8-U2**, Sit1

Uu

ultimate perfekt, vollendet **8-U2**, T2
umbrella Regenschirm **5-U0**, D
uncle Onkel **5-U1**, Song
uncomfortable unbequem **7-U5**, T1
under unter **5-U3**, T1
  under arrest, be verhaftet sein **8-U3**, T2
underground U-Bahn **6-U1**, WPB
understand verstehen **6-U6**, Sit1
undoubtedly zweifellos **7-U5**, Read
unfortunately unglücklicherweise **8-Rev4**
uniform Uniform **5-U1**, WPB
unit Unit, Lektion **5-U1**,

Index

United Kingdom Vereinigtes Königreich, UK **7-U1**, WP
university Universität **8**-Rev8
until bis **6-U5**, Sit2
up hinauf, herauf, nach oben **5-U0**, F
up-to-date aktuell, modern **6-U3**, WPD
upset aufgebracht **7-U5**, T2
urban städtisch, Stadt- **7-U1**, Read
urgent dringend **7-U1**, T2
us uns **5-U2**, Sit5
use gebrauchen, verwenden **5-U5**, WPB
useful nützlich **7-U5**, WP
user Benutzer/in **8**-Rev3
usually gewöhnlich **5-U5**, WPB

Vv

vacation Ferien **6-U7**, Sit1
valley Tal **6-U7**, WPA
van Lieferwagen **7-U1**, T2
vegetable Gemüse **8-U3**, T1
verb Verb, Tunwort **5-U5**, Ex1
very sehr **5-U1**, Sit1
vet Tierarzt, Tierärztin **6-U5**, WPD
victory Sieg **8-U3**, T2
video(cassette) Videokassette **5-U4**, T2
video recorder Videorekorder **7-U3**, Sit2
view Ausblick **5-U7**, T2
Viking Wikinger/in **7-U4**, Sit1
village Dorf **6-U2**, Sit3
vintage car Oldtimer **8**-Rev11
violence Gewalt **8-U1**, T2
violent gewalttätig **8-U1**, T2
violin Geige **7-U5**, Read
visa Visum, Sichtvermerk **8-U1**, Ex9
visit Besuch **7-U1**, TYE5
visit besuchen, besichtigen **5-U3**, Ex16
visitor Besucher/in **6-U6**, WPD
voice Stimme **6-U2**, T2
volleyball Volleyball **8-U2**, T1
vote wählen, Stimme abgeben für **8-U3**, WP
voyage Seereise **8-U1**, TYE4

Ww

wagon Wagen, Planwagen **8-U3**, TYE
wait warten **5-U5**, T2
wait Warten, Wartezeit **8-U1**, T1
wake up aufwachen, aufwecken **7-U3**, T2
walk Wanderung **7-U5**, T1
walk gehen, wandern **5-U2**, Sit3
walkman Walkman **5-U4**, T1
wall Mauer, Wand **5-U2**, T2
   wall chart Wandkarte **8**-Proj2
want wollen **5-U2**, T2
war Krieg **7-U3**, Com
wardrobe (Kleider)Schrank **5-U2**, WPC
warm warm **6-U3**, Sit1
warn warnen **6-U4**, T2
wash (sich) waschen **6-U2**, Sit2
   wash away wegspülen **6-U1**, Song
   wash up abspülen **6-U4**, Ex11
watch Uhr **5-U1**, T2
watch sehen, beobachten **5-U1**, Sit6
water Wasser **5-U4**, WPA

waterfall Wasserfall **6-U7**, WPA
wax Wachs **7-U1**, TYE5
waxwork Wachsfigur **6-U1**, Sit2
way Art und Weise **6-U1**, Ex4
way Weg **5-U1**, Sit7
   way of doing sth Art und Weise, etwas zu tun **8-U2**, Com
   way of life Lebensart, Lebensweise **8-U1**, T2
we wir **5-U1**, Sit1
weapon Waffe **7-U2**, T2
wear tragen **5-U4**, Sit3
weather Wetter **5-U7**, WPD
weather wetterfest sein; überstehen **7-U5**, Read
website Website **6-U3**, WPC
wedding Hochzeit(stag) **7-U5**, Sket2
Wednesday Mittwoch **5-U1**, Sit4
week Woche **5-U1**, Sit3
weekend Wochenende **5-U1**, Sit4
weigh wiegen **7-U2**, TYE
weight Gewicht **7-U5**, Sit3
welcome willkommen **6-U7**, T1
well gut **6-U6**, Sit3
well nun **5-U1**, Sit8
well-known berühmt **8**-Lit
Welsh walisisch **5-U7**, T1
west Westen **5-U1**, Sit1
   West Indian westindisch **7-U5**, TYE
western westlich, West- **7-U5**, Ex16
westward westwärts, nach Westen **8-U3**, TYE
wet nass, feucht **7-U4**, TYE
what was **5-U0**, A
   what for? wozu? **7-U1**, Read
   what if ... ? was ist, wenn ... ? **8-U4**, T2
   what's the matter? was ist los? **7-U2**, Read
whatever was auch immer **7-U5**, Read
wheel Rad **5-U3**, WPA
wheelchair Rollstuhl **5-U6**, T1
when wann **5-U4**, Ex14
when als **5-U6**, T1
when (immer) wenn **5-U7**, Sit4
where wo **5-U0**, J
whether ob **7-U5**, Read
which welche(r, s) **6-U1**, WPB
which der, die, das; welcher, welche, welches **7-U4**, Sit1
while während **7-U1**, T2
whisper flüstern **8-U4**, T2
white weiß **5-U0**, C
who wer **5-U1**, T2
whole ganz **7-U2**, Ex8
whose deren, dessen **7-U4**, Sit3
whose wessen **5-U6**, Sit3
why warum **5-U4**, T1
wide groß, weit **8-U3**, WP
widow Witwe **7-U4**, T2
wife Ehefrau **6-U1**, Sit1
wild wild, ungezügelt **6-U2**, T1
will werden **6-U5**, Sit1

win gewinnen **5-U4**, Sit1
wind Wind **8-U4**, T2
window Fenster **5-U0**, D
window-cleaner Fensterputzer/in **7-U5**, Rev
windshield Windschutzscheibe **8-U4**, Read
windsurfing Windsurfen **8-U4**, Sit1
wine Wein **6-U7**, WPA
wing Flügel **7-U2**, Read
winner Gewinner/in **8-U2**, T2
winter Winter **6-U4**, T2
witch Hexe **7-U2**, Read
with mit **5-U1**, Sit2
without ohne **6-U5**, T1
witness Zeuge, Zeugin **8-U2**, TYE4
witness Zeuge sein von **8-U2**, TYE4
woman Frau **5-U3**, Sit3
wonderful wunderbar **5-U7**, WPD
wood Holz **6-U1**, Song
wooden hölzern, aus Holz **8-U3**, TYE
word Wort **5-U0**, J
work arbeiten **5-U2**, Sit4
work Arbeit **5-U1**, Sit7
workman Handwerker **8-U3**, TYE
world Welt **6-U1**, T1
worldwide weltweit **8-U2**, T2
worried besorgt **7-U5**, T2
worry sich sorgen **6-U1**, T1
worse schlechter **6-U1**, Sit4
worst am schlechtesten **6-U1**, Sit4
worth wert **6-U6**, T2
would würde **8-U4**, Sit4
   would like möchte gern **5-U4**, WPA
   would like/love to do sth möchte gerne etwas tun **7-U1**, Com
wow Mann!, Wahnsinn! **6-U3**, T2
write schreiben **5-U3**, Com
writer Schriftsteller/in **8-U4**, T1
wrong falsch **5-U2**, Ex5

Yy

year Jahr **5-U1**, Sit3
yearbook Jahrbuch **8-U2**, T1
yell brüllen, laut schreien **8-U4**, T2
yellow gelb **5-U0**, C
yes ja **5-U0**, B
yesterday gestern **6-U2**, Sit1
yet, ... yet? schon **6-U4**, Sit3
   not... yet noch nicht **6-U4**, Sit3
yoghurt Joghurt **5-U4**, WPA
you du, ihr, Sie **5-U0**, A
young jung **6-U2**, WPB
your dein, deine, dein, ihr, ihre, ihr **5-U0**, A
yours deine(r, s) **6-U3**, Sit2
yourself dich, dir; selbst **8-U3**, Sit3
yourselves euch; selbst **8-U3**, Sit3
yummy lecker, schmackhaft **8-U2**, Sit1

Zz

zone Zone, Bereich **8-U4**, Sit2
zoo Zoo, Tierpark **5-U3**, Ex16

Activities / Extra Pages

Unit 1 Activities 1
to **spread** [spred]	verbreiten
to **long** [lɒŋ]	sich sehnen
to **stray** [streɪ]	(umher)streunen
heart [hɑːt]	Herz
heap [hiːp]	Haufen
blues [bluːz]	Trübsinn, Schwermut
to **melt** [melt]	schmelzen
brand new [ˌbrænd ˈnjuː]	brandneu
It's up to you. [ɪts ˌʌp tə ˈjuː]	Es liegt an dir.

Unit 1 Activities 2
freedom [ˈfriːdəm]	Freiheit
to **express** [ɪkˈspres]	ausdrücken
themselves [ðəmˈselvz]	sich, selbst
rapper [ˈræpə]	Rapper/in
slang [slæŋ]	Umgangssprache, Slang
African American [ˌæfrɪkən əˈmerɪkən]	afroamerikanisch; Afroamerikaner/in
beat [biːt]	Takt
shooting [ˈʃuːtɪŋ]	Schießerei
movement [ˈmuːvmənt]	Bewegung
dancer [ˈdɑːnsə]	Tänzer/in
jump [dʒʌmp]	Sprung
butterfly [ˈbʌtəflaɪ]	Schmetterling
over-sized [ˈəʊvəsaɪzd]	in Übergröße
pants [pænts]	Hose
belt [belt]	Gürtel
lace [leɪs]	Schnürsenkel
artist [ˈɑːtɪst]	Künstler/in

Unit 2 Activities 1
buffalo [ˈbʌfələʊ]	Büffel, Bison
pilgrim [ˈpɪlgrɪm]	Pilger/in
to **grow** [grəʊ]	anbauen; wachsen
vegetable [ˈvedʒtəbl]	Gemüse
harvest [ˈhɑːvɪst]	Ernte
pumpkin [ˈpʌmpkɪn]	Kürbis
corn [kɔːn]	Mais
cranberry [ˈkrænbəri]	Preiselbeere
common [ˈkɒmən]	gewöhnlich
however [haʊˈevə]	jedoch
extract [ˈekstrækt]	Auszug
speech [spiːtʃ]	Rede
celebration [ˌselɪˈbreɪʃn]	Feier
heart [hɑːt]	Herz
upon [əˈpɒn]	auf
to **welcome** [ˈwelkəm]	begrüßen
blueberry [ˈbluːbəri]	Blaubeere
egg [eg]	Ei
flour [ˈflaʊə]	Mehl
sour [ˈsaʊə]	sauer
cream [kriːm]	Sahne
salt [sɔːlt]	Salz
maple syrup [ˌmeɪpl ˈsɪrəp]	Ahornsirup
to **heat** [hiːt]	erhitzen
pan [pæn]	Pfanne
bowl [bəʊl]	Schüssel, Schale
batter [ˈbætə]	(Kuchen)Teig

Index

to **spread** [spred]	verteilen, ausbreiten

Unit 2 Activities 2
to **wonder** [ˈwʌndə]	sich fragen
grandmother [ˈgrænmʌðə]	Großmutter
surname [ˈsɜːneɪm]	Nachname
link [lɪŋk]	Internetlink
student [ˈstjuːdnt]	Schüler/in, Student/in

Unit 3 Activities 1
wise [waɪz]	weise, klug
landscape [ˈlændskeɪp]	Landschaft
pillow [ˈpɪləʊ]	Kopfkissen
twig [twɪg]	Zweig
wire [ˈwaɪə]	Draht
twine [twaɪn]	Schnur, Bindfaden
wooden [ˈwʊdn]	hölzern, aus Holz
bead [biːd]	Perle
feather [ˈfeðə]	Feder
hoop [huːp]	Reifen, Ring
to **tie** [taɪ]	binden

Unit 3 Activities 2
ebony [ˈebəni]	Ebenholz
ivory [ˈaɪvəri]	Elfenbein
harmony [ˈhɑːməni]	Harmonie
wherever [weərˈevə]	wo auch immer
student [ˈstjuːdnt]	Schüler/in, Student/in
topic [ˈtɒpɪk]	Thema
speech [spiːtʃ]	Rede
gospel [ˈgɒspl]	Gospel(lied)
soul [səʊl]	Seele; Soulmusik
African American [ˌæfrɪkən əˈmerɪkən]	afroamerikanisch; Afroamerikaner/in
reason [ˈriːzn]	Grund
percentage [pəˈsentɪdʒ]	Prozent
jobless [ˈdʒɒbləs]	arbeitslos
education [ˌedʒuˈkeɪʃn]	Ausbildung

Unit 4 Activities 1
to **prefer** [prɪˈfɜː]	vorziehen, lieber mögen
to **frighten** [ˈfraɪtn]	Angst einjagen
nut [nʌt]	Nuss

Unit 4 Activities 2
to **tumble** [ˈtʌmbl]	stürzen, fallen
jazz [dʒæz]	Jazz (Musik)

Unit 1 Extra Pages
shooting [ˈʃuːtɪŋ]	Schießen, Schießerei
incident [ˈɪnsɪdənt]	Vorfall, Zwischenfall
to **bully** [ˈbʊli]	tyrannisieren
stunt [stʌnt]	Kunststück
skateboard [ˈskeɪtbɔːd]	Skateboard
student [ˈstjuːdnt]	Schüler/in; Student/in
revolver [rɪˈvɒlvə]	Revolver
to **wound** [wuːnd]	verwunden
including [ɪnˈkluːdɪŋ]	einschließlich, inbegriffen

one hundred and fifty-nine **159**

Index

security [sɪ'kjʊərəti] — Sicherheit
victim ['vɪktɪm] — Opfer
blood [blʌd] — Blut
nightmare ['naɪtmeə] — Alptraum
to cause [kɔːz] — verursachen, hervorrufen
shocking ['ʃɒkɪŋ] — schockierend, fürchterlich
statistically [stə'tɪstɪkli] — statistisch gesehen
to shock [ʃɒk] — schockieren
to prevent [prɪ'vent] — verhindern, verhüten
to inspect [ɪn'spekt] — kontrollieren, überprüfen
schoolbag ['skuːlbæg] — Schultasche
metal detector ['metl dɪtektə] — Metallsuchgerät
safety ['seɪfti] — Sicherheit
snitch [snɪtʃ] — Petze
governor ['gʌvənə] — Gouverneur/in
loneliness ['ləʊnlinəs] — Einsamkeit
to solve [sɒlv] — lösen

Unit 2 Extra Pages

smokejumper ['sməʊkdʒʌmpə] — Feuerspringer/in
to rise [raɪz] — aufgehen, aufsteigen, (an)steigen
to destroy [dɪ'strɔɪ] — zerstören
square mile ['skweə maɪl] — Quadratmeile
temperature ['temprətʃə] — Temperatur
degree [dɪ'griː] — Grad
Fahrenheit ['færənhaɪt] — Temperatureinheit (Gefrierpunkt 32°C, Siedepunkt 212° C)
wide [waɪd] — groß, weit
wind [wɪnd] — Wind
height [haɪt] — Höhe
foot [fʊt] — Längenmaß (30,48 cm)
suit [suːt] — Anzug
helmet ['helmɪt] — Helm, Schutzhelm
parachute ['pærəʃuːt] — Fallschirm
clearing ['klɪərɪŋ] — Lichtung
workplace ['wɜːkpleɪs] — Arbeitsplatz
firefighter ['faɪəfaɪtə] — Feuerwehrmann/-frau
hell [hel] — Hölle
to spread [spred] — verbreiten, sich ausbreiten
impossible [ɪm'pɒsəbl] — unmöglich
to break out [breɪk 'aʊt] — ausbrechen
to rescue ['reskjuː] — retten
physical ['fɪzɪkl] — körperlich
deliberate [dɪ'lɪbərət] — absichtlich, bewusst
ditch [dɪtʃ] — Graben
sleep [sliːp] — Schlaf
to put out [pʊt 'aʊt] — löschen, ausmachen
to go on doing sth [gəʊ 'ɒn] — weitermachen mit
private ['praɪvət] — privat
to explode [ɪk'spləʊd] — explodieren
explosion [ɪk'spləʊʒn] — Explosion
roller coaster ['rəʊlə kəʊstə] — Achterbahn

Unit 3 Extra Pages

wind [wɪnd] — Wind
novel ['nɒvl] — Roman
cotton ['kɒtn] — Baumwolle

Extra Pages

last [lɑːst] — dauern, andauern
egg [eg] — Ei
supper ['sʌpə] — Abendessen
chicken ['tʃɪkɪn] — Huhn
to put off [pʊt 'ɒf] — verschieben
Yankee ['jæŋki] — Yankee, Nordstaatler; aus den Nordstaaten
Confederate [kən'fedərət] — Südstaatler; aus den Südstaaten
cabin ['kæbɪn] — Hütte
to intend to do sth [ɪn'tend] — beabsichtigen, etwas zu tun
unthinkable [ʌn'θɪŋkəbl] — unvorstellbar, undenkbar
nigger ['nɪgə] — beleidigende Bezeichnung für Afroamerikaner
hand [hænd] — Arbeiter
to drive [draɪv] — antreiben
mistress ['mɪstrəs] — Herrin
wood/woods [wʊdz] — Wald
willing ['wɪlɪŋ] — bereitwillig, gewillt
to faint [feɪnt] — ohnmächtig werden
to pretend to do sth [prɪ'tend] — vorgeben, etwas zu tun; so tun, als ob
grateful ['greɪtfl] — dankbar
silent ['saɪlənt] — stumm, still
illness ['ɪlnəs] — Krankheit
stalk [stɔːk] — Stengel, Stiel, Strunk
hope [həʊp] — Hoffnung
to rise (again) [raɪz] — auferstehen

Ex 3

similar ['sɪmələ] — ähnlich

Ex 5

fighter ['faɪtə] — Kämpfer/in
Oscar ['ɒskə] — Oscar (Filmpreis)

Unit 4 Extra Pages

headfirst [hed'fɜːst] — kopfüber
career [kə'rɪə] — Laufbahn, Karriere
following ['fɒləʊɪŋ] — folgend
frequently asked questions [friːkwəntli ɑːskt 'kwestʃənz] — häufig gestellte Fragen
vehicle ['viːəkl] — Fahrzeug
breakdown ['breɪkdaʊn] — Panne
ferry ['feri] — Fähre
sponsor ['spɒnsə] — Sponsor/in, Geldgeber/in
bench [bentʃ] — Sitzbank, Bank
disagreement [dɪsə'griːmənt] — Meinungsverschiedenheit
to quit [kwɪt] — aufgeben, aufhören mit
to keep going [kiːp 'gəʊɪŋ] — weitermachen
experience [ɪk'spɪərɪəns] — Erfahrung
whale [weɪl] — Wal
governor ['gʌvənə] — Gouverneur/in
cave [keɪv] — Höhle
to crawl [krɔːl] — kriechen, krabbeln
rock [rɒk] — Fels(en)
helpful ['helpfl] — hilfreich
contact ['kɒntækt] — Kontakt

Ex 3

glockenspiel ['glɒkənʃpiːl] — Glockenspiel

160 one hundred and sixty

Umschlag	Getty Images (Tony Stone)
Illustrationen	David Graham, Betty McCrae, Angus Montrose, Liz Roberts
Cartoons	Wendy Sinclair (*Raben*), Peter Muggleston
Textquellen	**Ebony and Ivory** Words and music by Mc Cartney, Paul / Wonder, Stevie 1982 by MPL Communications, MPL Music Verlag GmbH *S.49* **Gone with the Wind** Margaret Mitchell, MacMillan, London 1936 *S.75* **Headfirst into America** by Marlene Smith-Graham, Colcourt Publishing, 1998 *S.80* **New York, New York** Words and music by Ebb, Fred / Kander, John International Music Publications LTd., England *S.11* **The Lost Continent** by Bill Bryson, First Harper Perennial edition, 1990 *S.36*
Fotos	**Agence France Presse** *S.68* **AP Frankfurt / Ed Bailey** *S.11* **Archiv für Kunst und Geschichte, Berlin** *S.46, 47, 89* **All Action Pictures Limited, London** *S.64, 94* **Amana Colonies** *S.68* **Klaus Berold** *S.49* **Don Best / Best Impressions, Tillamook, OR** *S.25, inside front cover* **Tatjana Bielke** *S.85* **Burton Historical Collection, Detroit** *S.42* **Carolina Panthers** *S.83* **Cheryl and Dan Davy** *S.22, 23, 25, 81* **Udo Diekmann** *S.15, 39, 54, 86* **Gerlinde Eberhardt** *S.62* **Everglades National Park** *S.92, 93* **Firemans Fund Insurance Company** *S.84* **Henry Ford Museum** *S.60* **Das Fotoarchiv, Essen /Christopher Morris** *S.3, 73, 74 / Dan McComb* *S.73* **Getty Images** *S.3, 4, 5, 8, 11, 13, 14, 15, 17, 18, 19, 20, 21, 27, 28, 29, 30, 31, 34, 35, 37, 42, 43, 47, 52, 53, 54, 56, 57, 58, 63, 65, 66, 67, 75, 76, 82, 83, inside front cover* **Elise Graham** *S.65* **Brian D. Green** *S.61* **Philip Greenspun** *S.53* **Friedel Helmich** *S.22, 45* **Konrad Huber** *S.33, 56, 75, 79* **The Image Bank, München** *S.11, 35, 88* **John Jeggo / Staffordshire (UK) marquetry group** *S.42* **Jürgen Kanhäuser** *S.65* **Kennedy Space Center (NASA)** *S.56, inside cover* **Leavenworth Chamber of Commerce** *S.80* **Library of Congress, Washington** *S.18, 37, 44, 45, 51* **Miami Dolphins** *S.83* **MOMI/BFI stills** *S.37* **The Ocean County Columbus Day Parade Committee, Inc. Seaside Heights, N.J., USA (Mario A. Marano, Organizations and Groups Chairman, Michael Blandina, Parade Chairman)** *S.3, 21* **Pennsylvania Dutch Convention & Visitors Bureau** *S.35* **Plimoth Plantation, Inc.** *S.27, 38* **Picturefile / David Graham** *S.5, 6, 7, 9, 12 ,13, 14, 16, 24, 26, 28, 30, 33, 42, 49, 55, 56, 65, 79, 81, 94, inside front cover* **Picture Press, Hamburg / Bettmann** *S.46, 48 / Corbis Sygma* *S.57 / L. Kennedy* *S.73* **Retna Pictures Limited, London** *S.28* **Colin Ryder** *S.53* **Save the Manatee Club (website photo Patrick M. Rose)** *S.67* **2002 SeaWorld Orlando, All Rights Reserved / 2002 Discovery Cove, All Rights Reserved** *S.56, 58* **Elena Seibert** *S.87* **Craig and Marlene Smith-Graham** *S.78* **Tillamook County Creamery Association** *S.22* **Turner Entertainment Co.** *S.77* **Wilderness Adventure at Eagle Landing** *S.54* Nicht alle Copyrightinhaber konnten ermittelt werden; deren Urheberrechte werden hiermit vorsorglich und ausdrücklich anerkannt.
Acknowledgements	*The publishers wish to thank the staff, pupils, parents and friends of Alleyn's School, Dulwich, London and Carl-von-Linde-Realschule, Staatliche Realschule, Kulmbach for their continued help and assistance. They would also wish to express their thanks to the following organisations in the USA, for both their help and advice and for use of their stock photos: the Kennedy Space Center (NASA), the Everglades National Park, Seaworld and Discovery Cove, Orlando and to the Miami Dolphins and Carolina Panthers football teams for use of their logos, and to the the Save the Manatee organisation for use of their website. We would also thank the author Michael Crichton for the use of his photograph for publication.*
Danksagung	Wir danken den Lehrern und Lehrerinnen, den Schülern und Schülerinnen, ihren Eltern und den Freunden der Alleyn's School, Dulwich, London und der Carl-von-Linde-Realschule, Staatliche Realschule, Kulmbach für ihre andauernde Hilfe und Unterstützung. Außerdem möchten wir uns bei den folgenden Organisationen und Unternehmen in den USA für ihre Unterstützung und die Bereitstellung von Archivfotos bedanken: Kennedy Space Center (NASA), Everglades National Park, Seaworld und Discovery Cove, Orlando und bei den Miami Dolphins und den Carolina Panthers Football Teams für die Verwendung ihrer Logos, und bei der Save the Manatee Organisation für die Verwendung ihrer Website. Ebenfalls danken möchten wir dem Autor Michael Crichton für die Zustimmung zur Veröffentlichung seines Fotos.